McGraw-Hill Reading

WonderWorks

Mc
Graw
Hill
Education

Bothell, WA • Chicago, IL • Columbus, OH • New York, NY

Cover and Title Page: Nathan Love

www.mheonline.com/readingwonderworks

Send all inquiries to:
McGraw-Hill Education
Two Penn Plaza
New York, New York 10121

ISBN: 978-0-02-126882-5
MHID: 0-02-126882-7

Printed in the United States of America.

1 2 3 4 5 6 7 8 9 QVS 18 17 16 15 14 13   A

Program Authors

Douglas Fisher

Jan Hasbrouck

Timothy Shanahan

McGraw Hill Education

Bothell, WA • Chicago, IL • Columbus, OH • New York, NY

Unit 1

Think it Through

The Big Idea

(t) Valerie Sokolova; (b) Chris Vallo

Go Digital! www.connected.mcgraw-hill.com

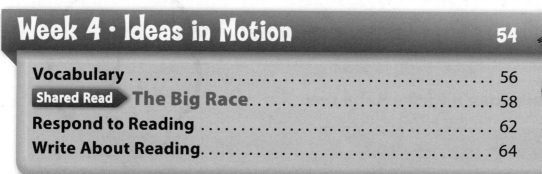

Amazing Animals

The Big Idea

Week 1 · Literary Lessons   80

Week 2 · Animals in Fiction   92

(t) Stephen Frink/Corbis; (c) James H. Robinson/Oxford Scientific/Getty Images Egmont Strigl/Imagebroker/SuperStock; (b) Alessandra Cimatoribus

Unit 3

THAT'S THE Spirit!

The Big Idea

(t) Richard Johnson; (b) Jeff Mangiat

Go Digital! www.connected.mcgraw-hill.com

4

(t) Paul Corbit Brown; (c) Division of Political History, National Museum of American History, Smithsonian Institute; (b) Annabelle Breakey/Digital Vision/Getty Images

FACT OR FICTION?

The Big Idea

Go Digital! www.connected.mcgraw-hill.com

Unit 5

Figure It Out

The Big Idea
What helps you understand the world around you? 264

Go Digital! www.connected.mcgraw-hill.com

Past, Present, and Future

The Big Idea

Week 1 · Old and New   328

Week 2 · Notes from the Past   340

 Go Digital! www.connected.mcgraw-hill.com

A C T
CCSS Access Complex Text

Some text can be hard to understand. It can be complex. But you can figure it out! Take notes as you read. Then ask yourself questions.

Vocabulary

☐ Did I look for context clues to help me figure out words I don't know?

☐ Did I use a dictionary to look up technical terms?

Make Connections

☐ Did I connect ideas from one part of the text to another?

☐ Did I connect two or more details in the text?

Text Features

☐ Are there illustrations or photos that help me understand the text?

☐ Is there a map or a diagram that gives me information?

Text Structure

☐ Did I look at how the text is organized?

☐ What kinds of sentences are in the text and what do they tell me?

Mike Moran

Text Evidence

The details in the text are the clues that will help you answer a question. These clues are called text evidence. Sometimes you will find answers right there in the text. Sometimes you need to look in different parts of the text.

It's Stated – Right There!

☐ Can I find the answer in one sentence?

☐ Do I need to look for details in more than one place in the text?

☐ Do the words in the text tell the exact answer?

☐ Did I use evidence to answer the question?

It's Not Stated – But Here's My Evidence

☐ Did I look for important clues in the text?

☐ Did I put the clues in my own words?

☐ Did I use clues to answer the question?

Talk About It

Talking with your classmates is a great way to share ideas and learn new things. Have a good idea? Share it! Not sure about something? Ask a question!

When I Talk

- ☐ Did I use complete sentences?
- ☐ Did I talk about one topic and describe the key details?
- ☐ Did I speak clearly?

When I Listen

- ☐ Did I listen carefully when others spoke?
- ☐ If I didn't understand something, did I ask a question?
- ☐ Did I ask questions about the topic so I could learn more?

Discussion Rules
- ☑ Be respectful.
- ☑ Speak one at a time.
- ☑ Listen to others with care.

Mike Moran

Write About Reading

A good way to think about what you have read is to write about it. You can write to tell what you think. You can write to share what you learned. Use evidence from the text to support your ideas and opinions.

Getting Ready to Write

☐ Did I look back at my notes about what I read?

☐ Did I find text evidence to support my opinions or ideas?

Writing Opinions

☐ Did I tell my opinion with a topic sentence?

☐ Did I use text evidence to support my opinion?

☐ Did I end with a strong conclusion?

Writing Informative Texts

☐ Did I start with a clear topic sentence?

☐ Did I use facts and definitions from the text to develop my topic?

☐ Did I end with a strong conclusion?

Think it Through

The Big Idea

How can a challenge bring out our best?

Talk About It

Essential Question

Where do good ideas come from?

Go Digital!

Write words that describe how people think of good ideas.

Ideas

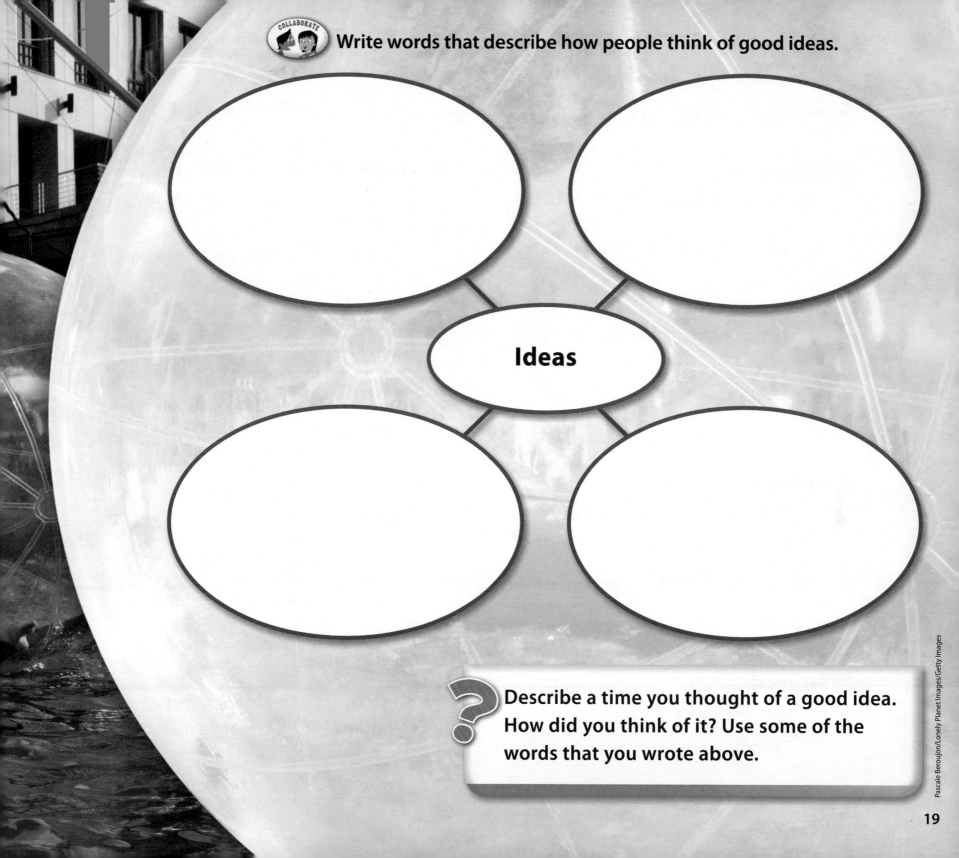

Describe a time you thought of a good idea. How did you think of it? Use some of the words that you wrote above.

CCSS Vocabulary

 Work with a partner to complete each activity.

1 gracious

Name one way you can be *gracious* to a friend.

_____

2 stale

What happens to bread when it gets *stale*?

_____

_____

3 muttered

When was a time that you *muttered* a few words?

_____

_____

4 frantically

List one thing you might search for *frantically*.

_____

5 official

Underline the example of an *official* document.

    poem   report card   list

6 brainstorm

The word brainstorm is a compound word.

▶ Underline the word *brain* in *brainstorm*.

▶ Draw a box around the word *storm* in *brainstorm*.

What do you do when you *brainstorm*?

_____

_____

_____

_____

7 original

Circle the word that means almost the same thing as *original*.

    new   old   last

8 **flattened**

Draw a box. Then draw a box that has been *flattened*.

High-Utility Words

Contractions

A contraction is a shortened form of two words.

Circle the contractions in the passage.

Dear Sue,

I'm so happy you're coming to visit me. We'll do a lot of fun things. I'll take you to the zoo. It's full of wild animals. And we'll meet my friends, Sid and Beth. They're really silly, and they'll make you laugh. I'll see you in two weeks!

Your friend,

Emma

Tara Moore/Getty Images

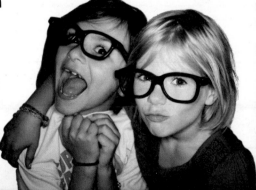

Read "The Dragon Problem."
Use this page to take notes.

_____

_____

_____

_____

_____

_____

_____

_____

_____

_____

_____

_____

22

CCSS **Shared Read** Genre • Fairy Tale

The Dragon Problem

? Essential Question

Where do good ideas come from?

Read how Liang gets a good idea.

Once upon a time, long before computers, there lived a young man named Liang. During the day, Liang helped his father. They built wood furniture. At night, Liang made unique, **original** toys. He made singing birds. With a sharp knife, he **carved** dragons with scales and claws out of wood. All the village children had one of Liang's dragons.

Liang knew a lot about dragons. One lived nearby on a mountain. A few times a year, the dragon would swoop into the village. He ate water buffalo. He ate pigs. He also ate any people who were around. The Emperor's summer palace was near Liang's village. But the Emperor had done nothing about the dragon.

One day in May, the Emperor and his family arrived. They were going to the summer palace. As they passed through the village, **gracious** Princess Peng smiled kindly at Liang. He fell instantly in love.

At dinner that night, Liang told his father about Princess Peng. He said he wanted to marry her. His father almost choked on the **stale**, hard rice ball he was eating.

"You're joking," said his father.

"I'm serious!" said Liang.

His father laughed so hard that his chair broke. He lay on top of the **flattened** chair still laughing.

Valerie Sokolova

❶ Expand Vocabulary

Carved is to have made or shaped something by cutting. **Draw a box** around what Liang *carved*.

❷ Sentence Structure A C T

Reread the third sentence in the third paragraph. **Underline** what happens as the Emperor goes through the village. Which word in the sentence tells you that two events are happening at the same time?

_____

❸ Comprehension
Sequence

Reread the third and fourth paragraphs. **Circle** the two events that happen after Liang sees the princess. When did Liang tell his father he wanted to marry Princess Peng?

_____

_____

Text Evidence

1 Expand Vocabulary

An **announcement** is a written or spoken statement that gives important information. **Draw a box** around the messenger's *announcement*.

2 Sentence Structure A C T

Reread the first sentence in the fourth paragraph. **Underline** the text that tells what Liang did after he heard the announcement. What word in the sentence tells you that two events are described?

_____

3 Comprehension
Sequence

Reread the last paragraph. **Circle** the events that happened after Liang got home. What word tells you that Liang went up the mountain after he found the cart?

_____

"I'll show him," Liang **muttered** angrily.

The next morning, the Emperor's messenger made an **official announcement**.

"Whoever gets rid of the dragon will marry Princess Peng."

When he heard the announcement, Liang raced to the palace. He was first to sign up. Then he looked for his friend Lee. He wanted to **brainstorm** ideas for getting rid of the dragon. But Lee was away. Liang sat on a bench frowning. Nearby, children were playing with the toy dragons he had made.

"Liang, what's wrong?" the children asked.

"I have to get rid of the dragon," he said.

"I have an idea," said little Ling Ling. "Carve a giant dragon. Leave it by the cave. It will scare away the real dragon."

"Perfect!" Liang shouted. He rushed home. Liang worked **frantically** for days and made a big, scary dragon's head. Finally it was finished. Liang found a cart. Then he went up the mountain. When he got near the cave, he put the head on a big rock. It looked like the dragon's body was behind the rock.

Valerie Sokolova

Liang hid. He gave a loud roar. "Who's there?" growled the dragon. He rushed out of his cave. Suddenly, he saw the huge dragon head looking at him. It glared angrily at him. "Go away, or I'll eat you!" the dragon commanded.

The huge dragon continued to glare at him. "He must be very strong. He's not afraid of me," thought the dragon. The dragon, like all bullies, was a **coward**. He quickly decided it was a good time to take a long trip.

"I'm leaving now. Make yourself at home," the dragon called as he flew away.

A year later, Liang and Princess Peng were married. They opened a toy shop and lived happily ever after.

Text Evidence

1 Expand Vocabulary

A **coward** is someone who is easily frightened. **Underline** the sentence that shows that the dragon is a *coward*.

2 Comprehension
Sequence

Reread the page. **Circle** the first thing the dragon did after he saw the huge dragon head. Write the last thing the dragon did.

_____

_____

3 Comprehension
Sequence

Reread the last paragraph. **Draw a box** around the text that tells when the end of the story takes place. What did Liang and Princess Peng do after they got married?

_____

_____

25

Respond to Reading

Discuss Work with a partner. Read the questions about "The Dragon Problem." Use the discussion starters to answer the questions. Write the page numbers to show where you found text evidence.

❓ Questions	💬 Discussion Starters	🔍 Text Evidence
1 Why does Liang want to find his friend Lee?	▶ Liang wants to find his friend Lee because… ▶ I read that…	Page(s): _____
2 What does little Ling Ling tell Liang to do?	▶ Little Ling Ling tells… ▶ I noticed that…	Page(s): _____
3 What idea does Liang use?	▶ Then Liang carved… ▶ I know the idea works because I read that…	Page(s): _____

Write Review your notes about "The Dragon Problem."
Then write your answer to the question below. Use text
evidence to support your answer.

Where did Liang get his idea for scaring the dragon?

_____

_____

_____

_____

_____

_____

_____

_____

_____

_____

Valerie Sokolova

27

Write About Reading

Shared Read

Read an Analysis **Story Structure** Read Ana's paragraph about "The Dragon Problem." Ana analyzes the events in the story. She tells how the events affect the characters and plot.

Student Model

Topic Sentence

Circle the topic sentence. What is Ana going to write about?

Evidence

Draw a box around the evidence that Ana includes. What other information from "The Dragon Problem" would you include?

Concluding Statement

Underline the concluding statement. Why is this sentence a good wrap up?

In "The Dragon Problem," the author uses the events to show how Liang is able to marry Princess Peng. In the beginning, Liang sees the beautiful Princess Peng. This event affects him. He falls in love with her. Then Liang hears an annoucement. Whoever gets rid of the dragon can marry Princess Peng. This event affects Liang, too. He decides to get rid of the dragon. Then he can marry the princess. Little Ling Ling gives him a good idea. Liang carves a big dragon head out of wood. This scares the dragon and he flies away. The events in the story helped me understand how Liang was able to marry the princess.

Leveled Reader

Write an Analysis **Story Structure** Write a paragraph about "Clever Puss." Analyze how the events helped you understand the plot and the characters?

_____

_____

_____

_____

_____

_____

_____

_____

_____

_____

_____

_____

Topic Sentence

☐ Include the title of the text you read.

☐ Tell how events help you understand the story.

Evidence

☐ Include important events from the story.

☐ Explain how they affect the plot.

Concluding Statement

☐ Restate how events helped you understand the story.

Talk About It

Weekly Concept Think of Others

Essential Question

How do your actions affect others?

Go Digital!

List two actions in the chart. Then write the effects of those actions on others.

Action		Effect
	→	
	→	
	→	

Describe a time you helped somebody. What effect did your action have on that person? Use the words you wrote above.

© Sean Justice/Corbis

Vocabulary

 Work with a partner to complete each activity.

1 accountable

List two things you are *accountable* for at home.

_____

_____

2 hesitated

The girl *hesitated* before diving into the pool. Why do you think the girl *hesitated*?

_____

3 desperately

I *desperately* tried to catch the ball.
Read the sentence out loud. Show how to try *desperately* to catch a ball.

4 advise

Write the name of a person who can *advise* you.

_____

5 self-esteem

How can you help a friend build *self-esteem*? List two ways.

_____

_____

6 humiliated

Read the synonyms below for *humiliated*. Write another synonym.
humiliated: foolish, ashamed,

_____

7 uncomfortably

▶ Underline the word *comfort* in *uncomfortably*.

▶ Circle the prefix, *un-*.

▶ Draw a box around the suffix, *-ly*.

▶ What does *uncomfortably* mean?

_____

_____

8 **inspiration**

Who or what is an *inspiration* to you? Tell why you feel this way. Draw a picture of that person or thing.

High-Utility Words

▶ **Time and Sequence**

Time and sequence words tell the order of events.

Circle the time and sequence words in the passage.

Bill woke up and jumped out of bed. First, he brushed his teeth. Next, he got dressed and combed his hair. Before he ate breakfast, he grabbed his books. He ate some toast, and then he ran out the door. Bill hurried to school. After school, Bill went to the park with Ed. Finally, he went home and played with his dog. It was a busy day.

33

My Notes

Read "The Talent Show."
Use this page to take notes.

_____

_____

_____

_____

_____

_____

_____

_____

_____

_____

_____

_____

THE Talent Show

? Essential Question

How do your actions affect others?

Read about how Tina's actions affect Maura.

"Tina, there is a school talent show in three weeks," I said. Tina is my best friend. I showed her the brightly colored poster for the talent show on the bulletin board.

"Maura, what kind of **act** will we perform in the talent show?" Tina asked.

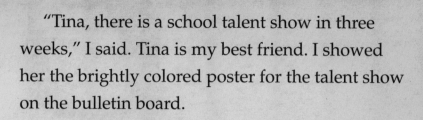

"Our act?" I said. I gripped my books tightly. I was learning to juggle and I wanted to do my own juggling act. "You want to do an act together?" I asked her.

"It will be fun," Tina said.

I **hesitated.** The grip on my books became **uncomfortably** tight. Then I tried to tell Tina about my act. "I have an idea."

Tina interrupted me. "Yeah, I have an idea too," she said. "Let's talk about our ideas at lunch."

I **desperately** wanted to win the talent show. But it was more than just about winning. I wanted to win with my own act.

Chris Vallo

35

Text Evidence

1 Expand Vocabulary

To be **resentful** means to feel angry because something is unfair. **Draw a box** around a clue that shows why Maura feels *resentful*.

2 Comprehension
Problem and Solution

Reread the second and third paragraphs. **Circle** details that show what Maura does at lunch. How does she try to solve her problem?

_____

_____

3 Genre ACT
Realistic Fiction

Reread the fourth paragraph. **Underline** what Tina says about juggling. How does Tina feel about Maura's idea?

_____

_____

During math, I tried to think of how to tell Tina what I wanted. Tina always took charge. We always ended up doing what she wanted. Sometimes I felt **resentful** and angry that I let Tina decide everything.

At lunch, Tina started to take charge again. "I have our act all planned. My **inspiration** came from a new TV show, 'You've Got Talent.' We can sing and dance to music. My mom can make us costumes."

"That is a good idea," I said. "But listen to my idea." I told her all about my juggling act.

"I don't think I can learn to juggle in three weeks," Tina said. "I might drop the balls in front of the audience. Then I would feel **humiliated**."

My grandmother picked me up after school. In the car, she asked me why I was so quiet. I told her about the talent show and Tina's idea.

"Maura, you cannot always do what your friends want," she said. "You have to stand up for yourself. I understand that Tina is your best friend, but remember, you are **accountable** for your own actions."

I thought about this. "So what should I do?"

"Respect your own ideas. I **advise** you to tell Tina the truth about what you want," my grandmother said. "It will be good for your **self-esteem**."

When I got home, I took a deep breath, called Tina, and told her the truth. I said I wanted to do my juggling act. She was **curt** and not very friendly on the phone. Tina barely said good-bye before she hung up. The rest of the night, I was worried that she was mad at me.

The next day, she described her act and her costume. I was surprised. She was not mad at all. But the biggest surprise came at recess. I chose the game to play, not Tina.

I guess standing up for myself did pay off.

Chris Vallo

❶ Comprehension
Problem and Solution

Maura takes action to solve her problem. **Draw a box** around the sentence that shows this. How does Maura solve her problem?

_____

_____

❷ Expand Vocabulary

Being **curt** means speaking to someone in a quick, rude way. **Circle** details that help you understand the meaning of *curt*.

❸ Genre A C T
Realistic Fiction

Reread the page. **Underline** details that show what Tina does the next day at school. What happens at recess?

_____

_____

 **Questions**  **Discussion Starters** **Text Evidence**

1 At the beginning of the story, what does Tina want Maura to do?

➤ Tina wants Maura to….

➤ Maura feels uncomfortable because Tina….

➤ I know this because I read….

Page(s): _____

2 Why is Maura quiet in the car after school?

➤ Maura is quiet because….

➤ I know this because I read….

Page(s): _____

3 At the end of the story, what happens to Tina and Maura?

➤ Maura tells Tina that….

➤ Maura is surprised because….

Page(s): _____

Write Review your notes about "The Talent Show." Then write your answer to the question below. Use text evidence to support your answer.

How did Tina's actions affect Maura?

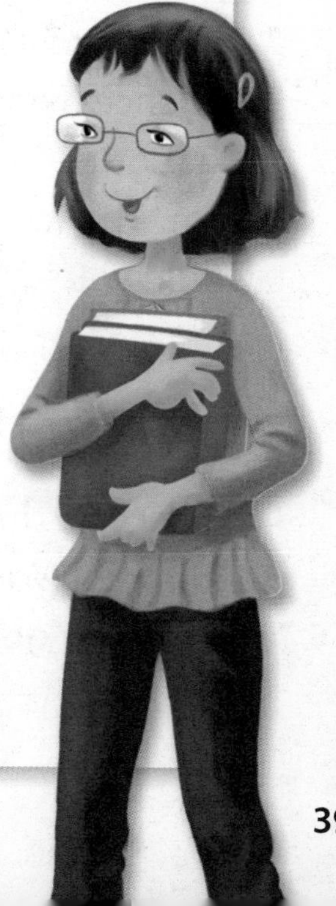

Chris Vallo

Shared Read

Read an Analysis **Story Structure** Read Kyra's paragraph about "The Talent Show." She writes her opinion about how the author uses realistic characters and events in the story.

Student Model

Topic Sentence

Circle the topic sentence. What is Kyra going to write about?

Evidence

Draw a box around the evidence Kyra includes. What other information from "The Talent Show" would you include?

Concluding Statement

Underline the concluding statement. Why is this sentence a good wrap up?

In "The Talent Show," I think the author does a good job of writing a realistic story. The characters, Maura and Tina, are like real kids. They are good friends and go to school together. Then Maura and Tina have a problem about the talent show. Maura doesn't want to do an act with Tina. Real friends have problems like this. They don't always want to do the same things. At the end of the story, Maura tells Tina how she feels. This is what real friends do, too. They talk about their feelings. I think the author showed how the characters solved their problem in a realistic way.

Leveled Reader

Write an Analysis > **Story Structure** Write a paragraph about "The Dream Team." Tell your opinion about how the authors uses realistic characters and events.

_____

_____

_____

_____

_____

_____

_____

_____

_____

_____

_____

_____

Topic Sentence

☐ Include the title of the text you read.

☐ Tell your opinion about how well the author uses realistic characters and events.

Evidence

☐ Include details the author uses to make the story realistic.

☐ Explain why the details are realistic.

Concluding Statement

☐ Restate your opinion.

☐ Tell how well the author used realistic characters and events.

Talk About It

Essential Question

How do people respond to natural disasters?

Go Digital!

COLLABORATE

Write words you have learned about responding to a natural disaster.

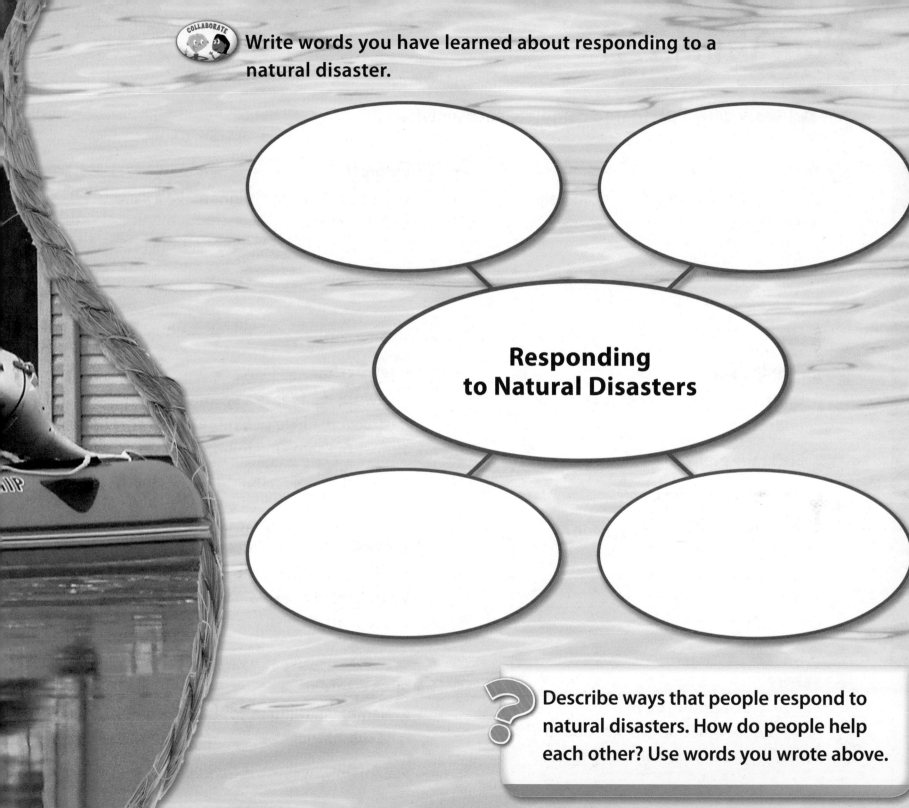

Responding to Natural Disasters

Describe ways that people respond to natural disasters. How do people help each other? Use words you wrote above.

CCSS Vocabulary

 Work with a partner to complete each activity.

1 **crisis**

Describe how a police officer can help during a *crisis*.

_____

_____

2 **unpredictable**

▶ Underline the word *predict* in *unpredictable*.

▶ Circle the prefix, *un*.

▶ Underline the suffix, *able*.

▶ What does *unpredictable* mean?

_____

_____

3 **severe**

I'm very disappointed in you.

Read the sentence above out loud in a *severe* way. Use your voice and face.

4 **collapse**

List two things that might make a sand castle *collapse*.

_____

_____

5 **destruction**

The word *damage* is a synonym for *destruction*. Circle two more words that have almost the same meaning.

destroy   build   smash

6 **hazard**

Pile three books on the floor. Then use the word *hazard* to explain why the books could cause harm.

7 **substantial**

▶ Name one thing in your classroom that is *substantial*.

▶ Explain why it is *substantial*.

8 alter

Draw a picture of a person's face. Then *alter* the face by changing it in some way.

High-Utility Words

Words That Compare

Words that compare are signal words that let readers know when comparisons are made in a text.

Circle the words that compare in the passage.

Snowstorms and blizzards are (both) winter storms. Like snowstorms, blizzards have snow. But blizzards also have lots of wind. Blizzard winds are strong. They blow at least 35 mph. The winds blow the snow around. It can be very difficult to see in a blizzard! Both blizzards and snowstorms keep people inside.

Corbis Bridge/Alamy

My Notes

Read "A World of Change." Use this page to take notes.

_____

_____

_____

_____

_____

_____

_____

_____

_____

_____

_____

_____

_____

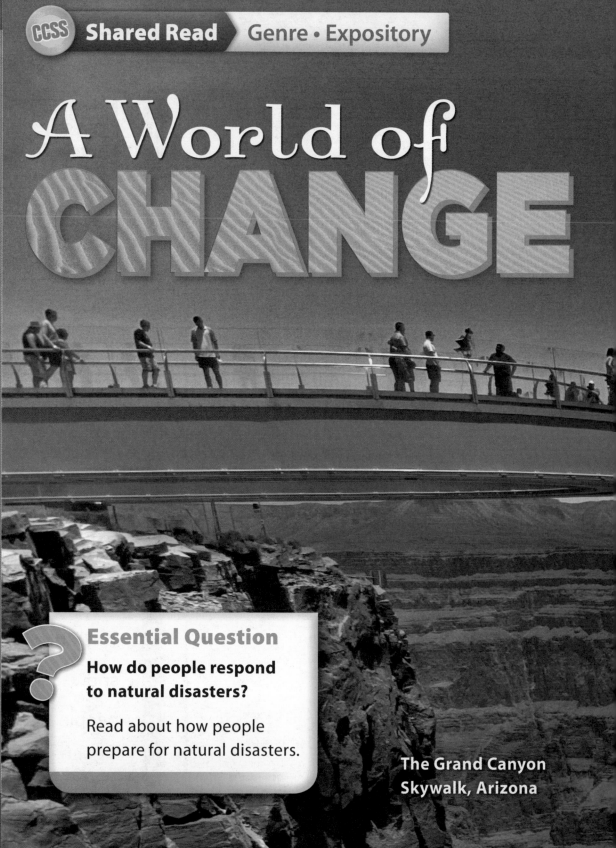

A World of CHANGE

? **Essential Question**

How do people respond to natural disasters?

Read about how people prepare for natural disasters.

The Grand Canyon Skywalk, Arizona

Earth is always changing. Natural changes take place every day. Some of those changes are slow. They happen over many years. Others are fast. They happen in minutes. Both kinds of changes **alter** the **surface** of Earth.

Natural Changes That Are Slow

Some changes on Earth can't be seen. They happen very slowly. Weathering, erosion, and deposition are all slow processes. They change Earth's surface. But they take years to do so.

Weathering happens when rain, snow, sun, and wind break down rocks. First the rocks break into small pieces. Then the pieces turn into dirt.

Erosion happens when dirt and rocks are taken away. It causes landforms to get smaller. Sometimes they even **collapse**, or fall down. Rivers are one cause of erosion. The Grand Canyon is an example of erosion. A strong river carved the land. It took thousands of years.

Deposition happens when dirt and rocks are dropped in new places. The dirt and rocks come from erosion. Over time, the dirt and rocks build up. Deposition by water can build up a beach. By wind, it can build up a **substantial** landform. One such landform is a sand dune.

Text Evidence

❶ Expand Vocabulary

The word **surface** means the outside of something. **Underline** the sentences that tell what kind of changes alter Earth's *surface* over time.

❷ Comprehension
Compare and Contrast

Reread the first paragraph. **Circle** words that tell you a comparison will be made. What two things will the text compare and contrast?

_____

_____

❸ Connection of Ideas Ⓐ Ⓒ Ⓣ

Reread the last two paragraphs. **Draw a box** around the sentences that show how deposition and erosion are connected. What is deposition?

Text Evidence

❶ Connection of Ideas (A C T)

Reread the second paragraph. **Underline** the sentence that tells you what people do to stop beach erosion. How do plants help to stop erosion?

_____

_____

❷ Expand Vocabulary

Sudden events that cause great harm are called **disasters**. **Draw a box** around two kinds of natural *disasters*.

❸ Comprehension
Compare and Contrast

Reread the third paragraph. **Circle** the text that shows how fast natural processes and slow natural processes are similar. How are fast natural processes and slow natural processes different?

_____

_____

Erosion is a slow process, but it can make big problems. Some kinds are dangerous. They can create a **hazard** for people.

How do people prevent erosion? They build seawalls to stop beach erosion. The walls block the ocean waves. People use big rocks to keep land in place. They also put in plants. The plant roots hold dirt in place.

Natural Changes That Are Fast

Fast natural processes are like slow processes. They both change Earth's surface. But fast processes are more powerful. They can cause great **destruction**. That is why fast natural processes are often called natural **disasters**. Volcanic eruptions and landslides cause fast changes in Earth's surface.

Volcanoes form around openings in Earth's crust. When pressure builds under Earth's surface, melted rock is forced upward. It flows through the volcano. Then it flows out through the opening. Eruptions can happen without warning and may cause a **crisis**.

Melted Rock

Like volcanic eruptions, landslides can also take place without warning. Landslides happen when heavy rains loosen the side of a hill or mountain. Suddenly rocks and dirt slide down. Some landslides are small. Others are large. Large landslides can cause **severe damage**.

Be Prepared

People can stop the effects of slow changes. But they cannot stop the effects of fast changes. So scientists try to predict when natural disasters will happen. Still, some disasters are **unpredictable**. They strike without warning. It is important to plan for them. An emergency plan can help save lives.

Natural processes change the surface of Earth. Some are slow. Others are fast. Both kinds of processes make Earth an amazing planet!

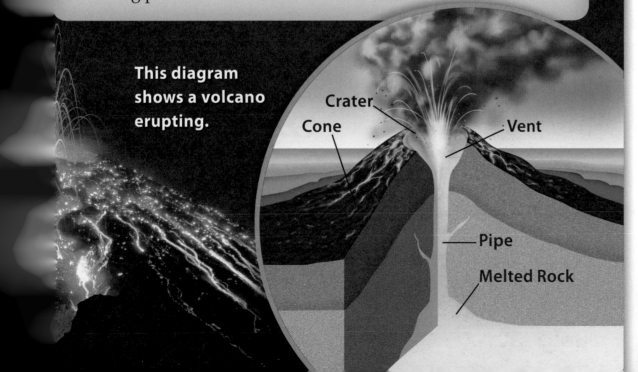

This diagram shows a volcano erupting.

Crater
Cone
Vent
Pipe
Melted Rock

Text Evidence

❶ Connection of Ideas **A** **C** **T**

Review the diagram. Reread "Natural Changes That Are Fast" on page 48. **Underline** the text that describes what the diagram shows. What kind of natural process is shown in the diagram?

_____

❷ Expand Vocabulary

The word **damage** means harm or an injury. **Draw a box** around the sentences that tell how landslides can cause *damage*.

❸ Comprehension
Compare and Contrast

Reread the last paragraph. How are slow natural processes and fast natural processes alike and how they are different?

_____

_____

_____

Respond to Reading

 **Discuss** Work with a partner. Read the questions about "A World of Change." Use the discussion starters to answer the questions. Write the page numbers to show where you found text evidence.

?Questions   **Discussion Starters**    **Text Evidence**

1 How do people protect a beach against erosion?	▶ People protect a beach by… ▶ I also read that they…	Page(s): _____
2 Why is it more difficult to prepare for a fast-moving disaster?	▶ One reason a fast-moving disaster is more difficult to prepare for is… ▶ A second reason…	Page(s): _____
3 How do people prepare for a fast-moving disaster?	▶ Scientists try to… ▶ I read that people…	Page(s): _____

Mike Moran

50

Write Review your notes about "A World of Change." Then write your answer to the question below. Use text evidence to support your answer.

How do people prepare for natural disasters?

_____

_____

_____

_____

_____

_____

_____

_____

_____

_____

_____

Write About Reading

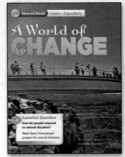

Shared Read

Read an Analysis **Illustrations** Read the paragraph below about "A World of Change." Sara tells how an illustration, such as a diagram, can add details about a topic.

Student Model

Topic Sentence

Circle the topic sentence. What is Sara going to write about?

Evidence

Draw a box around the evidence that Sara includes. What other information from "A World of Change" would you include?

Concluding Statement

Underline the concluding statement. Why is this sentence a good wrap up?

In "A World of Change," the author uses a diagram to help explain volcanoes. The diagram pictures the parts of a volcano. It shows what happens when a volcano erupts. The diagram has labels that name the parts of a volcano. This information is helpful. Some of the parts of the volcano are not mentioned in the text. By including a diagram, the author helps me understand what happens when a volcano erupts.

Neil Stewart

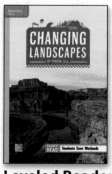

Leveled Reader

Write an Analysis > **Illustrations** Write a paragraph about "Changing Landscapes." How does the author use illustrations such as diagrams to explain the topic?

_____

_____

_____

_____

_____

_____

_____

_____

_____

_____

_____

Topic Sentence

☐ Include the title of the text you read.

☐ Tell about one illustration.

Evidence

☐ Describe the details you see in the illustration.

☐ Explain how these details tell you more about the topic.

Concluding Statement

☐ Restate how an illustration helped you learn more about the topic.

Talk About It

Essential Question

How can science help you understand how things work?

Go Digital!

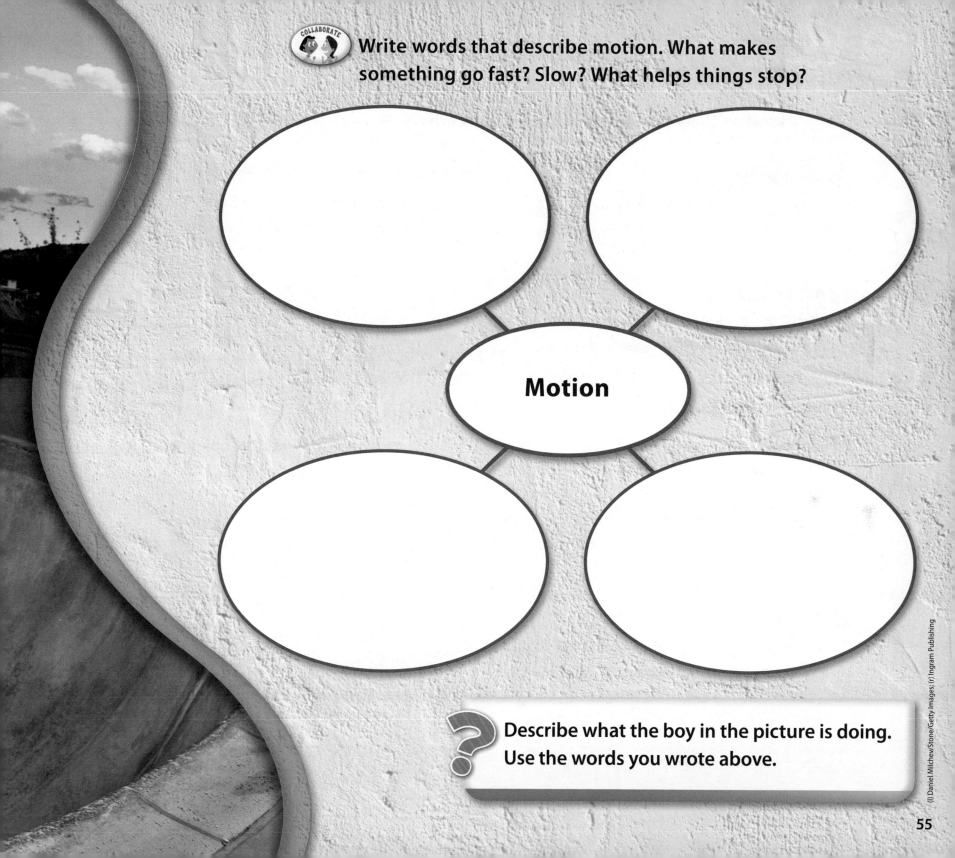

COLLABORATE

Write words that describe motion. What makes something go fast? Slow? What helps things stop?

Motion

Describe what the boy in the picture is doing. Use the words you wrote above.

 **Vocabulary**

 Work with a partner to complete each activity.

1 accelerate

Move a book to show how you can make it *accelerate*.

2 advantage

Circle the thing that what would give a soccer player an *advantage* in a game.

more practice   a sunny day

3 capabilities

What *capabilities* does a teacher need?

_____

_____

4 friction

When you use the brakes on a bike, you stop. How is this an example of *friction*?

_____

_____

5 gravity

Drop a pencil onto the floor. How is this an example of *gravity*?

_____

_____

_____

6 inquiry

List three jobs where people make *inquiries*, or ask questions.

_____

_____

_____

7 identity

Circle the person who might have a secret *identity*.

farmer   spy   doctor

8 thrilling

Draw a picture to show a *thrilling* moment in your life.

High-Utility Words

Prepositions

Prepositions are words that show a direction or location of something.

Circle the prepositions in the passage.

Vicky sat (in) her race car. Soon, she would ride down the biggest hill in town. Her dad stood behind the car. He put his hands on the back of it. The race began. He gave the car a big push. Vicky zoomed down the hill really fast. She passed two other cars. Vicky smiled as she drove over the finish line first.

My Notes

Read "The Big Race." Use this page to take notes.

Essential Question

How can science help you understand how things work?

Read how Alex and Liam want to use science to help them win a race.

58

I'm Clara. Welcome!

Alex and Liam wanted to build a car for the soap box derby. The boys had begun an **inquiry** into how to build a fast car. As a result, they had come to the science museum today for answers. A woman in a lab coat greeted them. She was wearing inline skates.

"Hi, I'm Clara. Are you the boys who want to know how to make a car go fast?"

"Yes, I'm Alex. He's Liam," Alex **responded**.

"Why are you wearing inline skates?" Liam asked.

"I'm a champion skater!" Clara claimed. She did a spin. Then she whispered, "That's not my true **identity**. I'm a scientist. Skates make it easier to get around. Follow me!"

IT'S ABOUT SPEED

They entered a large room. "Welcome to our *On the Move* exhibit," Clara said. "So, tell me about the race."

"There will be 20 cars in the race. We'll go down the steepest hill in town!" Alex said.

"Sounds **thrilling!** It's exciting to go fast!" Clara was at a machine. "This is a virtual race car. The screen shows you the racecourse. It also shows your speed. Speed is the distance an object moves in a certain amount of time."

Craig Phillips

Text Evidence

1 **Comprehension**
Cause and Effect

Reread the first paragraph. **Circle** the phrase *as a result*. Write the letter C above the cause. Write an E above its effect.

2 **Expand Vocabulary**

The word **responded** means answered. What did Alex say when he *responded* to Clara?

_____

_____

_____

_____

3 **Purpose** (A)(C)(T)

Reread the last paragraph. **Draw a box** around the sentence with a science fact. Does this fact inform you or entertain you?

_____

59

Text Evidence

❶ Expand Vocabulary

The word **apply** means to put into use. How does Clara *apply* force to a stool?

_____

_____

_____

❷ Comprehension
Cause and Effect

Reread the fourth paragraph. **Underline** the causes. **Draw a box** around the effects. What is the effect on the stool?

_____

_____

_____

❸ Purpose Ⓐ Ⓒ Ⓣ

Reread the last paragraph. **Circle** the sentences that tell how Alex and Liam will use science facts to make their car go faster.

60

FORCES AT WORK

A force is a push or a pull.

Alex and Liam climbed into the machine. Each seat had a steering wheel and a screen in front of it.

"To build a fast car," said Clara, "you need to know how forces affect motion."

"What's a force?" asked Liam.

"A force is a push or a pull," Clara explained. "Forces cause things to move. I **apply** force to this stool and it moves. Say you have two objects that are the same. The one that receives a bigger force will **accelerate**, or move faster." Clara pushed the two stools at the same time.

"Which stool received a bigger force?" Clara asked.

"The one that went farther," said Liam.

"So we should give our car a big push at the top of the hill. That will make it go fast," said Alex.

There's a sharp curve coming up!

I'm going to speed up now!

GRAVITY AND FRICTION

Clara smiled. "Right! Another force acting on your car is **gravity**. Gravity is a pulling force between two objects." Clara took a tennis ball out of her pocket. "I will drop this ball. Look. Gravity pulls it to the floor. Gravity will pull your car down the hill, too."

"So a big push gives us an **advantage** over other cars. Gravity will keep us going. How do we stop?" Liam asked.

"You'll need **friction**. Friction is a force between two surfaces. It slows things down. Or stops them from moving. See the rubber stoppers on my skates? The friction between them and the floor slows me down," said Clara.

"Thanks, Clara! I knew we had the skills and **capabilities** to win. Now we have science on our side, too," Liam **grinned**. Then everyone laughed.

You need friction.

Craig Phillips

Text Evidence

❶ Comprehension
Cause and Effect

Reread the first paragraph. **Underline** the detail that shows the effect of gravity on the tennis ball. What will the effect of gravity be on the boys' car?

_____

_____

❷ Purpose A C T

Reread the last two paragraphs. **Draw a box** around a science fact. **Circle** a sentence that shows this is a made-up story.

❸ Expand Vocabulary

To **grin** means to give a big smile. Reread the last two sentences. Why did Liam *grin*?

_____

_____

_____

Respond to Reading

Discuss Work with a partner. Read the questions about "The Big Race." Use the discussion starters to answer the questions. Write the page numbers to show where you found text evidence.

? Questions	Discussion Starters	
❶ Why do Liam and Alex visit the science museum?	▶ Liam and Alex visit … ▶ I read that …	Page(s): _____
❷ What do they learn from Clara about forces in motion?	▶ The boys learn that … ▶ I learned that …	Page(s): _____
❸ Why are gravity and friction important to Liam and Alex?	▶ Gravity and friction are … ▶ I learned that gravity … ▶ Friction is …	Page(s): _____

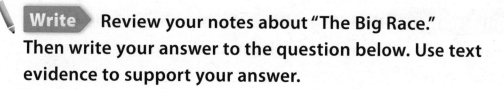

Write Review your notes about "The Big Race."
Then write your answer to the question below. Use text
evidence to support your answer.

How can science help you understand how things move?

_____

_____

_____

_____

_____

_____

_____

_____

_____

_____

Shared Read

Read an Analysis Headings Read the paragraph below about "The Big Race." Tony wrote about how headings help explain the topic.

Student Model

In "The Big Race," the author uses headings to organize information. Headings tell me what each section of text is about. For example, one of the headings in the text is "Gravity and Friction". So, I expect to read about gravity and friction in this part of the text. As I read, I find lots of information about gravity and friction. The author's use of headings helps me know what information will be in each section.

Topic Sentence

Circle the topic sentence. What is Tony going to write about?

Evidence

Draw a box around the evidence that Tony includes. What other information from "The Big Race" would you include?

Concluding Statement

Underline the concluding statement. Why is this sentence a good wrap up?

Leveled Reader

Write an Analysis **Headings** Write a paragraph about "George's Giant Wheel." Tell how the headings give information about the text.

_____

_____

_____

_____

_____

_____

_____

_____

_____

_____

_____

_____

Topic Sentence

☐ Include the title of the text you read.

☐ Tell whether the headings give information about the text.

Evidence

☐ Point out a heading.

☐ Explain how it helps you know what you will be reading.

☐ Support your ideas with details.

Concluding Statement

☐ Restate what the headings tell you about the text.

Talk About It

Weekly Concept Putting Ideas to Work

Essential Question

How can starting a business help others?

Go Digital!

GARLIC
SCAPES

SPRING
ONIONS

Write words that tell how a business can help others.

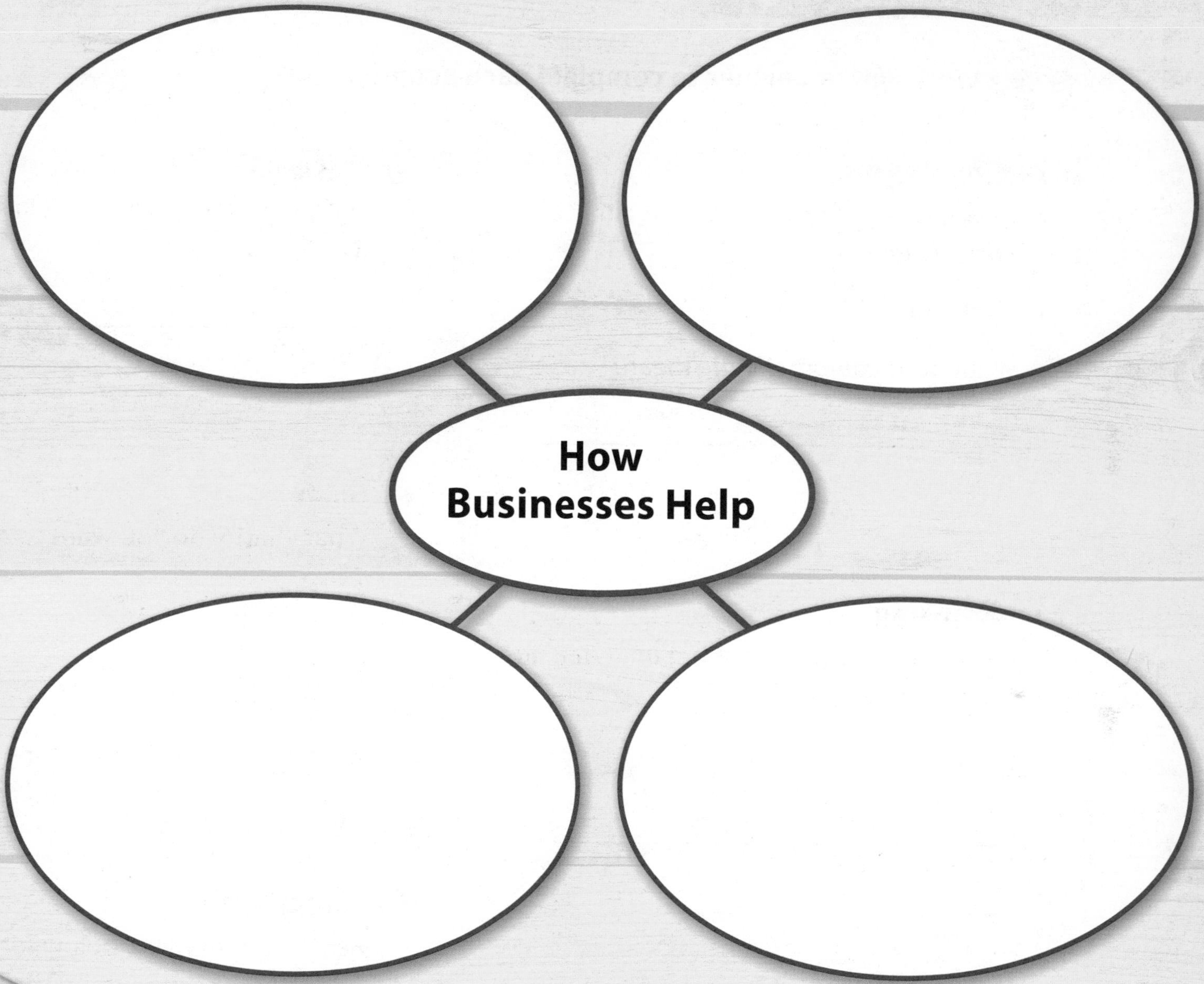

How
Businesses Help

Explain one way a business can give back to the community.

HEAD
LETTUCE
3.50 / HEAD

(l) Tom Williams/Roll Call/Getty Images; (r) Maria Toutoudaki/Photodisc/Getty Images

 Work with a partner to complete each activity.

1 compassionate

▶ Underline the word *compassion* in *compassionate*.

▶ Circle the suffix *-ate*.

▶ What does *compassionate* mean?

_____

_____

2 undertaking

Is cleaning up your room a big *undertaking*? Explain your answer.

_____

_____

3 innovative

In the future, what will be the most *innovative* way to travel? Circle your answer.

    car   horseback   space shuttle

4 enterprise

List a new *enterprise* that a kid can start if they like animals.

_____

_____

5 funds

What charity do you want to raise *funds* for?

_____

6 process

Act out the *process* of making a sandwich. Talk about each step as you act it out.

7 exceptional

Read the synonyms below for *exceptional*. Add another synonym to the list.

exceptional: special, outstanding,

_____

68

8 routine

Draw something you do as part of your daily classroom *routine*.

High-Utility Words

Homophones

Homophones are words that sound alike but are spelled differently and have different meanings.

Circle the homophones in the passage.

Cam and Tina plan to open a hat store some day. They know their store will be by the river because there are no hat stores there. The store will help the needy. For every two hats people buy, they're giving a dollar to charity. Will the sum of the funds be great? They hope so!

Caroline P. Digonis/Alamy

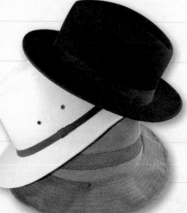

My Notes

Read "Dollars and Sense."
Use this page to take notes.

_____

_____

_____

_____

_____

_____

_____

_____

_____

_____

_____

_____

_____

_____

Essential Question

How can starting a business help others?

Read about how two companies are making a difference.

Dollars and $ENSE

Behind the success of these businesses is a desire to help others.

Good business is not about making the most money. A **compassionate** company knows that making money is only one way to measure success. Many businesses also help people.

Hearts and Soles

Blake Mycoskie had started four businesses. He needed a **break**. He wanted a change from his usual **routine**. In 2006, he went to Argentina, in South America. He visited poor villages and saw that very few children had shoes.

Mycoskie decided to help. "I'm going to start a shoe company. For every pair I sell, I'm going to give one pair to a kid in need," he said.

For this new **undertaking**, Mycoskie used his own money. He named the business TOMS: Shoes for Tomorrow. The shoes are like the shoes worn by Argentine workers.

Mycoskie's one-for-one program is **innovative**. TOMS gives away a pair of shoes for each pair sold. By 2011, TOMS had donated one million pairs.

Text Evidence

1 Expand Vocabulary

To take a **break**, is to stop working and do something different. **Circle** the detail that tells why Mycoskie needed a *break*.

2 Organization **A C T**

Reread the section, "Hearts and Soles." **Draw a box** around the details that tell what Mycoskie decided to start. What did Mycoskie name his company?

_____

3 Comprehension
Main Idea and Key Details

Reread "Hearts and Soles." **Underline** the details about how Mycoskie's new business will help kids. What happens when TOMS sells a pair of shoes?

_____

_____

_____

Text Evidence

1 Expand Vocabulary

When something has **expanded**, it has grown larger. How did Mycoskie's company *expand*?

_____

_____

_____

2 Organization (A C T)

Reread the third paragraph. **Circle** the detail that tells what new enterprise was started by the Hard Rock company in 1990. How are this company and TOMS alike?

_____

_____

3 Comprehension
Main Idea and Key Details

Reread "Giving Back Rocks!" **Underline** the details that tell about one way that the company raises funds.

TOMS' employees give away shoes.

The company has grown. It has **expanded** to sell eyeglasses. One pair of eyeglasses is donated for every pair sold.

Mycoskie is pleased. He is surprised. He can make money and give it away. "I never thought I could do both," Mycoskie says.

Giving Back Rocks!

Have you ever seen a Hard Rock Cafe? The Hard Rock company owns restaurants and hotels. In 1990, it began a new **enterprise.** It raises money and gives it to charities.

Since then, the company has given millions of dollars to different causes.

One way the company raises **funds** is by selling T-shirts. The **process** starts with rock stars. They design the art for the shirts. Then the shirts are sold on the Internet. Part of the money from sales is given to charity.

Hard Rock Cafes give back to the community.

(t) Kwaku Alston/Stockland Martel; (b) Thomas A. Kelly/CORBIS

Top Five Biggest Charities

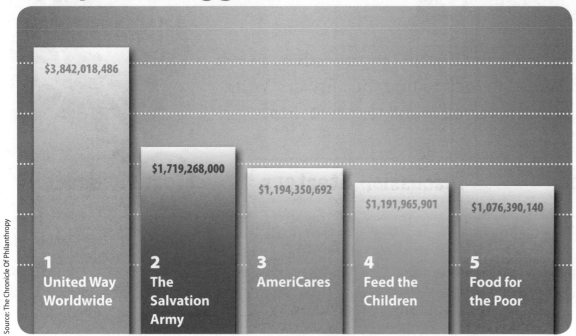

Source: The Chronicle Of Philanthropy

- 1 **United Way Worldwide** — $3,842,018,486
- 2 **The Salvation Army** — $1,719,268,000
- 3 **AmeriCares** — $1,194,350,692
- 4 **Feed the Children** — $1,191,965,901
- 5 **Food for the Poor** — $1,076,390,140

This graph shows five charities. It shows how much money each charity raised in a year.

At all of the Hard Rock Cafe locations, employees are encouraged to raise money for charity.

The Hard Rock Cafe in Hollywood, Florida, worked with some **exceptional** high school students. They had a big event. It was to raise money for the Make-A-Wish Foundation. The foundation fills the wishes of children who are very sick.

A Different Kind of Profit

Every day, companies think of new ways to help. Sponsoring a sports team is one way businesses give back to a community. If you own a business, making a **profit** is important. However, helping others is as important as making money. Helping others is good business!

Text Evidence

1 Organization A C T

Reread the graph "Top Five Biggest Charities" and its caption. **Draw a box** around the charity that has raised the most money. Which charity raised the smallest amount of money?

_____

2 Expand Vocabulary

A **profit** is the amount of money you make after your expenses. **Circle** the phrase that means the same thing as *profit*.

3 Comprehension
Main Idea and Key Details

Reread the last paragraph. **Underline** details that tell what some companies are doing today. According to the article, what is as important as making money?

_____

_____

 **Discuss** Work with a partner. Discuss the questions below about "Dollars and Sense." Reread to find the answers. Write page numbers to show where you found text evidence.

?Questions | **Discussion Starters** |  **Text Evidence**

❶ How does Blake Mycoskie's company, TOMS, help others?	▶ TOMS gives away a pair of shoes when …. ▶ The company also gives away …. ▶ I noticed that Mycoskie ….	Page(s): _____
❷ How does the company that owns the Hard Rock Cafes help others?	▶ The company sells T-shirts that …. ▶ Part of the money from the shirts …. ▶ Hard Rock Cafe employees are also encouraged to ….	Page(s): _____
❸ Why do companies like TOMS and Hard Rock help others?	▶ Companies like TOMS and Hard Rock know that helping others is …. ▶ I know this because I read ….	Page(s): _____

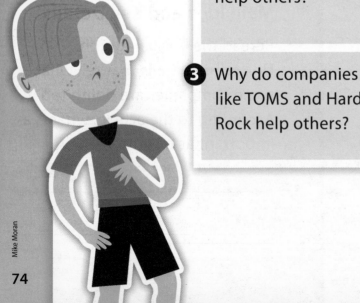

Write Review your notes about "Dollars and Sense." Then write your answer to the question below. Use text evidence to support your answer.

How do the two companies in "Dollars and Sense" help others?

John Lund/Blend Images LLC

CCSS # Write About Reading

Shared Read

Read an Analysis **Main Idea and Key Details** Madeline wrote about "Dollars and Sense." She analyzed how the author used key details to support the main idea.

Student Model

Topic Sentence

Circle the topic sentence. What is Madeline going to write about?

Evidence

Draw a box around the evidence that Madeline includes. What other information from "Dollars and Sense" would you include?

Concluding Statement

Underline the concluding statement. Why is this sentence a good wrap up?

In "Dollars and Sense," the author uses key details to support the main idea that helping others is good for business. For example, Blake Mycoskie started a business. The business donates one pair of shoes to children in need for every pair it sells. It also donates one pair of eyeglasses for every pair it sells. The company that owns Hard Rock Cafe also helps people in need. They sell T-shirts. Some of the money from the sales of these shirts goes to charity. These details all support the idea that it is important for businesses to give back to the community.

Leveled Reader

_____

_____

_____

_____

_____

_____

_____

_____

_____

_____

_____

Topic Sentence

☐ Include the title of the text you read.

☐ Tell whether the author used key details to support the main idea.

Evidence

☐ Provide examples from the text.

☐ Explain how these examples support the main idea.

Concluding Statement

☐ Restate how the author used key details to support the main idea.

Amazing Animals

The Big Idea

What can animals teach us?

Talk About It

Essential Question

What are some messages in animal stories?

Go Digital!

80

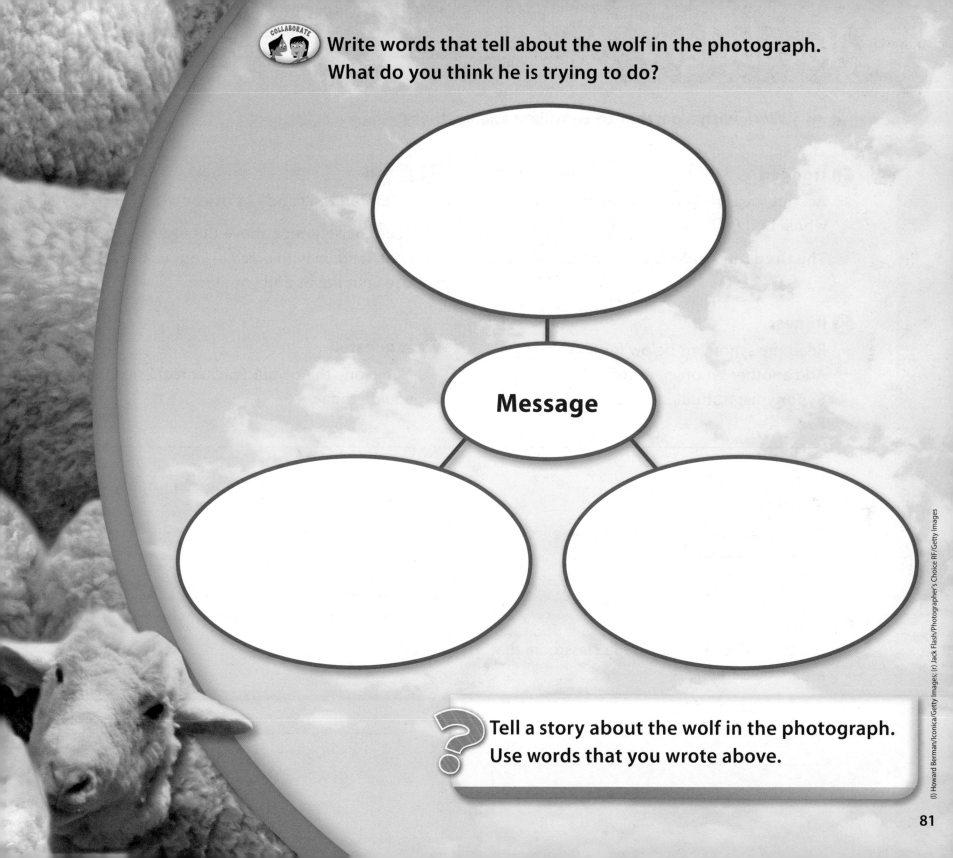

Write words that tell about the wolf in the photograph. What do you think he is trying to do?

Message

Tell a story about the wolf in the photograph. Use words that you wrote above.

Vocabulary

 Work with a partner to complete each activity.

1 **trudged**

Act out the sentence below. Use your whole body.

The tired boy *trudged* through the snow.

2 **honest**

Read the synonyms below for *honest*.
Add another synonym to the list.
Synonyms: truthful, sincere,

_____

3 **dazzling**

Show how you would protect your eyes in *dazzling* sunlight.

4 **fabric**

List two things you see in the classroom that are made of *fabric*.

_____

_____

5 **greed**

I want all the candy in the bowl!

Read the sentence above out loud.
Read it again with *greed* in your voice.
Use your hands and your face.

6 **requested**

Name one thing your teacher *requested* that you do today.

_____

_____

_____

7 **attracted**

Write the name of a food that you are *attracted* to.

_____

_____

8 **soared**

Think of something that can *soar* above your head. Draw a picture of it.

High-Utility Words

Possessive nouns show who or what owns something. Possessive singular nouns end in an apostrophe and an *s*.

Circle the singular possessive nouns in the passage.

Long ago, a woman caught a fish. She took it back to her (mother's) home. She used her husband's knife to clean the fish and her sister's pan to cook it. Then she put the fish on the table. Suddenly, her daughter's cat jumped up and ate the fish! All that was left was the fish's tail. The woman's family was very hungry that day.

My Notes

Read of "The Fisherman and the Kaha Bird." Use this page for notes.

The Fisherman and the Kaha Bird

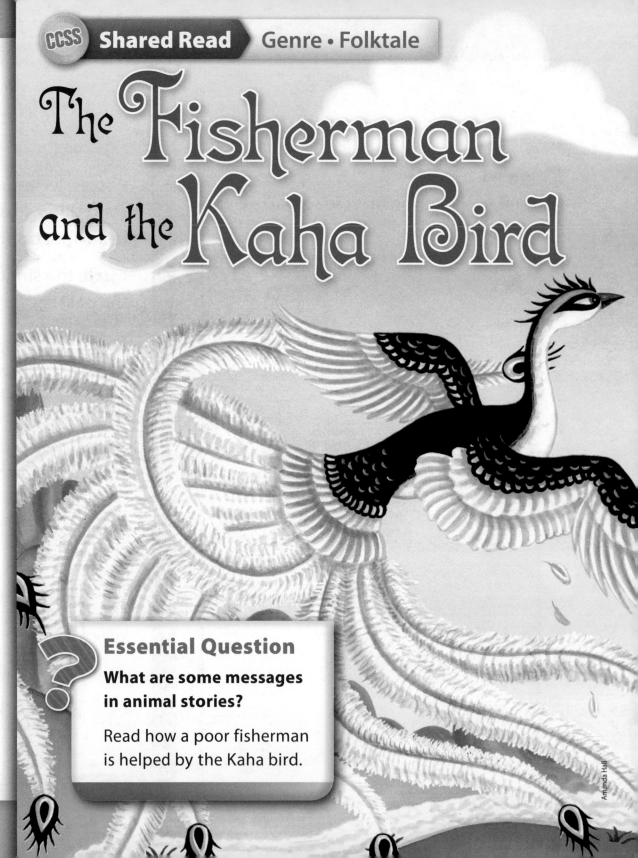

? Essential Question

What are some messages in animal stories?

Read how a poor fisherman is helped by the Kaha bird.

Amanda Hall

Long ago there lived an old fisherman. He made his living catching fish. All day he sat on the riverbank. But he never got more than a few small fish to sell at the market. He and his wife were always hungry.

One morning, the tired old fisherman **trudged** slowly to the river. Suddenly a great bird settled in the tree above him. It had bright, **dazzling** silver feathers. The fisherman was delighted. He knew this was the Kaha, a glittering bird that sometimes helped the poor or the sick.

"You work for little **reward**," the Kaha said. "I wish to help. Every day I will bring you a large fish. You can sell it at the market."

As the days passed, the **honest** Kaha kept her promise. The fisherman sold the fish. He came home with food. He came home with clothing made from silk **fabric** for his wife.

At the market one day, the king's crier made an announcement. "Find the great Kaha for our Shah! Receive a reward of fifty bags of gold!"

Text Evidence

1 Expand Vocabulary

A **reward** is something given in return for work or achievement. **Draw a box** around the word that tells what size *reward* the fisherman worked for.

2 Comprehension
Theme

Reread the third and fourth paragraphs. **Underline** the text that tells how the Kaha will help the fisherman. What does the fisherman do after he sells the fish?

_____

_____

3 Connection of Ideas A C T

Reread the page. **Circle** details that tell about the fisherman's life before the Kaha. How did his life change after he met the Kaha?

_____

_____

85

Text Evidence

❶ Expand Vocabulary

To **betray** someone is to cause them harm. **Draw a box** around the details that tell what made the fisherman *betray* the Kaha.

❷ Comprehension
Theme

Reread the first paragraph. **Underline** why the fisherman wants the gold. What did the fisherman's greed make him forget about the Kaha?

_____

_____

❸ Connection of Ideas Ⓐ Ⓒ Ⓣ

Reread the last paragraph. **Circle** the sentence that tells how the Kaha felt when the fisherman invited her to dinner. Why was the Kaha surprised?

_____

_____

The fisherman thought, "That gold will make me rich! But how can I **betray** the bird?" Finally, his **greed** for gold blinded him to the generosity of the Kaha.

He told the Shah's crier about the Kaha. He **requested** four hundred men to help him catch her.

That evening, four hundred servants followed the fisherman home. They hid among the trees as the fisherman set out a feast. When the Kaha landed in a tree, the fisherman said, "Come dine with me, friend. I wish to express my gratitude, my thanks."

The Kaha was touched by the fisherman's kindness. **Attracted** to the meal, she flew down to join him. Suddenly, the fisherman grabbed the Kaha by the feet. He called to the servants to help. The surprised Kaha spread her wings. She began to fly up with the fisherman. A servant caught the fisherman by the feet. The bird rose higher. A second and third servant grabbed onto the first. Soon four hundred servants hung by one another's feet. The Kaha **soared** upward.

The fisherman looked down. He could barely see the river below. If he hadn't betrayed the Kaha, he would not be in this trouble now. There was but one thing to do. The fisherman let go of the bird's feet. The servants and the fisherman **tumbled** from the sky. They landed in the river.

It was many weeks before the fisherman had healed enough to fish again. Every day he looked in the sky for the beautiful silver bird. But the Kaha was never seen again.

Amanda Hall

Text Evidence

1 Expand Vocabulary

To **tumble** means to fall suddenly. **Circle** the sentence that tells why everyone *tumbled* into the river.

2 Connection of Ideas Ⓐ Ⓒ Ⓣ

Reread the last paragraph. **Underline** the details that show what the fisherman does every day. Think about the story's beginning. Why does he do this?

_____

_____

3 Comprehension
Theme

Reread the last paragraph. **Draw a box** around what happened to the fisherman after he fell into the water. What lesson did the fisherman learn about greed?

_____

_____

Respond to Reading

COLLABORATE

Discuss Work with a partner. Read the questions about "The Fisherman and the Kaha Bird." Use the discussion starters to answer the questions. Write page numbers to show where you found text evidence.

 Questions    Discussion Starters   Text Evidence

	Questions	Discussion Starters	Text Evidence
❶	At the beginning of the story, how does the Kaha help the fisherman?	▶ Each day, the Kaha… ▶ I noticed that the fisherman now had…	Page(s): _____
❷	Why does the fisherman tell the Shah's crier about the Kaha?	▶ The fisherman tells the… ▶ I know this because I read…	Page(s): _____
❸	At the end of the story, what happens to the fisherman after he tricks the Kaha?	▶ After the fisherman tricks… ▶ Every day the fisherman…	Page(s): _____

Mike Moran

Write Review your notes about "The Fisherman and the Kaha Bird." Then write your answer to the question below. Use text evidence to support your answer.

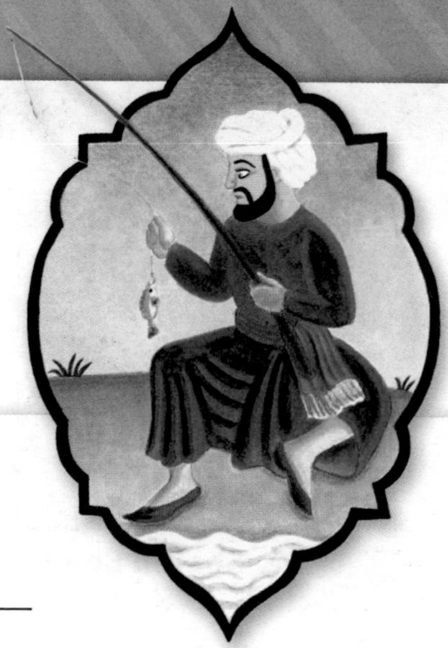

What is the message or lesson in "The Fisherman and the Kaha Bird"?

Amanda Hall

Shared Read

Read an Analysis ▸ Theme Read Mario's paragraph about "The Fisherman and the Kaha Bird." He wrote his opinion about how well the author used the characters' actions to express the theme of the story.

Student Model

Topic Sentence

Circle the topic sentence. What is Mario going to write about?

Evidence

Draw a box around the evidence that Mario includes. What other information from "The Fisherman and the Kaha Bird" would you include?

Concluding Statement

Underline the concluding statement. Why is this sentence a good wrap up?

In "The Fisherman and the Kaha Bird," I think the author does a good job of expressing the theme of the story through the characters' actions. The Kaha helps a poor fisherman by bringing him fish to sell. The fisherman can now buy food. Then the Shah offers gold to anyone who catches the Kaha. The fisherman tricks the Kaha because he wants the gold. The fisherman and the Shah's soldiers grab the Kaha bird's feet. The Kaha flies up high and the fisherman and soldiers fall into the river. The theme is that greed leads to loss. I think the characters' actions helped me to understand the story's theme.

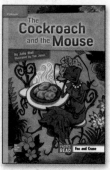

Leveled Reader

_____

_____

_____

_____

_____

_____

_____

_____

_____

_____

_____

_____

_____

_____

Topic Sentence

☐ Include the title of the text you read.

☐ State your opinion about how well the author shows the theme.

Evidence

☐ Include characters' words or actions that help show the theme.

☐ Tell what the theme is.

Concluding Statement

☐ Restate your opinion.

Talk About It

Essential Question

How do animal characters change familiar stories?

 Go Digital!

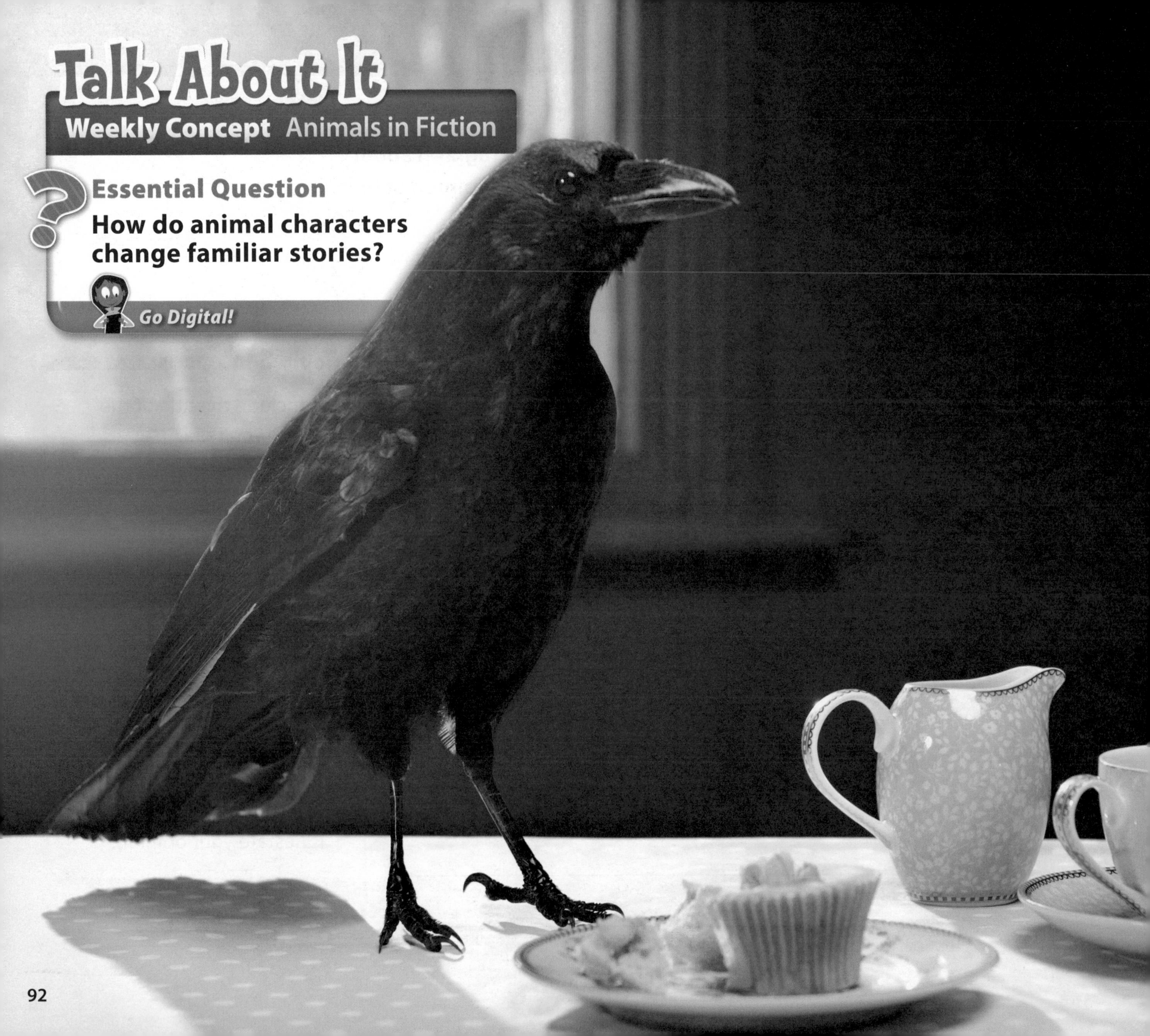

Write words that tell about traits of different animals.

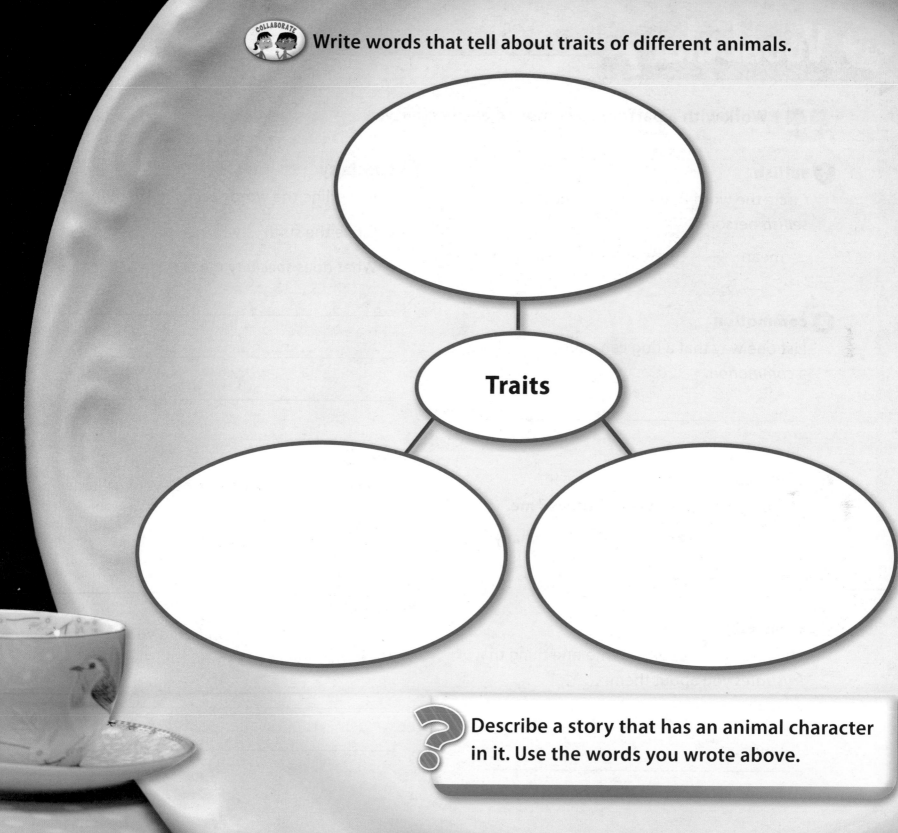

Traits

Describe a story that has an animal character in it. Use the words you wrote above.

CCSS Vocabulary

 Work with a partner to complete each activity.

1 selfish

Circle the word that does not describe a *selfish* person.

mean greedy helpful

2 commotion

List one way that a dog can cause a *commotion*.

_____

3 annoyed

The bug's buzzing really *annoyed* me.

Read the sentence out loud. Show what you do when a buzzing bug *annoys* you.

4 frustrated

Think about rainy days. Write one thing that *frustrates* you about them.

_____

_____

5 specialty

▶ Underline the word *special* in *specialty*.

▶ Circle the suffix, *-ty*.

▶ What does *specialty* mean?

_____

_____

_____

6 attitude

Circle the word that describes your *attitude* when you have no homework to do.

upset cheerful sad

7 familiar

Name a story that is *familiar* to you. Write the title of the story.

_____

_____

94

8 **cranky**

Draw a picture of a happy face. Then draw a *cranky* face.

High-Utility Words

▶ Contractions

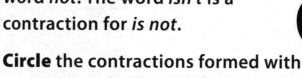

Some contractions are formed with a verb plus the word *not*. The word *isn't* is a contraction for *is not*.

Circle the contractions formed with a verb plus *not* in the passage.

One rainy day, Hare and Turtle had a bike race. Hare knew Turtle (wasn't) fast. He thought Turtle couldn't win. So Hare didn't rush. He stopped often to brush water off his fur. But Turtle kept going. "Rain doesn't bother me, so I don't have to stop!" said Turtle. Hare didn't win the race after all. Turtle won.

My Notes

Read "The Ant and the Grasshopper." Use this page to take notes.

_____

_____

_____

_____

_____

_____

_____

_____

_____

_____

_____

_____

_____

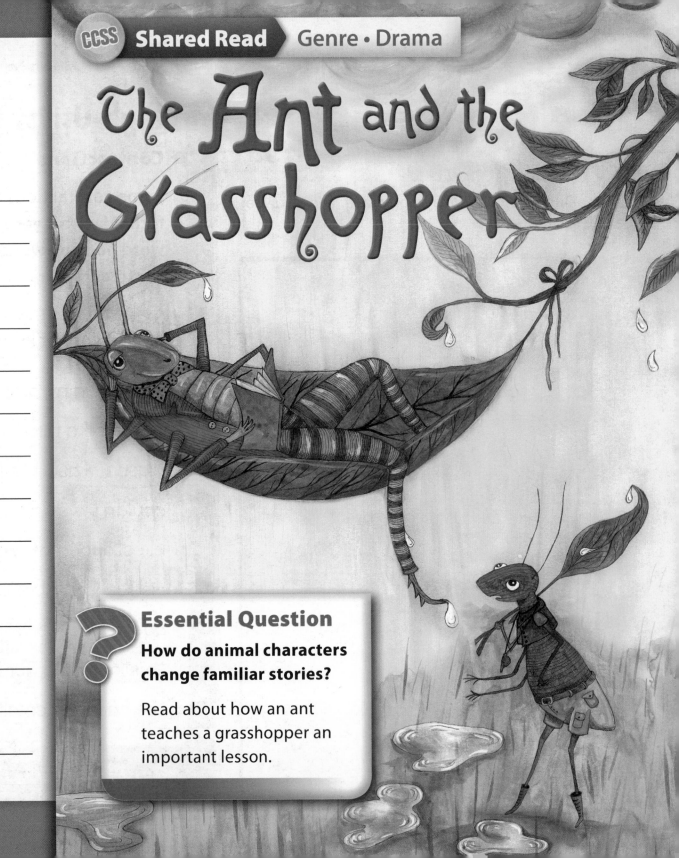

The Ant and the Grasshopper

Essential Question

How do animal characters change familiar stories?

Read about how an ant teaches a grasshopper an important lesson.

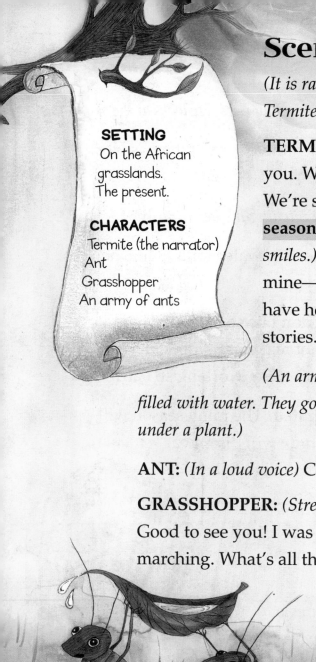

Scene I

(It is raining on the African grasslands. Termite turns and sees the audience.)

SETTING
On the African grasslands.
The present.

CHARACTERS
Termite (the narrator)
Ant
Grasshopper
An army of ants

TERMITE: *(Happily)* Yipes! I didn't see you. Welcome to the plains of Africa! We're soggy now because it's the rainy **season** of the year. Sorry. *(She shrugs and smiles.)* Today, we'll visit two friends of mine—Ant and Grasshopper. Maybe you have heard of them from other **familiar** stories. Let's see what they are up to!

(An army of ants marches in, carrying leaves filled with water. They go up to Grasshopper, who is napping under a plant.)

ANT: *(In a loud voice)* Company, halt! *(The ants stop.)*

GRASSHOPPER: *(Stretching and yawning)* Ant, old pal! Good to see you! I was just napping when I heard you marching. What's all the **commotion**?

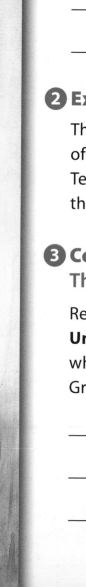

Emily Carew Woodard

Text Evidence

❶ Genre A**C**T

Reread the text under Scene I. **Circle** the details that tell about the setting of the play. Where does the play take place?

_____

_____

❷ Expand Vocabulary

The word **season** means a time of the year. **Draw a box** around Termite's word that names the *season*.

❸ Comprehension
Theme

Reread the Grasshopper's lines. **Underline** the text that tells you what Grasshopper is doing. Is Grasshopper working or resting?

_____

_____

_____

97

Text Evidence

① Comprehension
Theme

Reread the end of Scene I. **Circle** two things that Ant says to Grasshopper about doing work. What kind of worker is Ant?

_____

_____

② Expand Vocabulary

To **toil** means to work hard. **Draw a box** around the word that tells what Grasshopper thinks of *toil*.

③ Comprehension
Theme

Reread the end of Scene I. **Underline** the warning Ant gives Grasshopper. What detail tells you Grasshopper does not believe Ant?

_____

_____

_____

ANT: *(Looking **annoyed**)* Grasshopper, have you seen what falls from the sky?

(Ant points up at a cloud. Grasshopper sleepily rises. He looks at the sky.)

ANT: Rain, Grasshopper! And when there is rain, there is work to be done.

GRASSHOPPER: *(Smiling, then scratching his head)* Huh?

ANT: *(Sighing)* You should be collecting water for a time when we need it.

GRASSHOPPER: *(Laughing)* Oh, don't be so serious! There is lots of water now. Relax! Why not make napping your new **specialty,** instead of all this silly **toil**? Stop working so hard!

ANT: *(Shaking his head. He is **frustrated**)* The rainy season will not last forever. Your carefree **attitude** will disappear with the water. Soon you will be regret being lazy.

(The ants march off. Grasshopper continues to laugh.)

Scene II

(It is a few months later. The plains are now dry, and brown. Grasshopper, looking weak, knocks on Ant's door. Ant opens the door.)

GRASSHOPPER: (*Nervously*) Hi there, pal…. Boy, it's hot! I was wondering … if you had some water. . . for your old friend.

(*Ant tries to close the door. Grasshopper quickly grabs it.*)

GRASSHOPPER: (*Begging wildly*) PLEASE, Ant! I am so thirsty! There isn't a drop of water anywhere!

ANT: (*After a pause*) We ants worked hard to get this water. But we can't let you suffer. (*Gives Grasshopper a sip of water*) Do not think us **selfish**, but we can share only a few drops. I warned you. If you had collected water, you would not be in this difficult **situation**.

(*Grasshopper walks slowly away. Termite watches him.*)

TERMITE: Ant has done a good deed, but tired, **cranky** Grasshopper must still search for water. Grasshopper learned an important lesson. Next time, he will follow Ant's advice!

Emily Carew Woodard

Text Evidence

❶ Genre ⒶⒸⓉ

Reread Grasshopper's dialogue at the top of the page. **Circle** the stage direction that tells how Grasshopper speaks. Why is Grasshopper nervous?

_____

_____

❷ Expand Vocabulary

A **situation** is the way things are at a certain time. How does Ant describe the *situation* Grasshopper is in? **Draw a box** around the word that describes it.

❸ Comprehension
Theme

Reread Termite's dialogue. Think about Scene I. What important lesson did Grasshopper learn in Scene II?

_____

_____

99

Respond to Reading

Discuss Work with a partner. Read the questions about "The Ant and the Grasshopper." Use the discussion starters to answer the questions. Write the page numbers to show where you found text evidence.

? Questions	Discussion Starters	Text Evidence
1 In Scene I, what type of person does Ant act like?	▶ Ant acts like a person who… ▶ I know this because I read…	Page(s): _____
2 In Scene I, what type of person does Grasshopper act like?	▶ Grasshopper's character traits are… ▶ I know this because I read…	Page(s): _____
3 In Scene II, how does Ant treat Grasshopper?	▶ In Scene II, Ant… ▶ I read that Ant does this even though Grasshopper…	Page(s): _____

Write Review your notes about "The Ant and the Grasshopper." Then write your answer to the question below. Use text evidence to support your answer.

How do Ant and Grasshopper act like real people?

_____

_____

_____

_____

_____

_____

_____

_____

_____

_____

Shared Read

Read an Analysis **Genre** Read Jan's paragraph about "The Ant and the Grasshopper." She writes her opinion about how well the author uses the elements of a play to tell a story.

Student Model

Topic Sentence

Circle the topic sentence. What is Jan going to write about?

Evidence

Draw a box around the evidence that Jan includes. What other evidence would you include from "The Ant and the Grasshopper"?

Concluding Statement

Underline the concluding statement. Why is this sentence a good wrap up?

The author of "The Ant and the Grasshopper" does a good job of using the elements of a play to tell a story. The stage directions show how the setting changes and what a hard worker Ant is. The dialogue also shows that Ant was working hard to collect water. Grasshopper's dialogue shows that he thought Ant was silly to work hard. He tells Ant to relax. I think the author does a good job of using dialogue and stage directions to tell the story. At the end of the play, I understood that Grasshopper wished he had collected water instead of being so lazy.

Leveled Reader

Write an Analysis **Genre** Write a paragraph about "Saving the Green Bird." Tell your opinion of how well the author uses the elements of a play to tell a story.

_____

_____

_____

_____

_____

_____

_____

_____

_____

_____

_____

Topic Sentence

☐ Include the title of the play you read.

☐ Give your opinion of how well the author uses the elements of a play.

Evidence

☐ Include the elements that best help to tell the story.

☐ Explain what the dialogue helped you understand.

Concluding Statement

☐ Restate your opinion.

103

Talk About It

? Essential Question

How are all living things connected?

Go Digital!

COLLABORATE

Write words that describe the connections between animals. How do they help each other?

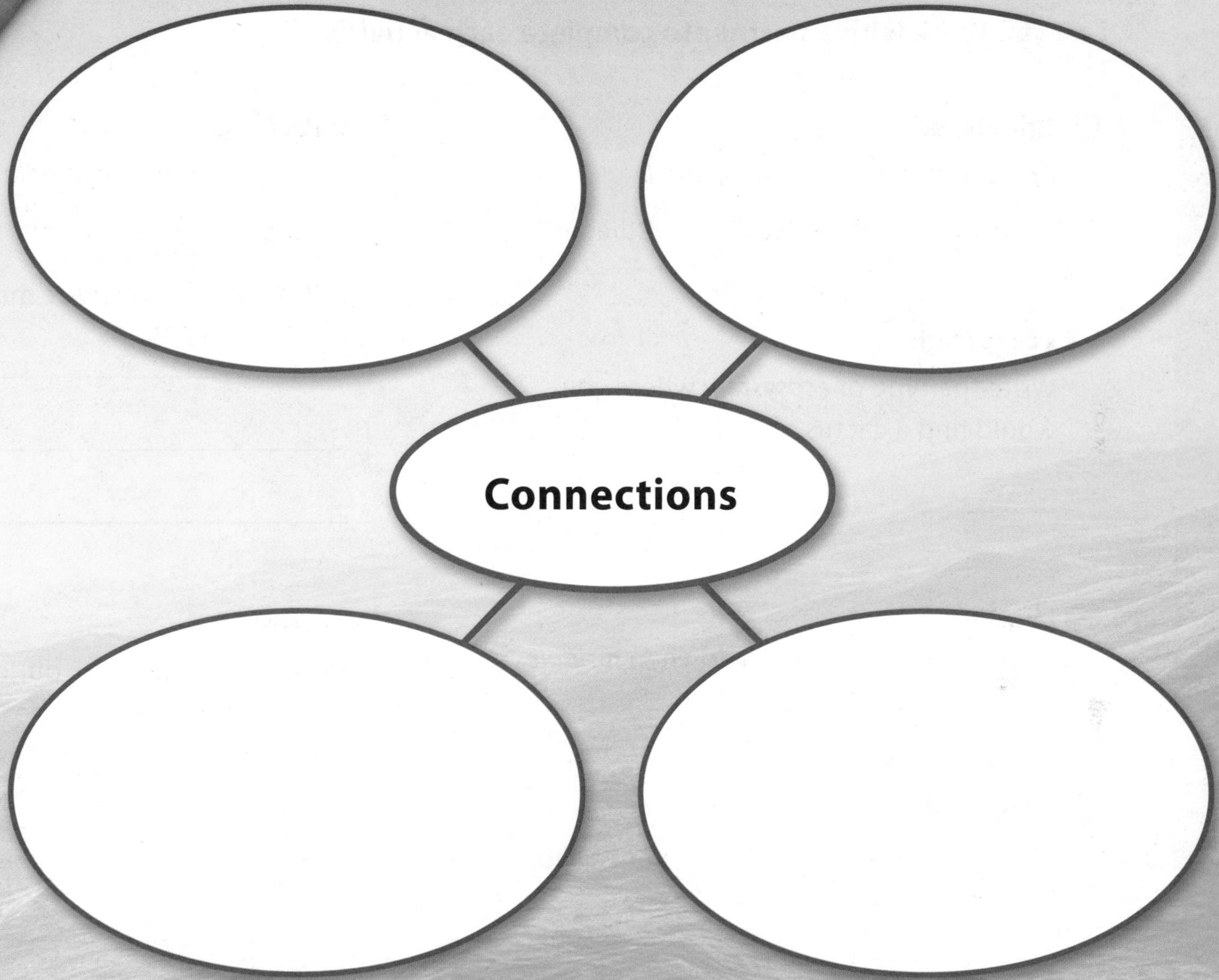

Connections

Tell how two animals help each other. Use words you wrote above.

Vocabulary

 Work with a partner to complete each activity.

1 flourished

Circle an antonym for *flourished*.

    grew   did well   died

2 ecosystem

Write the type of *ecosystem* where you would find a cactus.

_____

3 ripples

Show how tall grass moves when it *ripples*. Use your hands and your body.

4 crumbled

If you *crumbled* a dried leaf in your hand, what did you do?

_____

_____

_____

5 imbalance

▶ Underline the word *balance* in *imbalance*.

▶ Circle the prefix, *im-*.

▶ What does *imbalance* mean?

_____

_____

_____

6 droughts

How does a field look during a *drought*? List three words that describe it.

_____

_____

_____

7 extinct

Circle the animal that is *extinct*.

    dog   dinosaur   cow

8 fragile

Draw a picture of a glass and a rock. Then draw an arrow pointing to the one that is most *fragile*.

High-Utility Words

Suffixes

A suffix is a word part. It is added to the end of a word. It changes a word's meaning. The suffix -*er* changes a word to mean *someone who does something*.

Circle words that end with the suffix -*er* in the passage.

Jane is a scuba diver. She is also an explorer of coral reefs. Tom is a writer and a photographer. Once, Tom joined Jane on a dive to take pictures of sea creatures. A big fish swam by him. "That fish was a fast swimmer!" Tom said. "But this crab is a slow mover. I can get plenty of photos."

My Notes

Read "Rescuing Our Reefs." Use this page to take notes.

CCSS **Shared Read** Genre • Narrative Nonfiction

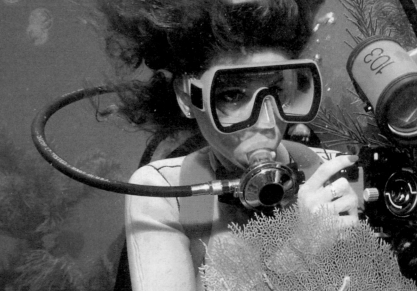

Rescuing Our Reefs

Essential Question

How are all living things connected?

Read how plants and animals are connected in a coral reef ecosystem.

The photographer sits on the side of the boat. She fixes her mask. Then she dives into the waters of the Florida Keys. A colorful coral reef lies below. It is home to sea anemones, **gaudy**, colorful parrotfish, and other animals. This reef has **flourished** and grown.

Parrotfish

Coral Reef Connections

The photographer learned about this reef **ecosystem**. She knows the plants and animals need each other to survive. Reefs are made up of tiny animals called coral polyps. Plant-like algae live inside the coral. The algae use a process called photosynthesis to turn energy from the sun into food. They make food for themselves. They make food for the coral, too. In return, the coral gives the algae a home. It also gives the algae carbon dioxide for photosynthesis. In a food chain, algae are called producers. Producers make their own energy.

The photographer sees a parrotfish. She takes a picture. The parrotfish nibbles the coral. It wants the algae inside. In a food chain, the parrotfish is a consumer. Consumers cannot make their own energy. The parrotfish eats the algae. Energy from the algae is passed along to the fish.

The photographer notices a long silver fish. It is a barracuda. The seagrass **ripples**. It sways back and forth. It almost hides the hungry predator. The photographer snaps a photo. Then she swims on.

(tr) Tim Grollimund; (bkgd) Stephen Frink/Corbis

Text Evidence

1 Expand Vocabulary

Something that is **gaudy** is bright and showy. Read the details about the parrotfish. Look at the photo of it. Why is the parrotfish gaudy?

_____

_____

_____

2 Purpose A C T

Reread the first paragraph. **Circle** who the story is about. What topic does the story give facts and information about?

_____

_____

3 Comprehension
Main Idea and Details

Reread the second paragraph. **Underline** the key details that tell how the algae make food.

Text Evidence

1 **Expand Vocabulary**

To be **bleached** is to be made whiter or lighter in color. **Circle** the sentence that tells what happens to *bleached* coral.

2 **Comprehension**
Main Idea and Details

Reread the second paragraph. **Underline** key details that tell what can happen to coral when there is an imbalance.

3 **Purpose** A C T

Look at the flow chart. **Draw a box** around the sentence that tells about the flow chart. What does the flow chart show?

_____

_____

_____

_____

110

Coral Bleaching

The photographer sees some **bleached** coral. Once colorful, it is now white. It looks like pieces of a **crumbled** castle.

Coral needs a natural balance. Climate change and pollution can cause an **imbalance**. Some areas have dried up from **droughts** while other areas have had more rain. Too much sun and warmer oceans can cause coral bleaching.

Pollution and warm water hurt the relationship between coral and algae. The algae stop making food. Then the coral gets rid of it. The algae give the coral its color, so the coral turns white. Without algae, the coral starves.

Many plants and animals depend on the reef. They need it for food and shelter. As more and more coral reefs die, plants and animals also die. They may become **extinct**. The beautiful reef the photographer saw earlier would change. It would look like the white, crumbling reef that she sees now.

Energy is passed along in a food chain.

Sun gives energy. | Plants use energy to grow. | Animals eat plants. | Animals eat animals.

Rescuing Reefs

The photographer swims back to the boat. She will send her photographs to the Nature Conservancy. It is an organization that saves **fragile** reefs. Scientists there are trying to **rebuild** reefs. They attach pieces of staghorn coral to concrete blocks. The staghorn helps grow new coral. Once the coral grows, the blocks are planted in reefs.

The photographer hopes her pictures will help save reefs. They show the connection between pollution, climate change, and coral bleaching. She breaks through the water's surface. She climbs into the boat.

"I have some good shots!" she says. "They show the healthy reef. They show the sick reef, too!" She begins putting her photos on her laptop.

Text Evidence

❶ Expand Vocabulary

To **rebuild** means to build again, or to fix something that has been damaged. **Draw a box** around the details that tells how scientists try to *rebuild* the reefs.

❷ Comprehension
Main Idea and Details

Reread "Rescuing Reefs." **Circle** three key details in the text that tell how scientists rescue reefs.

❸ Purpose Ⓐ Ⓒ Ⓣ

Reread the last paragraph on page 110. How is it different from the last paragraph on this page?

_____

_____

_____

_____

_____

Respond to Reading

Discuss Work with a partner. Read the questions about "Rescuing Our Reefs." Use the discussion starters to answer the questions. Write page numbers to show where you found text evidence.

?Questions	Discussion Starters	Text Evidence
1 Why do algae in a reef need coral to survive?	▶ Algae in a reef need coral to survive because… ▶ I know this because I read…	Page(s): _____
2 Why do coral and parrotfish in a reef need algae to survive?	▶ Coral needs algae to survive because… ▶ I noticed that parrotfish…	Page(s): _____
3 Why do plants and animals depend on the coral in a reef?	▶ Plants and animals depend on the coral because… ▶ If the coral dies,…	Page(s): _____

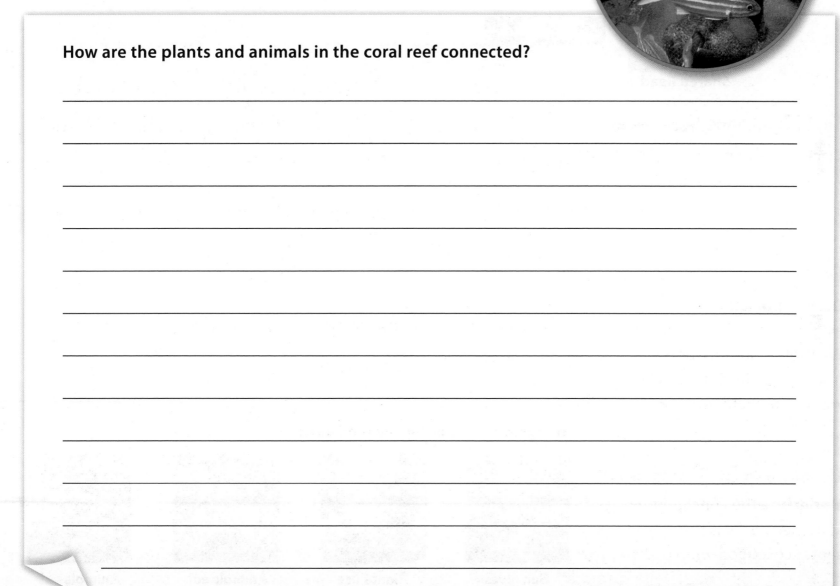

Write Review your notes about "Rescuing Our Reefs." Then write your answer to the question below. Use text evidence to support your answer.

How are the plants and animals in the coral reef connected?

_____

_____

_____

_____

_____

_____

_____

_____

_____

_____

Write About Reading

Shared Read

Read an Analysis **Text Features** Read Cody's paragraph about "Rescuing Our Reefs." He analyzes how the author uses a text feature to give more details about a topic.

Student Model

Topic Sentence

Circle the topic sentence. What is Cody going to write about?

Evidence

Draw a box around the evidence that Cody includes. What other information from "Rescuing Our Reefs" would you include?

Concluding Statement

Underline the concluding statement. Why is this sentence a good wrap up?

In "Rescuing Our Reefs," the author uses a flow chart to give more information about the topic. The text tells about the coral reef ecosystem. It talks about what part algae and fish play in the food chain. The flow chart shows how energy moves from the sun to plants to the animals that eat them. The flow chart helped me to understand how a coral reef works because it helped me to see how a food chain works.

Energy is passed along in a food chain.

| Sun gives energy. | Plants use energy to grow. | Animals eat plants. | Animals eat animals. |

(bl) Dan Sherwood/Design Pics; (bcl, bkgd) Darryl Leniuk/Radius Images/Corbis; (bcr) Stephen Frink/Corbis; (br) Richard Carey/Alamy

114

Leveled Reader

Write an Analysis **Text Features** Write a paragraph about "Saving San Francisco Bay." Analyze how the author uses a text feature to give more information about the topic. Include evidence from the text.

_____

_____

_____

_____

_____

_____

_____

_____

_____

_____

Topic Sentence

☐ Include the title of the text you read.

☐ Include the text feature you want to write about.

Evidence

☐ Explain what part of the text the feature goes with.

☐ Explain how the text feature gives more information.

Concluding Statement

☐ Restate how the author's use of a text feature gives more information about the topic.

Talk About It

Weekly Concept Adaptations

Essential Question

What helps an animal survive?

Go Digital!

116

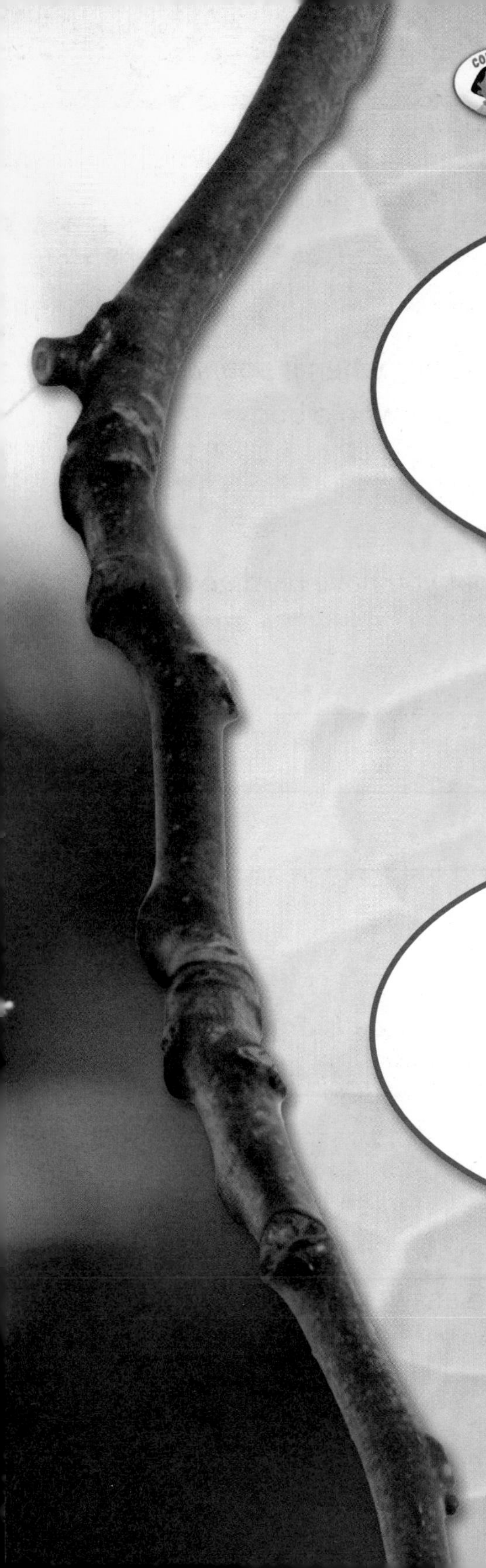

Write words that describe the adaptations that help animals and insects to survive.

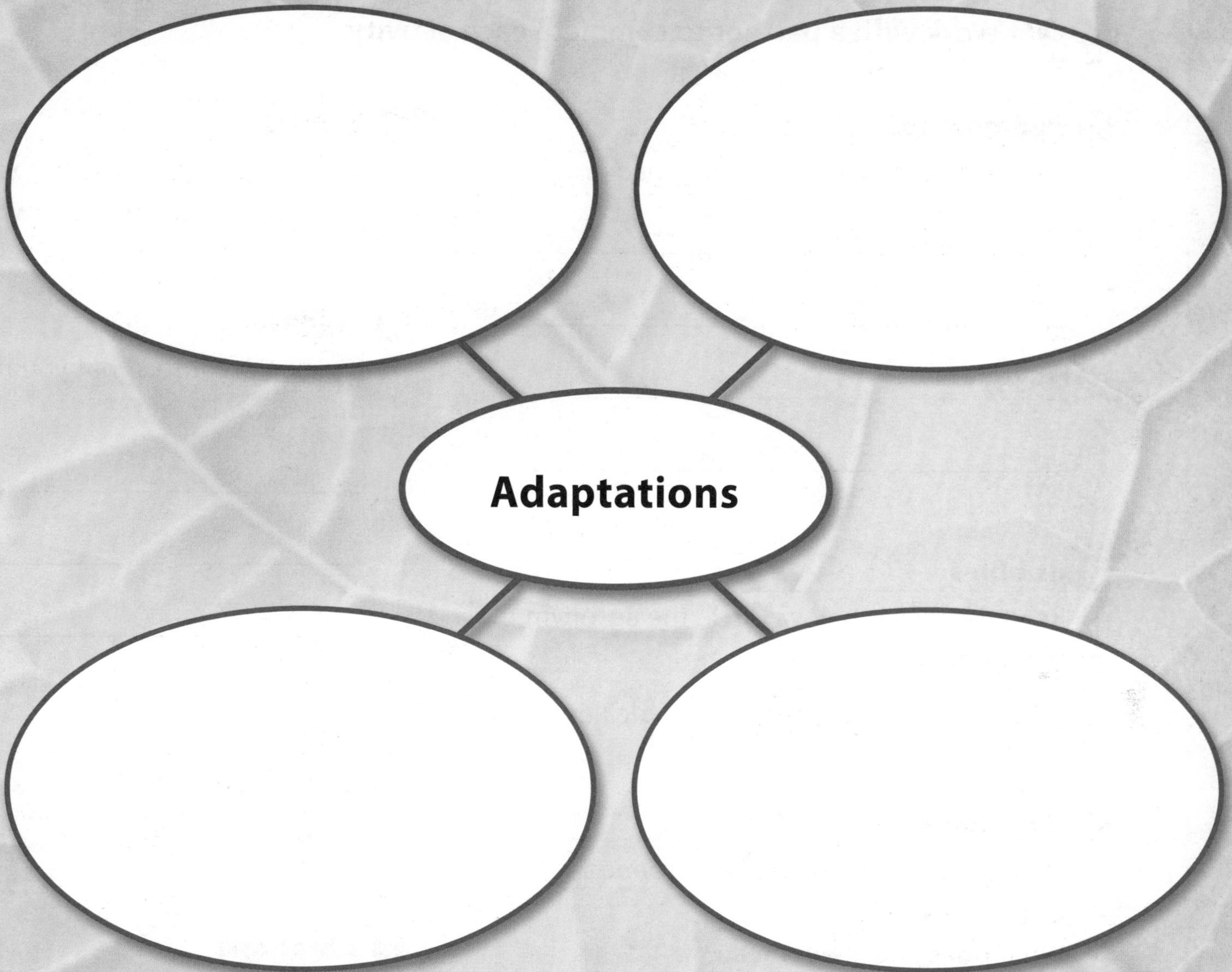

Adaptations

Tell about an animal and its adaptations. Use the words you wrote above.

Vocabulary

 Work with a partner to complete each activity.

1 camouflaged

Why is it hard to see a *camouflaged* insect?

_____

_____

_____

2 dribbles

Read the words below. Circle the antonym for *dribbles*.

drips   gushes   trickles

3 poisonous

Underline the root word in *poisonous*.
Circle the suffix, *-ous*.
What does *poisonous* mean?

_____

_____

_____

4 pounce

Show what a cat looks like when it *pounces* on a toy mouse. Use your whole body.

5 predator

List two *predators* that you have read about or seen on TV.

_____

_____

_____

6 prey

Which of these might be a cat's *prey*?

tree   bird   rock

7 vibrations

Which of these things would cause the most *vibrations*? Circle the answer.

closing your eyes   beating on a drum

8 **extraordinary**

Imagine an *extraordinary* animal. Think about how it looks. Now draw a picture of this *extraordinary* animal.

High-Utility Words

▶ **Homophones**

Homophones are words that sound the same but are spelled differently. They also have different meanings.

Circle the homophones in the passage.

Butterflies from everywhere live in the butterfly house. It is like (their) natural habitat (there.) I studied one I'd read about that had red wings. When it closed its wings, it looked like a leaf. Then a new butterfly arrived on the scene. I'd seen it in a book and knew it was a swallowtail.

Read "Animal Adaptations."
Use this page to take notes.

_____

_____

_____

_____

_____

_____

_____

_____

_____

_____

_____

_____

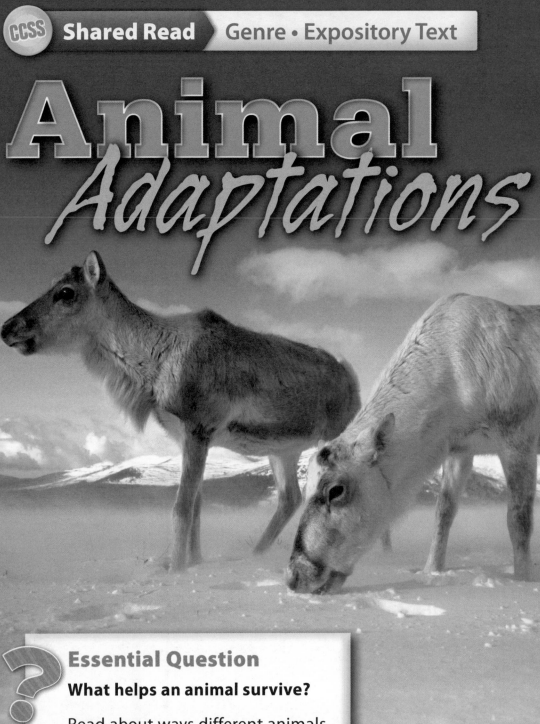

Animal Adaptations

Essential Question

What helps an animal survive?

Read about ways different animals adapt to their environments.

What would you do if you saw a skunk lift its tail? Hopefully, you would run! Skunks have protection. They can blast a **predator** with a stinky spray from under their tails.

A skunk's smelly spray can travel up to 10 feet.

Animals have special ways to survive called adaptations. Adaptations can be physical ones such as the skunk's spray. Some animals have bright colors. The colors warn predators that they are **poisonous**. Some animals can sense **vibrations** in the ground. Others can hear sounds from far away. Adaptations can also affect behavior. Birds fly south every winter. They do this to avoid **harsh**, severe temperatures.

Staying Warm

Imagine living in the Arctic tundra. The usual temperature is an **extraordinary** 10 to 20° F. This is the home of the caribou. To stay warm, caribou have two layers of fur. Under the fur is a layer of fat. Caribou have compact bodies. Only 5 feet long, caribou can weigh over 500 pounds.

The caribou's nose and mouth is covered in short hair. This hair warms the air before it goes into their lungs. It keeps them warm as they push snow aside to find food.

(bkgd) blickwinkel/Alamy; (r) Comstock/PunchStock

Text Evidence

1 Expand Vocabulary

A **harsh** temperature is one that is extremely hot or extremely cold. **Underline** the text that tells you how birds avoid *harsh* temperatures.

2 Comprehension
Main Idea and Key Details

Reread the section, "Staying Warm." **Circle** key details that tell why caribou are able to stay warm.

3 Sentence Structure A C T

Reread the last paragraph. In the last sentence, what word does the pronoun *it* stand for? **Draw a box** around the word. What do the words *them* and *they* stand for?

_____

_____

_____

_____

121

Text Evidence

① Expand Vocabulary

When things **decline**, they become less. **Underline** the sentence that tells what caribou do when their food sources *decline*.

② Sentence Structure (A)(C)(T)

Reread the last sentence of the first paragraph. **Draw a box** around the part of the sentence that tells when it is time for the caribou to return up north. What word in the sentence signals time?

③ Comprehension
Main Idea and Key Details

Reread "Insects in Disguise." **Circle** key details that tell you about phasmids' adaptations or special features.

Finding Food

Every day, a caribou eats over six pounds of lichen! Caribou have unusual stomachs. They are designed to digest lichen. Lichen is one of the few foods they can find in winter. But even caribou have a tough time in the coldest part of winter. Their food sources **decline**. They have to leave the tundra and go to large forest areas. Food is easier to find there. When the melting snow **dribbles** into streams, they can return up north.

Lichen grows in cold temperatures.

Insects in Disguise

Look closely at the picture of the tree branch. Can you spot the insect? It is a phasmid. Some phasmids are also called leaf insects or walking sticks. They look like leaves or twigs. These insects can change colors. They blend in with their surroundings so they are **camouflaged** from predators. They disappear! Phasmids are active at night. This helps them avoid predators, too. They are hard to spot in daylight. They are even harder to spot at night.

This phasmid is called a walking stick. It looks like a stick with legs.

(t) Global Warming Images/Alamy; (bl) James H. Robinson/Oxford Scientific/Getty Images Egmont Strigl/Imagebroker/SuperStock; (r) Pete Oxford/Minden Pictures

An alligator's log-shaped body is an adaptation. It's hard to spot an alligator in the water.

Water, Please!

In the Florida Everglades, the dry season is **brutal** for many plants and animals. Alligators have a way to survive the harsh dry season. They use their feet and snouts to clear dirt from the holes in bedrock. The holes can then hold water. So when the ground dries up, the alligators drink from their water holes.

Other species use these water holes, too. Plants grow there. Other animals find water there. Animals that visit the alligator holes are easy **prey**. The alligator may **pounce** on them without warning. But alligators only eat a few times each month. So, the animals take their chances. They visit the alligator holes when they need water. In the end, it's all about survival!

Text Evidence

❶ Expand Vocabulary

To be **brutal** is to be severe or very unpleasant. **Draw a box** around the animal that can survive this *brutal* dry season.

❷ Sentence Structure Ⓐ Ⓒ Ⓣ

Reread the last sentence on the page. **Circle** the phrase that tells the reader that this is the end of the article.

❸ Comprehension
Main Idea and Key Details

Reread the last paragraph. **Underline** the sentences that tell why it is dangerous for the animals to visit the water holes. Why do animals go to the water holes, anyway?

_____

_____

_____

_____

Respond to Reading

 Discuss Work with a partner. Read the questions about "Animal Adaptations." Use the discussion starters to answer the questions. Write page numbers to show where you found text evidence.

?Questions	Discussion Starters	Text Evidence
1 How do caribou stay warm in the Arctic tundra?	▶ Caribou stay warm because… ▶ I also read that…	Page(s): _____
2 How does having an unusual stomach help the caribou survive ?	▶ A caribou's stomach… ▶ I also read that lichen…	Page(s): _____
3 Where do caribou go in the winter?	▶ Caribou go… ▶ I noticed that…	Page(s): _____

Mike Moran

Write Review your notes about "Animal Adaptations." Then write your answer to the question below. Use text evidence to support your answer.

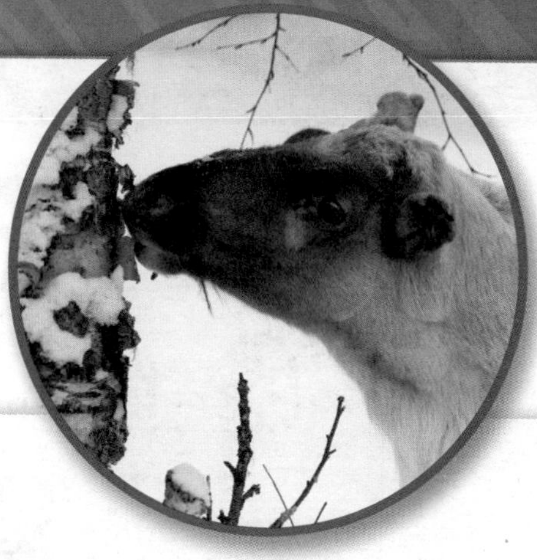

How do adaptations help caribou survive in the Arctic tundra?

Global Warming Images/Alamy

Write About Reading

Shared Read

Read an Analysis ▶ **Photographs and Captions** Read Tandi's paragraph about "Animal Adaptations." She writes her opinion about how well the author uses photographs and captions.

Student Model

Topic Sentence

Circle the topic sentence. What is Tandi going to write about?

Evidence

Draw a box around the evidence that Tandi includes. What other information from "Animal Adaptations" would you include?

Concluding Statement

Underline the concluding statement. Why is this sentence a good wrap up?

In "Animal Adaptations," I think the author did a good job using photographs and captions. The text tells about how skunks protect themselves with a bad smelling spray. The photograph shows a skunk with its tail up. It looks like the skunk will spray. The caption says that a skunk's spray can go as far as 10 feet. The photograph and caption gave me more information about the skunk. I liked the fact that this detail is not in the text.

Leveled Reader

Text Features Write a paragraph about "Extreme Animals." Tell your opinion about how well the author uses photographs and captions.

_____

_____

_____

_____

_____

_____

_____

_____

_____

_____

_____

Topic Sentence

☐ Include the title of the text you read.

☐ Give an opinion about how well the author uses photographs and captions.

Evidence

☐ Give an example of a photograph and caption.

☐ Make sure your example supports your opinion.

☐ Explain how the photograph and caption help you understand the text.

Concluding Statement

☐ Restate your opinion.

Talk About It

Essential Question

How are writers inspired by animals?

Go Digital!

128

Think of different kinds of animals. Write words that describe their characteristics.

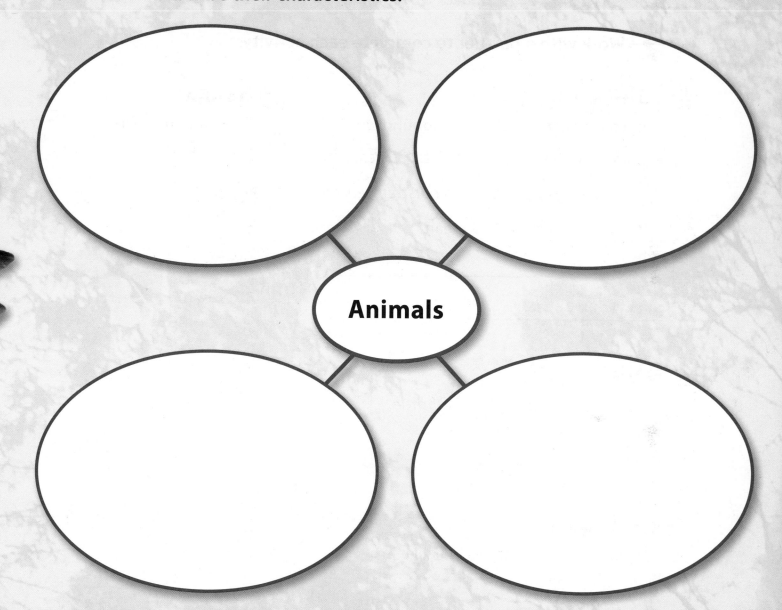

Animals

 Describe an animal that you would like to write about. Use the words that you wrote above.

Work with a partner to complete each activity.

1 outstretched

The word *outstretched* is a compound word.

▶ Underline the word *out* in *outstretched*.

▶ Circle the word *stretched* in *outstretched*.

▶ What does *outstretched* mean?

_____

_____

2 brittle

Read the antonyms below for *brittle*.
Add another antonym to the list.

brittle: solid, tough, _____

3 descriptive

Describe what your shoes look like in a
descriptive way.

_____

_____

_____

4 creative

Draw a T-shirt. Then draw a *creative* design
on the shirt.

Read the descriptive poem. With a partner, complete each activity.

RAINBOW CROW

The crow is a kite, black and dark.

She glides above us in the park.

And when she sings, her loud caw

is like the rasp of a rusty saw.

Look closely at her shining back,

A rainbow glistens in the black.

SUNDAY AFTERNOON

The cats are sleeping.

Two glossy, furry puddles

In a sunlit patch.

5 simile

A simile compares two things using *like* or *as*. **Circle** a simile in "Rainbow Crow."

6 rhyme

Two words *rhyme* when they sound the same. **Draw a box** around two rhyming words in "Rainbow Crow."

7 meter

A poem's *meter* is the pattern of stressed and unstressed syllables in each line. How does the meter affect the rhythm of "Rainbow Crow?"

_____

_____

8 metaphor

"The crow is a kite" is a *metaphor* because it compares two unlike things. **Underline** a metaphor in "Sunday Afternoon."

My Notes

Read the poems. Use this page to take notes.

Dog

A brown boomerang,
my dog flies off, arcs his way
back into my arms.

— Jeffrey Boyle

? Essential Question

How are writers inspired by animals?

Read how poets use creative thinking to write about animals.

THE EAGLE

He clasps the crag with crooked hands;
Close to the sun in lonely lands,
Ring'd with the azure world, he stands.

The wrinkled sea beneath him crawls;
He watches from his mountain walls,
And like a thunderbolt he falls.

— Alfred, Lord Tennyson

Alessandra Cimatoribus

Text Evidence

1 Literary Elements
Metaphor

Reread "Dog." **Circle** the object that the dog is being compared to in the poem.

2 Genre A C T

Reread "Dog." **Underline** the line that has seven syllables.

3 Comprehension
Point of View

Reread the first stanza of "The Eagle." **Draw a box around** the pronouns. Does the poem have a first-person narrator or a third-person narrator?

_____

4 Literary Elements
Simile

Reread the last stanza. What is the eagle is being compared to?

_____

Text Evidence

1 Literary Elements
Rhyme

Reread the poem. **Draw a box** around each of the words that rhyme in the first stanza.

2 Comprehension
Point of View

Circle the pronouns in the first stanza. Who is the speaker in this poem?

_____

_____

3 Genre ACT

Reread the last stanza. **Underline** the details that tell how the speaker eats the bugs. Is the poet being serious or funny? Explain.

_____

_____

_____

CHIMPANZEE

From branch to branch on outstretched arms,
From tree to ground I leap.
When I want to eat a snack,
I stick a stick in termite heaps.

I use my teeth to rip off leaves
And make the branch all bare,
Then find the hole the bugs come out
And patiently wait there.

My skinny branch becomes a bridge,
As brittle bugs climb up the stick.
I pick them off one by one
And crunch them like potato chips!

— Ellen Lee

Rat

Teeth like jackhammers,
I chew through concrete for fun,
bring the outdoors in!

— Rosa Sandoval

Alessandra Cimatoribus

Text Evidence

1 Literary Elements
Simile

Reread the poem. **Circle** the simile. What two unlike things are being compared?

_____

_____

2 Genre A C T

What picture does the poet create with this haiku?

_____

_____

3 Comprehension
Point of View

Underline the pronoun that lets you know that the rat is the speaker in the poem. Why does the rat chew through concrete?

_____

_____

135

Respond to Reading

 **Discuss** Work with a partner. Discuss the questions below about the poem "Rat." Reread to find the answers. Write page numbers to show where you found text evidence.

? Questions | **Discussion Starters** | **Text Evidence**

1 In "Rat" what object does the poet compare the rat's teeth to?	▶ The rat's teeth are compared to… ▶ I know this because I read...	Page(s): _____
2 In the poem "Rat" who is the speaker?	▶ In "Rat," the speaker is… ▶ I noticed that...	Page(s): _____
3 Why does the rat chew through concrete?	▶ The rat chews through concrete because… ▶ The rat wants to bring… ▶ I know this because I read....	Page(s): _____

Write Review your notes about the poem "Rat." Then write your answer to the question below. Use text evidence to support your answer.

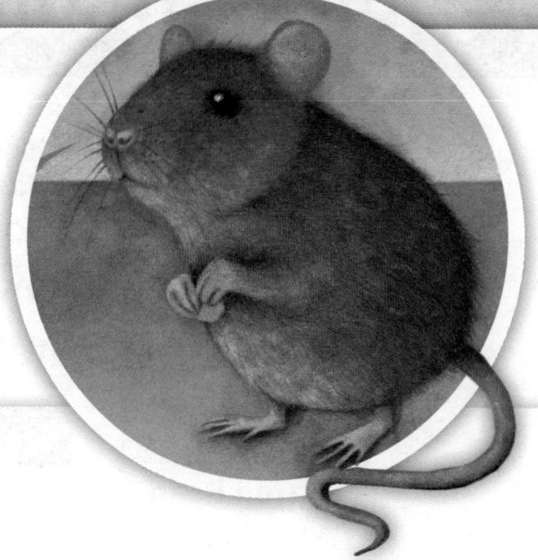

How does the poet show us what a rat is like?

Alessandra Cimatoribus

Shared Read

Read an Analysis **Precise Language** Zora wrote about the poems "The Eagle" and "Dog." She analyzed how the author used precise language in the poems to describe the animals.

Student Model

Topic Sentence

Circle the topic sentence. What is Zora going to write about?

Evidence

Draw a box around the evidence that Zora includes. What other information from the poems would you include?

Concluding Statement

Underline the concluding statement. Why is this sentence a good wrap up?

In the poems "The Eagle," and "Dog" the authors use precise language to create a picture in the reader's mind. In "The Eagle," the author uses the verb "clasps." This word describes how the eagle grabs onto the edge of the cliff. It helped me to picture the Eagle's strong claws holding onto the cliff. In "Dog," the author uses the verb "arcs." This word tells how the dog jumps into its owner's arms. The word also made me think about the arc of a boomerang. These examples show how the authors used precise language to create detailed pictures in the reader's mind.

Leveled Reader

Write an Analysis   **Precise Language**   Write a paragraph about "Putting on an Act." Analyze the author's use of precise language.

_____

_____

_____

_____

_____

_____

_____

_____

_____

_____

_____

Topic Sentence

☐ Include the title of the text you read.

☐ Tell whether the author uses precise language.

Evidence

☐ Describe examples of precise language.

☐ Explain how the precise language helps to create a picture in the reader's mind.

☐ Support your ideas with details.

Concluding Statement

☐ Restate how the author uses precise language.

UNIT 3

THAT'S THE Spirit!

140

THE Big Idea

How can you show your community spirit?

Talk About It

Essential Question
How can you make new friends feel welcome?

Go Digital!

142

Write words that describe how you can help somebody feel welcome.

Welcome

 Describe how you would help a new student at your school. Use the words you wrote above.

CCSS Vocabulary

 Work with a partner to complete each activity.

1 acquaintance

Show how you would greet an *acquaintance*. Now show how you would greet your best friend.

2 cautiously

When do you walk *cautiously*?

_____

_____

3 logical

Give your partner *logical* directions from your classroom to the gym.

_____

_____

4 scrounging

Pretend you are *scrounging* for a pencil in your desk.

5 trustworthy

Read the antonyms below for *trustworthy*. Add another antonym to the list.
trustworthy: unreliable, irresponsible,

_____

6 scornfully

▶ Underline the base word *scorn* in *scornfully*.

▶ Draw a circle round the suffix *-ful*.

▶ Draw a box around the suffix *-ly*.

▶ What does *scornfully* mean?

_____

_____

7 complementary

How are shoes and socks *complementary*?

_____

_____

_____

144

8 **jumble**

Draw a picture that shows a *jumble* of shoes and boots.

High-Utility Words

▶ **Adverbs**

Adverbs that end with -*ly* can tell *how* or *when* something is done.

Circle adverbs with -*ly* in the passage.

Frank (recently) moved to a new town. He swiftly unpacked. Then he immediately went for a walk in the park. "Welcome to our town," a voice said cheerfully.

A tiny chipmunk quickly hopped onto Frank's shoulder. "I hope you'll like it here," the chipmunk said. Frank laughed loudly at the unusual welcome.

My Notes

Read "At the Library." Use this page to take notes.

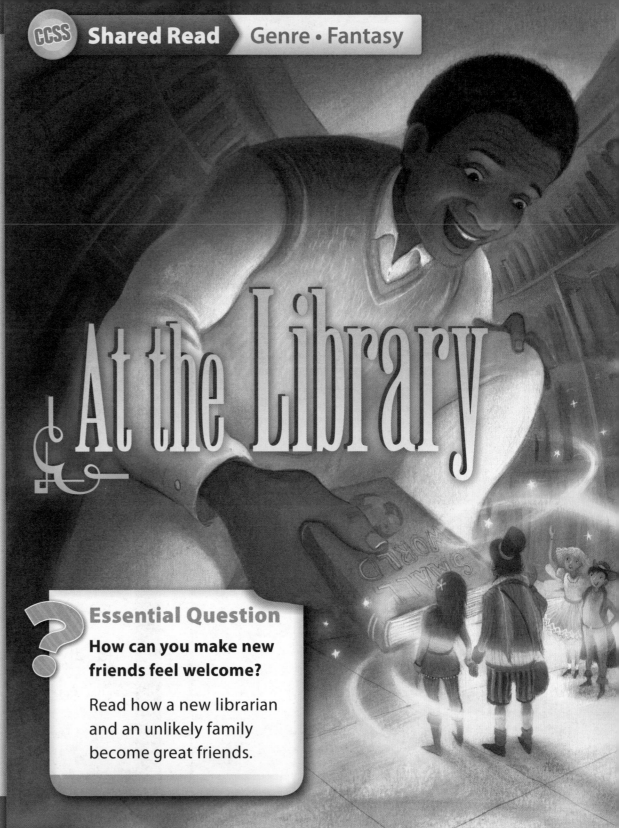

At the Library

? Essential Question

How can you make new friends feel welcome?

Read how a new librarian and an unlikely family become great friends.

Rick Dodson admired the pink and orange sky as he locked the library door. The sun began its **descent** behind the mountains as Rick walked towards his office. Seeing a **jumble** of books on a table, he sighed. He began to gather them up.

"Not tonight," he said and put the books back on the table.

The librarian never left books out, but today was his birthday. That meant a walk to the Cupcake Café for a birthday treat.

That evening, Rick sat in his book-filled living room, thinking about his old friends. They had called to say happy birthday. If only this job had not required him to move halfway across the country … After six months, he had made an **acquaintance** or two, but no real friends.

"Books are my friends," he thought, which reminded him of the jumble of books. "I might as well go back tonight and shelve them."

He entered the library and turned on the lights. A book, *Small World*, was face-down on the floor. "What's going on?" he muttered. He **cautiously** lifted it up. "Ahhh!" he yelled and dropped the book.

Four tiny figures scrambled about as the book hit the floor.

"Mr. Dodson," exclaimed a breathless voice, "we are enchanted to meet you."

"What … who …" Rick stammered.

Text Evidence

❶ Expand Vocabulary

When something makes a **descent**, it moves from a higher place to a lower place. **Circle** the details that tell where the sun began its *descent*. Is the sun setting or rising?

_____

❷ Comprehension
Point of View

Reread the first paragraph. **Underline** the pronouns. What is the narrator's point of view in this story?

_____

❸ Sentence Structure Ⓐ Ⓒ Ⓣ

Reread the fourth paragraph. **Draw a box** around the sentence with ellipses. What words could you use to finish this sentence?

_____

_____

147

Text Evidence

1 Sentence Structure Ⓐ Ⓒ Ⓣ

Reread the fourth paragraph.
Underline the text in quotation
marks. Who is speaking?

_____

2 Expand Vocabulary

A **rodent** is a small mammal that
chews with its front teeth. **Draw
a box** around the kind of *rodents*
Harry meets on his nightly patrol.

3 Comprehension
Point of View

Reread the last two paragraphs.
Circle the details of what Rick is
thinking about. How do we know
what he is thinking?

_____

_____

_____

"We're the Bookers! I'm William. This is Emily. These are our
children, Harry and Clementine. By the way, happy birthday!"

"You know it's my birthday?"

"It's only **logical** that we'd want to learn about the new
librarian. So naturally, we read your file."

"You were **scrounging** through my files?" Rick collapsed
into a nearby chair.

The Bookers began climbing up the table.
"We're absolutely **trustworthy**," Emily assured him.

"Haven't you heard of Bookers?" William asked.
"Every library has Bookers!"

"We ensure everything runs smoothly,"
said Emily. "Seen any mice around?"

Rick slowly shook his head.

"I do nightly **rodent** patrols," Harry said.
"Those nasty mice run at the sight of me,"
he added **scornfully**.

"Do your chairs ever squeak?" inquired Clementine.
"No! That's because we oil them!"

Rick thought about the past six months. He hadn't
seen one mouse, his chairs never squeaked, and
his pencils were never dull.

"The pencils?" he asked.

"We sharpen them nightly," William replied.

"But why?" asked Rick.

"Look around!" exclaimed William. "We work and read. Bookers and libraries are **complementary**. We belong together."

"Mr. Dodson," said Emily, "we would like to be friends."

Rick grinned. "Call me Rick. And I'd love to be friends."

Rick made other friends, but he spent many nights with the Bookers. He got a toy car for Harry's rodent patrol. He read books to Clementine. And every birthday, he shared cupcakes with his friends.

Richard Johnson

1 Comprehension
Point of View

Reread the page. **Circle** the details that tell how Rick responds when Emily says they want to be friends.

2 Sentence Structure A C T

Reread the last sentence. **Draw a box** around what Rick does on his birthday. What word in the sentence tells you this happens each year?

_____

3 Comprehension
Point of View

Reread the page. Think about the story. How has Rick's life changed from the beginning of the story?

_____

_____

_____

149

Discuss Work with a partner. Read the questions about "At the Library." Use the discussion starters to answer the questions. Write the page numbers where you found text evidence.

? Questions	Discussion Starters	Text Evidence
1 How did Rick meet the Bookers?	▶ Rick first saw the Bookers when … ▶ I noticed that the Bookers said …	Page(s): _____
2 What do the Bookers tell Rick that they do at the library?	▶ The Bookers tell Rick … ▶ The Bookers also explained …	Page(s): _____
3 What did Emily say to Rick that made him grin?	▶ Emily told Rick that … ▶ I know this made Rick happy because he said…	Page(s): _____

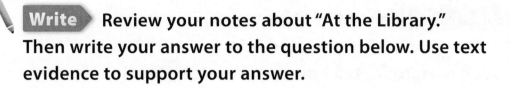

Write Review your notes about "At the Library."
Then write your answer to the question below. Use text
evidence to support your answer.

How did the Bookers make Rick Dodson feel welcome?

_____

_____

_____

_____

_____

_____

_____

_____

_____

_____

_____

Richard Johnson

Shared Read

Read an Analysis ▸ **Point of View** Read Erin's paragraph about "At the Library." She analyzed how the author used a third-person narrator to tell how the characters feel in the story.

Student Model

Topic Sentence

Circle the topic sentence. What is Erin going to write about?

Evidence

Draw a box around the evidence that Erin includes. What other information from "At the Library" would you include?

Concluding Statement

Underline the concluding statement. Why is this sentence a good wrap up?

In "At the Library," the author uses a third-person narrator to tell the story. From the narrator, I learn that Rick is a librarian. He moved across the country six months ago. It is Rick's birthday. Rick's friends all call to wish him a happy birthday. I can tell Rick misses his old friends because he feels he has made no new friends. That night at the library, Rick meets four tiny people, the Bookers. They live in the library. Rick grins when the Bookers ask to be his friends. I learn how Rick feels about these events through the author's use of a third-person narrator.

Leveled Reader

Write an Analysis **Point of View** Write a paragraph about "A New Bear in the Forest." Analyze how the author uses a first-person narrator to tell about the characters and events in the story.

_____

_____

_____

_____

_____

_____

_____

_____

_____

_____

_____

Topic Sentence

☐ Include the title of the text you read.

☐ Explain how the author used a first-person narrator to tell about the characters and events.

Evidence

☐ Describe the details you learned from the first-person narrator.

Concluding Statement

☐ Restate how the author's use of a first-person narrator helped you understand the characters and events.

153

Talk About It

Essential Question

In what ways can you help your community?

Go Digital!

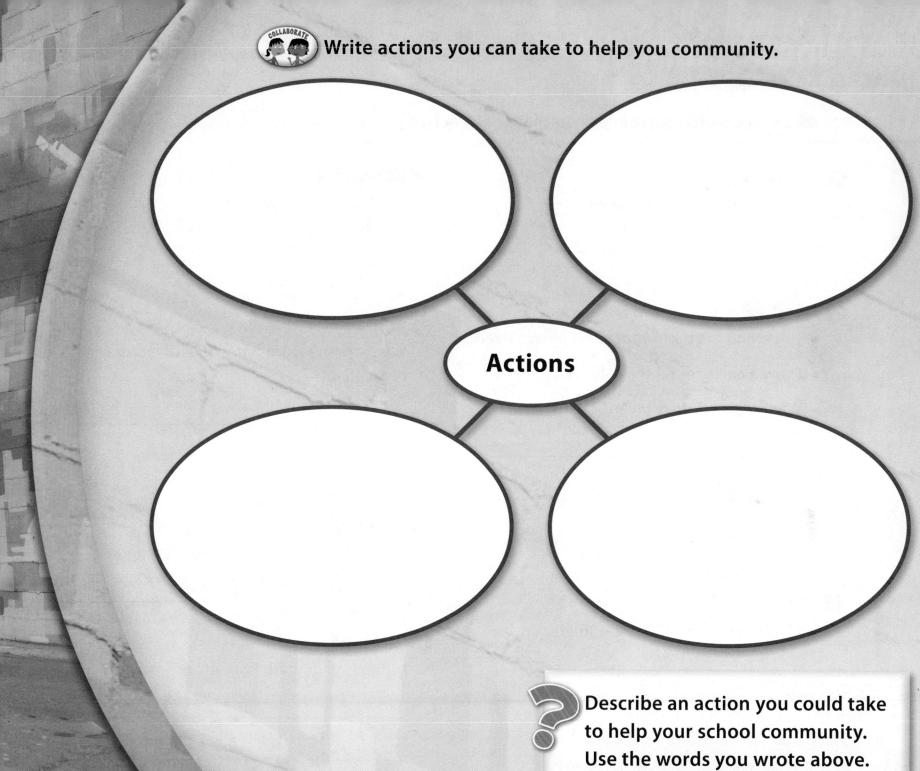

Write actions you can take to help you community.

Actions

Describe an action you could take
to help your school community.
Use the words you wrote above.

Blend Images/Alamy

155

 Work with a partner to complete each activity.

1 residents

Who is a *resident* in your home?

_____

2 selective

▶ Underline the base word *select* in *selective*.

▶ Draw a circle round the suffix *-ive*.

▶ What does *selective* mean?

_____

_____

_____

3 organizations

Describe what kind of *organization* you want to raise money for.

_____

_____

_____

4 generosity

Read the words below. Circle the synonym for *generosity*.

greediness   selfishness   kindness

5 mature

What are the words *childish* and *mature* an example of?

_____

_____

6 gingerly

Pretend that you are *gingerly* petting a friend's cat. Use your face to show expression.

7 assigned

When is your math homework *assigned*?

_____

_____

8 scattered

Draw a picture of leaves *scattered* on the grass.

High-Utility Words

▶ **Linking Words**

Linking words link the main part of a sentence to another group of words.

Circle the linking words in the passage.

Maggie got busy (when) the food bank asked for help. She collected food in her neighborhood. She started there because her neighbors wanted to help. Then she set up a donation box at school after she asked her teacher for permission. The box filled quickly since the students liked to help. Maggie kept collecting until the food bank had enough.

Read "Remembering Hurricane Katrina." Use this page to take notes.

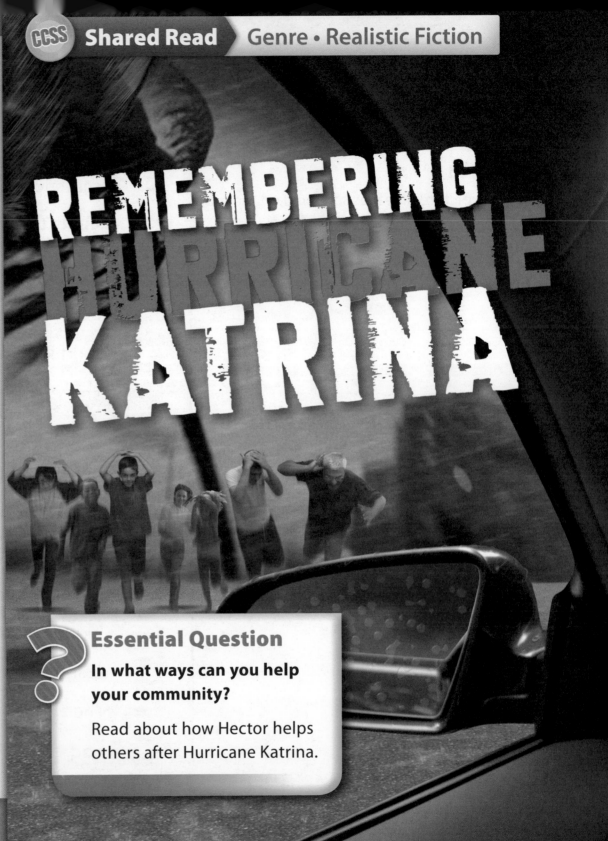

REMEMBERING HURRICANE KATRINA

Essential Question

In what ways can you help your community?

Read about how Hector helps others after Hurricane Katrina.

Leaning over my steering wheel, I watched the heavy clouds roll in. The sky became dark gray. Raindrops were soon **scattered** across my windshield. A storm was coming. Looking at the boxes of clothes in the back seat, I smiled.

A torrential downpour of rain began beating against my windshield. Lightning flickered. I pulled off the road until my visibility improved. People on the sidewalk held purses and briefcases over their heads in a **futile** effort to keep from getting wet. Children danced in the downpour. The rain reminded me of another storm ten years earlier.

Hurricane Katrina slammed into the Gulf Coast when I was nine. The powerful storm caused severe damage.

One of my strongest memories was watching the evening news with my aunt. A reporter inside the Houston Astrodome was surrounded by thousands of people. They all had the same weary expression. Many wore torn and dirty clothes. Some had no shoes. They slowly shuffled along, their faces full of sadness.

(bkgd) Jim Reed/Digital Vision/Getty Images; (l) Lisette Le Bon/Purestock/SuperStock; (bl) Thomas Barwick/Photodisc/Getty Images; All other images by Jeffrey Mangiat

Text Evidence

❶ Organization ACT

Reread the second paragraph. **Draw a box** around the sentence that tells you the narrator is thinking about an event from the past. When did the event happen?

_____

❷ Expand Vocabulary

When something is **futile**, it is useless. **Circle** the details that describe people's *futile* efforts to stay dry.

❸ Comprehension
Point of View

Reread the last two paragraphs. **Underline** the details that the narrator uses to describe the people he sees on the news. How does the narrator feel watching them?

_____

_____

_____

159

Text Evidence

1 Comprehension
Point of View

Reread the first four paragraphs. **Underline** the name of the narrator. What does he think when he sees the little boy on TV?

_____

_____

2 Organization (A)(C)(T)

Reread the third and fourth paragraphs. **Draw a box** around the paragraph that gives information about Katrina. What sentence brings you back to Hector and his aunt watching TV?

_____

_____

_____

3 Expand Vocabulary

If you **devised** something, you thought it up. **Circle** who helped Hector *devise* a plan.

"Are they here because of the hurricane?" I asked softly.

Aunt Lucia nodded. "*Sí*, Hector. They are from New Orleans, Louisiana. Hurricane Katrina destroyed their homes. They lost everything. Now they are temporary **residents** of the Astrodome. They'll stay until it's safe to go home."

I knew a lot about Katrina. The storm had formed in hot tropical weather and then had traveled north. It had come so close to Texas that I worried it would strike Houston. It missed us. But other cities were not so lucky.

The TV reporter looked around. People tried to speak to her, but she was **selective** about whom she would interview. I noticed a little boy behind her, hugging an old teddy bear. Watching him, I knew I had to do something.

The next day, my friends joined me at our volunteer club, the Houston Helpers. Together we **devised** a plan. We wanted to collect toys and give them to the kids at the Astrodome. Donating the toys would give a little joy to these families.

Anxious to get started, we made lists of things to do. Then each of us was **assigned** a task.

We spread the word to our schools and other **organizations**. Soon the donation bins were overflowing with toys!

I'll never forget that day at the Astrodome. Kids flew at us from all sides. Smiles lit up their faces as we pulled toys from our bags. Parents thanked us for our **generosity**. They told our group leaders how thoughtful and **mature** we all were.

BZZZZ. My cell phone jolted me back to the present. I noticed that the storm had passed.

"Hector?"

"*Sí*, yes, hi, Jeannie."

"Do you have the donations? We need them for the victims of yesterday's tornado."

"Yes, I have the clothing donations. The storm **delayed** me, but I'll be there soon!"

I **gingerly** eased my car into the busy traffic. It felt good to know that I was making a difference again.

❶ Organization Ⓐ Ⓒ Ⓣ

Reread the first three paragraphs. **Draw a box** around the sentence that shows a change in time. Where is Hector when his cell phone rings?

_____

_____

❷ Expand Vocabulary

Someone who is **delayed** is made late by something. **Circle** what *delayed* Hector.

❸ Comprehension
Point of View

Reread the last two paragraphs. **Underline** the words that show how Hector feels about helping others. How is Hector helping people?

_____

_____

_____

Respond to Reading

Discuss Work with a partner. Read the questions about "Remembering Hurricane Katrina." Use the discussion starters to answer the questions. Write the page numbers to show where you found text evidence.

? Questions	Discussion Starters	Text Evidence
1 What did Hector and his friends want to do?	▶ Hector and his friends wanted… ▶ Hector and his friends are members of…	Page(s): _____
2 What plan did the Houston Helpers devise?	▶ The Houston Helpers decided to… ▶ I read that they also…	Page(s): _____
3 Why was their plan successful?	▶ Their plan was successful… ▶ I know this because I read…	Page(s): _____

Write Review your notes about "Remembering Hurricane Katrina." Then write your answer to the question below. Use text evidence to support your answer.

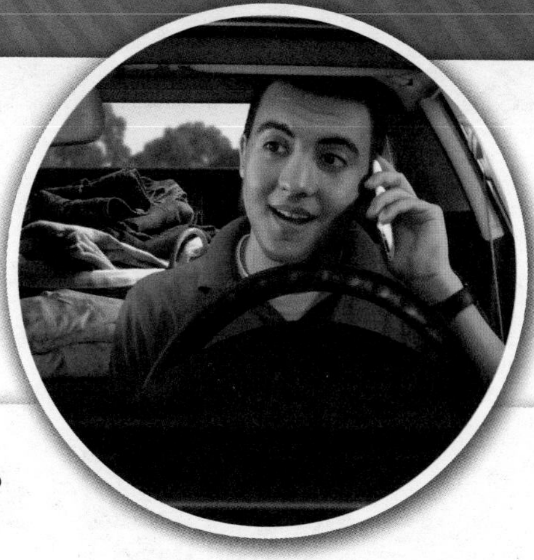

How did Hector and his friends help people after Hurricane Katrina?

Jeff Mangiat

Shared Read

Read an Analysis **Genre** Read Yoshi's paragraph below about "Remembering Hurricane Katrina." She writes her opinion about how well the author used details to create realistic characters and events.

Student Model

In "Remembering Hurricane Katrina," the author did a good job of making the characters and the story events realistic. As the story begins, Hector is driving a car. He has to pull over because of a bad storm. The storm makes him remember Hurricane Katrina. Hector was just a kid then. He and his friends helped the people who were homeless because of the hurricane. They collected toys and gave them to the kids. I liked how Hector and his friends found a way to help. The story felt realistic because collecting toys is something my friends and I would do.

Topic Sentence

Circle the topic sentence. What is Yoshi going to write about?

Evidence

Draw a box around the evidence that Yoshi includes. What other information from "Remembering Hurricane Katrina" would you include?

Concluding Statement

Underline the concluding statement. Why is this sentence a good wrap up?

John Lund/Drew Kelly/Blend Images; Royalty-Free/Corbis; Purestock/PunchStock

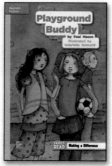

Leveled Reader

Write an Analysis **Genre** **Write a paragraph about "Playground Buddy." Tell your opinion about how the author uses details to create realistic characters and events.**

Topic Sentence

- ☐ Include the title of the text you read.
- ☐ Tell your opinion about how well the author used realistic characters and events.

Evidence

- ☐ Describe the details the author provided.
- ☐ Explain how these details were realistic.

Concluding Statement

- ☐ Restate why the characters and events seemed real.

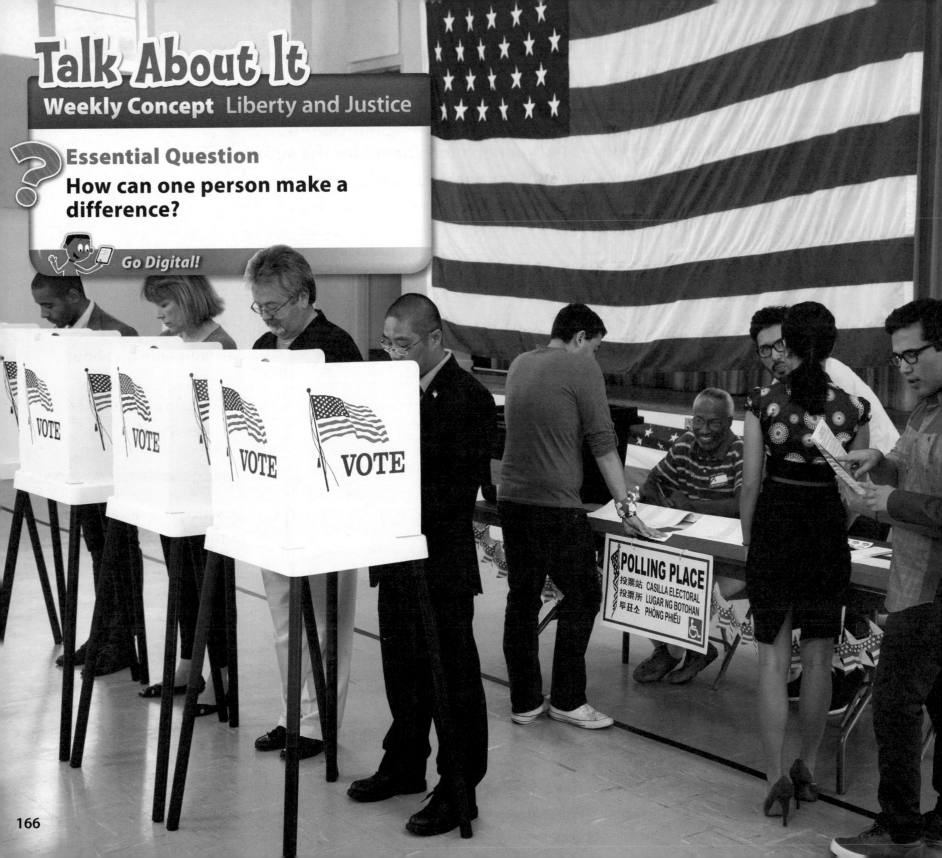

Talk About It

Essential Question

How can one person make a difference?

Go Digital!

POLLING PLACE
投票站 CASILLA ELECTORAL
投票所 LUGAR NG BOTOHAN
투표소 PHÒNG PHIẾU

Write words that tell what one person can do to make a difference.

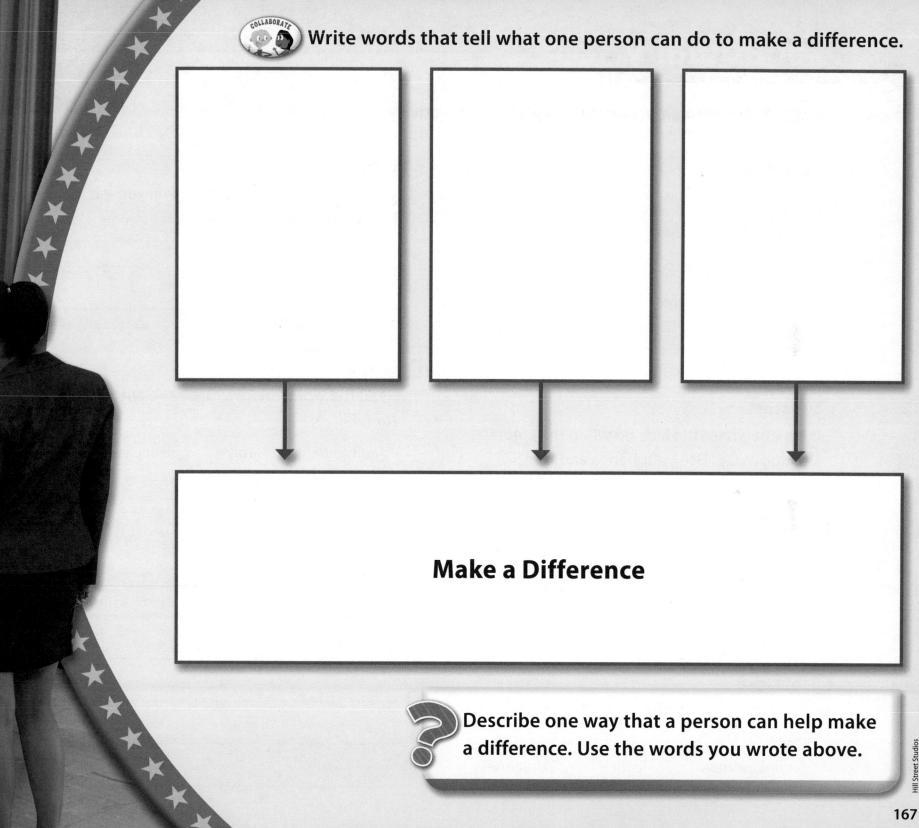

Make a Difference

Describe one way that a person can help make a difference. Use the words you wrote above.

Hill Street Studios

CCSS Vocabulary

 Work with a partner to complete each activity.

1 mistreated

▶ Underline the base word *treat* in *mistreated*.

▶ Circle the prefix *mis-*.

▶ Circle the ending *-ed*.

▶ What does *mistreated* mean?

_____

2 protest

Act out what little kids do when they *protest* taking a nap. Use your hands and face.

3 qualified

Is a doctor *qualified* to take care of animals or people?

_____

4 injustice

Read the words below. Circle two synonyms for *injustice*.

   unkindness   justice   unfairness

5 boycott

You decide to *boycott* candy. Will you eat a lot of candy or no candy?

_____

_____

6 fulfill

Read the words below. Circle the antonym for *fulfill*.

   achieve   fail   succeed

7 registered

What school activity do you want to *register* for?

_____

_____

_____

_____

168

8 **encouragement**

Draw a picture of one student giving *encouragement* to another student.

High-Utility Words

▶ Homophones

Homophones are words that sound alike but have different spellings and meanings.

Circle the homophones in the passage.

A store often sold old milk (to) people. Chris had returned sour milk at least (two) times. He talked to the owners, but their excuses were weak. So Chris and four neighbors protested. In a week, there was fresh milk on the shelves. It was a win for all of the customers.

My Notes

Read "Judy's Appalachia."
Use this page to take notes.

Judy's APPALACHIA

A mountaintop is leveled to mine for coal in Appalachia.

 Essential Question

How can one person make a difference?

Read about how one person decided to take a stand.

(l) George Steinmetz/Corbis; (br) Paul Corbit Brown

Judy Bonds's grandson stood in a creek in West Virginia. He held up a handful of dead fish. "What's wrong with these fish?" he asked. All around him, dead fish floated in the water. That day became a turning point for Judy Bonds. She decided to fight against the coal mining companies. They were poisoning her home.

Marfork, West Virginia

The daughter of a coal miner, Judy was born in Marfork, West Virginia. The people of Marfork had been coal miners for **generations**. Coal mining provided entire families with jobs. Coal helped light and warm their homes.

Marfork was in a leafy green valley surrounded by the Appalachian Mountains. Judy grew up there. She swam and fished in the river. She raised a daughter there.

Mountaintop Removal Mining

An energy company came to Marfork in the 1990s. It began to do mountaintop removal mining. Using dynamite, the company blew tops off mountains to get to the coal underneath. The process was quicker than underground mining. But it caused problems. Whole forests were destroyed.

Judy Bonds spoke out against mountaintop removal mining.

Text Evidence

1 Comprehension
Author's Point of View

Reread the first paragraph. **Circle** the sentence that tells why that day was a turning point. Why did Judy decide to fight the mining companies?

_____

_____

2 Expand Vocabulary

A **generation** is the time between when parents are born and when their children are born. **Underline** the words that tell what people in Marfork had been for *generations*.

3 Organization A C T

Reread the last two paragraphs. **Draw a box** around the sentence that describes Marfork before the 1990s. What was Marfork like after the energy company came?

_____

_____

171

Text Evidence

① Expand Vocabulary

Blasts that blow things up are called **explosions**. **Circle** the details that tell what the effects of the *explosions* were.

② Comprehension
Author's Point of View

Reread the third paragraph. **Underline** details that describe what Judy did to fight against the mining. What did Judy want?

_____

_____

_____

③ Organization ⓐⓒⓣ

Look at the time line. **Draw a box** around the year Judy was born. What information does the time line give?

_____

_____

Dust from the **explosions** filled the air. Dust settled over the towns. Coal sludge made of mud, chemicals, and coal dust got into the water.

Pollution from the mountaintop removal mining began making people sick. Where Judy lived, coal sludge flowed into rivers and streams. As a result, people packed up and left. Judy was very sad. The land she loved was being **mistreated**. The valley that had always been her home was poisoned. It was no longer a safe place to live. Judy's family had to leave.

Working for Change

Something had to be done about the pollution. Judy decided it was important to **protest** against the mining. She wanted the mining to stop. Judy felt **qualified** to talk to groups. She could tell them about the **injustice** of whole towns being forced to move. She could tell how mountains and forests had been destroyed because of strip mining. After all, she had grown up in a mining family.

1952	**2001**	**2003**	**2011**
Judy is born in West Virginia.	Judy's family leaves Marfork.	Judy is awarded the Goldman Environmental Prize.	Judy dies at age 59.

Judy worked as a volunteer for the Coal River Mountain Watch. The group fought against mountaintop removal mining. Finally, Judy became the group's leader. She **registered**, or signed up, to take part in protests

Judy Bonds spoke at protests.

against mining companies. At the protests, Judy faced angry people. Many coal miners were not against mountaintop removal mining. They liked it because they needed the jobs. Judy knew it would be impossible to **boycott** the mining companies. Coal miners could not **afford** to leave their jobs. They needed the money. Instead, she asked for changes in the mining process. Slowly, small changes were made to protect mining communities. In 2003, Judy was given the Goldman Environmental Prize for her efforts as an activist.

Encouraging Others

Sadly, Judy could not **fulfill** all of her goals. She was diagnosed with cancer. In 2011, Judy died. But her success provided **encouragement** to other activists. Her work will help protect the Appalachian Mountains and help others remain in their homes.

The Monongahela National Forest in West Virginia

(bkgd) Panoramic Images/Getty Images; (bc) Courtesy Goldman Environmental Prize; (br) Mark Schmerling; (tr) Paul Corbit Brown

Text Evidence

❶ Organization Ⓐ Ⓒ Ⓣ

Reread the first paragraph. **Underline** the details that tell you about Judy's job. What award was Judy given for her efforts?

_____

_____

❷ Expand Vocabulary

To **afford** means to be able to do something without bad results. **Circle** the words that tell what the coal miners could not *afford* to do.

❸ Comprehension
Author's Point of View

Reread the last paragraph. **Draw a box** around the details that tell how Judy's work helped others. How does the author feel about Judy Bonds?

_____

_____

Discuss Work with a partner. Read the questions about "Judy's Appalachia." Use the discussion starters to answer the questions. Write the page numbers where you found text evidence.

 **Questions**    **Discussion Starters**   **Text Evidence**

	Questions	Discussion Starters	Text Evidence
1	What did Judy decide to fight against?	▶ Judy decided to… ▶ I know this because I read that…	Page(s): _____
2	What did Judy Bonds protest against?	▶ Judy Bonds protested against… ▶ She wanted…	Page(s): _____
3	What type of changes did Judy push for?	▶ Judy pushed for changes in… ▶ As a result,…	Page(s): _____

Write Review your notes about "Judy's Appalachia." Then write your answer to the question below. Use text evidence to support your answer.

How did Judy Bonds make a difference in West Virginia?

_____

_____

_____

_____

_____

_____

_____

_____

_____

_____

Shared Read

Topic Sentence

Circle the topic sentence. What is Shari going to write about?

Evidence

Draw a box around the evidence that Shari includes. What other information from "Judy's Appalachia" would you include?

Concluding Statement

Underline the concluding statement. Why is this sentence a good wrap up?

Read an Analysis **Author's Point of View** Read Shari's paragraph below about "Judy's Appalachia." She analyzes details to identify the author's point of view.

Student Model

In "Judy's Appalachia," I can tell the author admires how Judy Bonds stood up to the mining companies. Judy grew up in Marfork. In the 1990s, a company came to Marfork. They used a process called mountaintop removal mining. Whole forests were destroyed. Sludge got into the rivers. The pollution made people sick. Judy Bonds spoke at protests. She worked for changes in the mining process. Slowly the mining companies started to make small changes. These details support the author's opinion that Judy Bond was a brave person who made a difference in people's lives.

Leveled Reader

Write an Analysis **Author's Point of View** Write a paragraph about "Jacob Riis: Champion of the Poor." Use details from the text to identify the author's point of view.

_____

_____

_____

_____

_____

_____

_____

_____

_____

_____

_____

Topic Sentence

☐ Include the title of the text you read.

☐ Identify the author's point of view.

Evidence

☐ Include details that support the author's point of view.

☐ Explain why these details are important.

Concluding Statement

☐ Restate the author's point of view.

How can words lead to change? Describe the ways that people use words to create change.

Powerful Words

How could your words lead to change? Use the words you wrote above.

Vocabulary

 Work with a partner to complete each activity.

1 tension

Circle a synonym for *tension*.

stress   calm   relief

2 address

You give an *address* to the class about littering. Your teacher says that he likes your speech. How are the words *address* and *speech* related?

_____

_____

3 opposed

Would you be *opposed* to an earlier bedtime? Why or why not?

_____

_____

4 perish

Read the words below. Circle the word that is an antonym for *perish*.

expire   live   die

5 proclamation

As King, I *proclaim* October 3 to be a holiday!

Read the *proclamation* above out loud. Use your voice to make it sound official.

_____

6 haste

Circle the words that complete the sentence: He wanted to make *haste*, so _____.

▶ he stood still

▶ he walked quickly

▶ he walked slowly

7 shattered

A glass fell and *shattered*. How does it look?

_____

_____

_____

8 divided

Draw a picture of a circle. Then draw a line to *divide* it in half.

High-Utility Words

▶ **Possessives**

Adding 's to a name or a noun makes it a possessive. It shows ownership.

Circle the possessives in the passage.

John liked his (teacher's) idea about growing a vegetable garden. They could use one of the school's fields. Some kids in John's class did not like the idea. Even his best friend's opinion was that it was a bad idea. John made a speech about knowing where one's food comes from. His words changed the class's attitude.

My Notes

Read "Words for Change."
Use this page to take notes.

_____

_____

_____

_____

_____

_____

_____

_____

_____

_____

_____

_____

Words for Change

 Essential Question

How can words lead to change?

Read how Elizabeth Cady Stanton's words helped bring about change for women.

The Early Years

Elizabeth Cady Stanton and her daughter

In 1827, Elizabeth Cady Stanton was eleven. Her father told her, "Oh, my daughter, I wish you were a boy." Elizabeth was **shattered**. Then she decided to prove that women deserved the same rights as men.

Elizabeth's father was a lawyer, judge, and congressman. Women came to him for legal advice. Elizabeth listened **eagerly** and with excitement to his advice, but she was often disappointed. Her father could not help them. Women did not have the same rights as men. Married women could not own property or vote. Later, Elizabeth said that she felt sorry for these women. She thought the laws were unfair.

Elizabeth found these unfair laws in her father's law books. First she drew lines through the laws she **opposed**. Then she planned to cut these pages out. Her father had a better idea. He told her that she should get lawmakers to pass new laws. Then the unfair laws would **perish** and disappear. As a result, women's lives would be changed.

Women march in a parade in New York City.

Text Evidence

1 Connection of Ideas (A)(C)(T)

Reread the first paragraph. **Underline** what Elizabeth's father says. How did these words affect Elizabeth?

_____

_____

2 Expand Vocabulary

To do something **eagerly** is to do it with excitement. **Draw a box** around a word that means almost the same thing as *eagerly*.

3 Connection of Ideas (A)(C)(T)

Reread the last two paragraphs. **Circle** the details that tell what Elizabeth did to her father's law books. What did her father tell her to do instead?

_____

_____

_____

Text Evidence

1 Expand Vocabulary

An **issue** is a problem that people have different ideas about. **Circle** the *issue* that Elizabeth and Henry worked on.

2 Comprehension
Author's Point of View

Reread the first paragraph. **Underline** the words the author uses to describe Elizabeth.

3 Connection of Ideas ⒶⒸⓉ

Draw a box around the sentence that tells what the Declaration of Rights and Sentiments was about. What document did Elizabeth use as her model?

_____

_____

_____

_____

Working for Change

Elizabeth was just as passionate about the rights of African Americans. She fought for people's right to be free. The country was **divided** in two by the **issue**, or problem, of slavery. Elizabeth met Henry Stanton, who was also working to end slavery. The got married in 1840. When they married, Elizabeth did not follow tradition. She did not say "promise to obey" in her wedding vows.

The Seneca Falls Convention

Elizabeth tried to be a good wife and mother but she wanted to be an activist and work for change. She took her father's advice, and she wrote a **proclamation**. It was called the Declaration of Rights and Sentiments. It was modeled after the Declaration of Independence. It said that women should be able to vote and have the same rights as men.

Elizabeth presented this document in 1848 at America's first women's rights convention. It was held in Seneca Falls, New York. Elizabeth and her friend Lucretia Mott organized this important event. Elizabeth gave the **address** at the convention. In her speech, she said women should have "all the rights and privileges which belong to them as citizens of the United States."

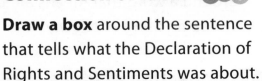

List of attendees at the convention

A Winning Team

Three years later, Elizabeth met Susan B. Anthony. The two made an unstoppable team. Elizabeth was a passionate speaker and writer. Susan was a gifted leader and organizer. In 1869, they formed the National Woman Suffrage Association. This group worked to get women the right to vote. Congress was slow, and showed no **haste** to change the law. Elizabeth traveled around the country. She spoke about change and a woman's right to vote. She did not care if her speeches caused **tension**. They often made people angry, but Elizabeth believed in her cause.

Susan B. Anthony and Elizabeth Cady Stanton

Victory at Last

Elizabeth Cady Stanton never got to vote. She died on October 26, 1902. Yet her bold words had a lasting **impact**. Women finally got the right to vote on August 18, 1920. Elizabeth Cady Stanton's passion for equal rights paved the way. And women's lives were changed forever.

Text Evidence

1 **Comprehension**
Author's Point of View

Reread the first paragraph. **Underline** the details the author uses to describe Elizabeth and Susan.

2 **Expand Vocabulary**

An **impact** is something that has a strong effect. **Circle** the sentence that tells how Elizabeth's words had an *impact*.

3 **Comprehension**
Author's Point of View

Reread the last paragraph. **Draw a box** around the words the author uses to tell how Elizabeth helped women. What is the author's opinion of her?

_____

_____

_____

_____

Respond to Reading

 Discuss Work with a partner. Read the questions about "Words for Change." Use the discussion starters to answer the questions. Write the page numbers where you found text evidence.

 Questions    Discussion Starters   **Text Evidence**

Questions	Discussion Starters	Text Evidence
1 What is the Declaration of Rights and Sentiments?	▶ Elizabeth Cady Stanton wrote… ▶ The declaration said…	Page(s): _____
2 What did Elizabeth and Susan B. Anthony do?	▶ Elizabeth and Susan B. Anthony… ▶ I know this because I read…	Page(s): _____
3 What did Elizabeth speak about?	▶ Elizabeth spoke about… ▶ Elizabeth believed in…	Page(s): _____

Mike Moran

186

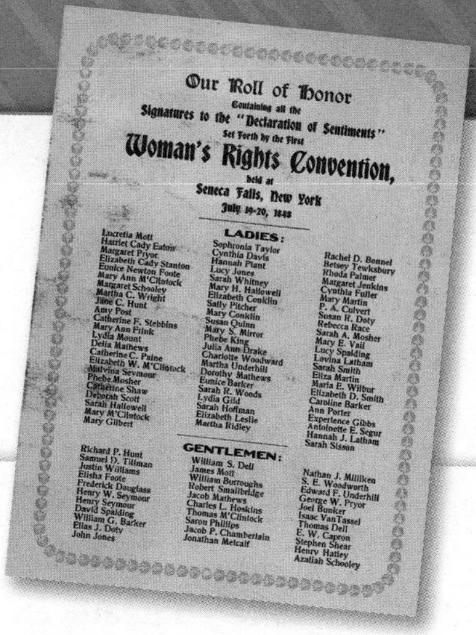

Our Roll of Honor
Containing all the
Signatures to the "Declaration of Sentiments"
Set Forth by the First
Woman's Rights Convention,
held at
Seneca Falls, New York
July 19-20, 1848

LADIES:

Lucretia Mott
Harriet Cady Eaton
Margaret Pryor
Elizabeth Cady Stanton
Eunice Newton Foote
Mary Ann M'Clintock
Margaret Schooley
Martha C. Wright
Jane C. Hunt
Amy Post
Catherine F. Stebbins
Mary Ann Frink
Lydia Mount
Delia Mathews
Catherine C. Paine
Elizabeth W. M'Clintock
Malvina Seymour
Phebe Mosher
Catherine Shaw
Deborah Scott
Sarah Hallowell
Mary M'Clintock
Mary Gilbert

Sophronia Taylor
Cynthia Davis
Hannah Plant
Lucy Jones
Sarah Whitney
Mary H. Hallowell
Elizabeth Conklin
Sally Pitcher
Mary Conklin
Susan Quinn
Mary S. Mirror
Phebe King
Julia Ann Drake
Charlotte Woodward
Martha Underhill
Dorothy Mathews
Eunice Barker
Sarah R. Woods
Lydia Gild
Sarah Hoffman
Elizabeth Leslie
Martha Ridley

Rachel D. Bonnel
Betsey Tewksbury
Rhoda Palmer
Margaret Jenkins
Cynthia Fuller
Mary Martin
P. A. Culvert
Susan R. Doty
Rebecca Race
Sarah A. Mosher
Mary E. Vail
Lucy Spalding
Lovina Latham
Sarah Smith
Eliza Martin
Maria E. Wilbur
Elizabeth D. Smith
Caroline Barker
Ann Porter
Experience Gibbs
Antoinette E. Segur
Hannah J. Latham
Sarah Sisson

GENTLEMEN:

Richard P. Hunt
Samuel D. Tillman
Justin Williams
Elisha Foote
Frederick Douglass
Henry W. Seymour
Henry Seymour
David Spalding
William G. Barker
Elias J. Doty
John Jones

William S. Dell
James Mott
William Burroughs
Robert Smallbridge
Jacob Mathews
Charles L. Hoskins
Thomas M'Clintock
Saron Phillips
Jacob P. Chamberlain
Jonathan Metcalf

Nathan J. Milliken
S. E. Woodworth
Edward F. Underhill
George W. Pryor
Joel Bunker
Isaac VanTassel
Thomas Dell
E. W. Capron
Stephen Shear
Henry Hatley
Azaliah Schooley

Write Review your notes about "Words for Change." Then write your answer to the question below. Use text evidence to support your answer.

How did Elizabeth Cady Stanton help women get the right to vote?

The Library of Congress, Manuscript Division

Write About Reading

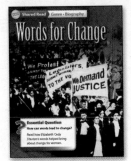

Shared Read

Topic Sentence

Circle the topic sentence. What is Molly going to write about?

Evidence

Draw a box around the evidence that Molly includes. What other information from "Words for Change" would you include?

Concluding Statement

Underline the concluding statement. Why is this sentence a good wrap up?

Read an Analysis **Reasons and Evidence** Read Molly's paragraph below about "Words for Change." She analyzes how the author supports her point of view.

Student Model

In "Words of Change," the author supports her point of view that Elizabeth Cady Stanton helped women win the right to vote. Elizabeth wrote a paper based on the Declaration of Independence. It said that women should have the same rights as men and the right to vote. The paper was presented at the first women's rights convention. Elizabeth also gave many speeches about women's rights. These reasons and evidence support the author's point of view that Elizabeth fought for women's rights.

Leveled Reader

Write an Analysis **Reasons and Evidence** Write a paragraph about "Nellie Bly: Reporter for the Underdog." Tell how the author used details to support a specific point of view.

_____

_____

_____

_____

_____

_____

_____

_____

_____

_____

Topic Sentence

☐ Include the title of the text you read.

☐ Identify the author's point of view.

Evidence

☐ Use details that support the author's point of view.

☐ Be sure to include only the important details.

Concluding Statement

☐ Restate how the details used by the author supported her point of view.

Talk About It

Essential Question

In what ways can advances in science be helpful or harmful?

Go Digital!

190

Write words that describe advances in science that have helped people.

Scientific Advances

 Talk about one way that science has helped people. Use the words you wrote above.

(l) Angelo Cavalli/Digital Vision/Getty Images; (r) Image Source/Veer

CCSS Vocabulary

 Work with a partner to complete each activity.

1 characteristics

What are two *characteristics* of a rabbit?

_____

_____

2 inherit

Circle two things a puppy can *inherit* from its mother.

long tail   fur color   dog food

3 resistance

Circle the best answer.
Tiffany has a *resistance* to the flu because

▶ she had a flu shot.

▶ she eats apples.

4 agriculture

List a crop that people who work in *agriculture* might grow.

_____

5 advancements

▶ Underline the word *advance* in *advancements*.

▶ Circle the suffix *-ment*.

▶ What does *advancements* mean?

_____

_____

6 disagreed

Think about a time when you *disagreed* with a friend. What did you *disagree* about?

_____

_____

_____

7 concerns

Underline two words below that are synonyms for *concerns*.

worries   fears   jokes

8 prevalent

Draw a picture of an insect that is *prevalent* in the summer.

Compound Words

Compound words are made up of two or more smaller words.

Circle the compound words in the passage.

On Saturdays, farmers bring fruits and vegetables to an (outdoor) marketplace. Mom and I go there every weekend. This Saturday, Mom bought apples to make applesauce. She bought blueberries and homemade jam, too. Some of the fruits and vegetables were unusual. I saw a tiny watermelon. It was just the right size for one person!

Blend Images/SuperStock

My Notes

Essential Question

In what ways can advances in science be helpful or harmful?

Read about how science has helped to make better food crops.

194

Food Fight

Is it safe to change Mother Nature?

An amazing thing is happening to our food. It's called genetic modification. Scientists are changing the genes inside seeds to make **superior**, or better, food crops. Genes are inside all living things. A seed's genes decide what **characteristics** it will **inherit** when it grows into a plant.

For centuries, farmers have worked to make crops better. They bred the sweetest melon plants with the biggest melon plants. This made plants that produced big, sweet melons.

But this kind of crossbreeding can take years.

Now, scientists have a shortcut. They can put a gene from one living thing into another.

That living thing could be a plant. It could be a virus or even be an animal. The foods created from genetic modification are called GM foods. GM foods are made to survive insects, bad weather, or to grow faster. But are these **advancements** in **agriculture** good for us?

Text Evidence

1 Connection of Ideas A C T

Reread the first paragraph. **Circle** the details that tell what genetic modification is. Why do you think scientists want to change a seed's genes?

_____

_____

2 Expand Vocabulary

Something that is **superior** is better than others. Reread the second paragraph. **Underline** the sentence that tells how the crossbred melons are *superior*.

3 Comprehension
Author's Point of View

Reread the last paragraph. **Draw a box** around the question the author asks. What will the author discuss in the rest of the article?

_____

_____

Text Evidence

1 Comprehension
Author's Point of View

Reread the first two paragraphs. **Underline** the details that tell how Bt corn resists insects. Why does the author think Bt corn is good?

_____

_____

2 Expand Vocabulary

Foods that are **nutritious** are good for you. They have nutrients you need to stay healthy. **Circle** the word that means almost the same thing as *nutritious*.

3 Connection of Ideas Ⓐ Ⓒ Ⓣ

Reread the last paragraph. **Draw a box** around the details that tell how many genes were used to modify golden rice. What makes this kind of golden rice healthful?

_____

_____

Support for Superfoods

Scientists have created GM crops with a **resistance** to insects and disease. Bt corn is one such crop.

It has an insect-killing gene. Farmers who grow Bt corn use less chemicals. That is good for farmers. It is also good for the environment.

Some superfoods are extra **nutritious**, and healthful.

GM potatoes that resist disease were first sold in the 1990's.

Golden rice has been modified with three different genes. The new genes help make a special rice. The rice has a nutrient that can help prevent blindness.

Superfoods

These foods have been genetically modified. They now have special powers.

Rice

Rice contains phytic acid. Too much of it can be bad for people. A new kind of rice has been bred that has less of this acid.

Salmon

To create supersized salmon, scientists changed a growth gene. These new kind of salmon grow twice as fast as wild salmon.

Tomatoes

Modified tomatoes can be picked ripe and will not bruise when shipped. One company wanted to make a tomato that could survive frost. They used a gene from an arctic fish. The fish-tomato did not work.

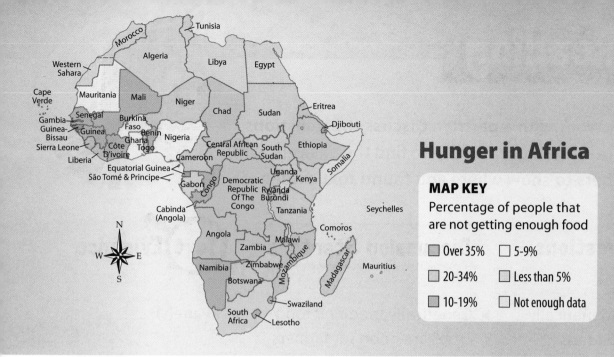

Hunger in Africa

MAP KEY
Percentage of people that are not getting enough food

- ⬛ Over 35%
- ⬜ 5–9%
- ⬜ 20–34%
- ⬜ Less than 5%
- ⬛ 10–19%
- ⬜ Not enough data

Safety Issues

Many people have **disagreed** with the idea of making GM foods. They think these foods will hurt the environment. Plants with new genes will crossbreed with weeds. That will make pesticide-resistant weeds. Another worry is that GM foods may cause allergies.

Genetically modified crops are **prevalent**. They are grown in many different places.

Some people won't buy them because of health **concerns**. Many companies **avoid** using GM foods in their products. However, there is no proof that GM foods are unhealthy.

Time Will Tell

Genetically modified foods have not hurt anyone. If there are problems, researchers think they will be easy to manage. It is important to keep researching GM foods. These foods can help to feed the world.

Text Evidence

① Connection of Ideas Ⓐ Ⓒ Ⓣ

Reread "Safety Issues." **Underline** the details that tell why people don't like GM foods. Why won't some people buy GM foods?

_____

_____

② Expand Vocabulary

When you **avoid** something, you keep away from it. What do some companies *avoid* using in their products?

_____

_____

③ Comprehension
Author's Point of View

Reread the last paragraph. **Draw a box** around what the author says is important. What does the author think GM foods can do?

_____

Respond to Reading

Discuss Work with a partner. Discuss the questions below about "Food Fight." Reread to find the answers. Write page numbers to show where you found text evidence.

 **Questions**  **Discussion Starters** **Text Evidence**

❶ Why are genetically modified foods good for farmers?	▶ Genetically modified food crops are good for farmers because… ▶ I read that. . .	Page(s): _____
❷ What are two kinds of GM foods that have been improved?	▶ Two kinds of GM foods that have been improved are… ▶ I noticed that…	Page(s): _____
❸ Why is it important to keep researching genetically modified foods?	▶ One place where people are not getting enough food is… ▶ I know this because I read…	Page(s): _____

Write Review your notes about "Food Fight." Then write your answer to the question below. Use text evidence to support your answer.

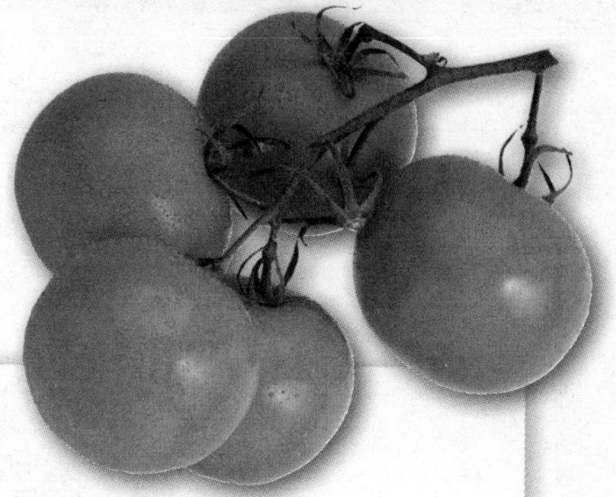

What are some good things about genetically modified foods?

Stockbyte/Getty Images

Write About Reading

CCSS

Shared Read

Read an Analysis **Text Structure** Jay wrote about "Food Fight." He states his opinion about how well the author used a compare-and-contrast text structure.

Student Model

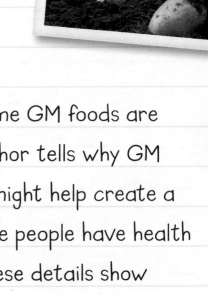

Topic Sentence

Circle the topic sentence. What is Jay going to write about?

Evidence

Draw a box around the evidence that Jay includes. What other information from "Food Fight" would you include?

Concluding Statement

Underline the concluding statement. Why is this sentence a good wrap up?

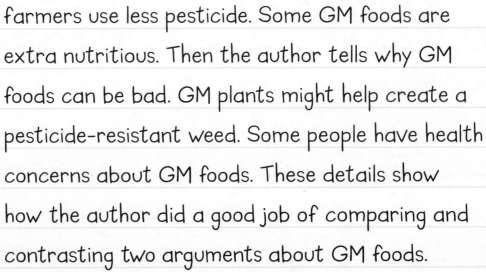

I think the author of "Food Fight" did a good job of using a compare-and-contrast text structure. First, the author talks about the good aspects of GM foods. For example, farmers use less pesticide. Some GM foods are extra nutritious. Then the author tells why GM foods can be bad. GM plants might help create a pesticide-resistant weed. Some people have health concerns about GM foods. These details show how the author did a good job of comparing and contrasting two arguments about GM foods.

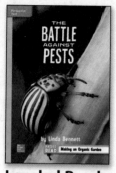

Leveled Reader

Write an Analysis **Text Structure** Write a paragraph about "The Battle Against Pests." Tell your opinion about how well the author uses a compare-and-contrast text structure.

Topic Sentence

- ☐ Include the title of the text you read.
- ☐ Tell whether the author did a good job of using a compare-and-contrast text structure.

Evidence

- ☐ Explain how the author used a compare-and-contrast text structure.
- ☐ Support your ideas with details.

Concluding Statement

- ☐ Restate you opinion about the author's use of text structure.

FACT OR FICTION?

THE BIG IDEA
How do different writers treat the same topic?

COLLABORATE Write words that describe the different jobs that people do when they work for the government.

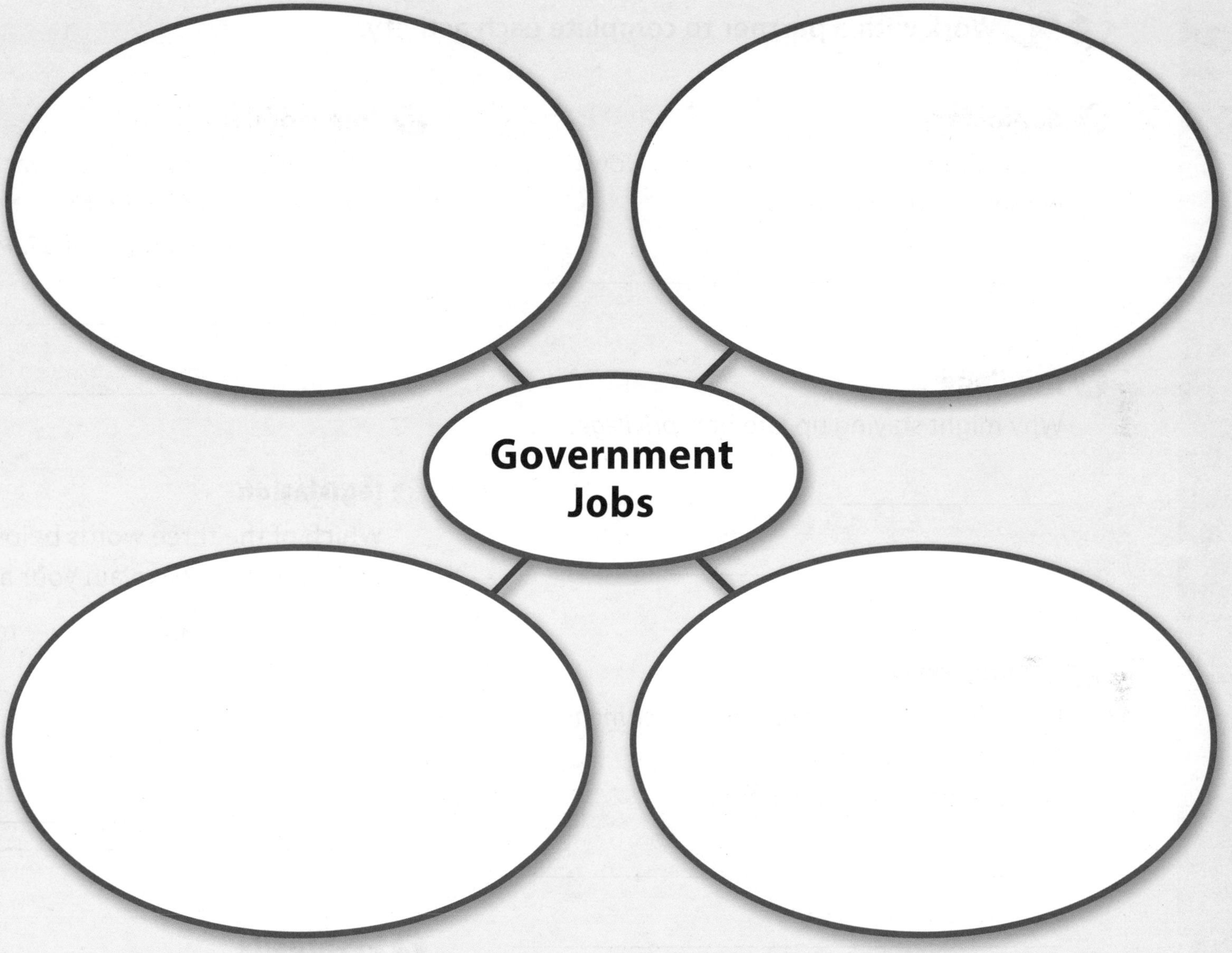

Government Jobs

Talk about why we need police officers. Use words that you wrote above.

Vocabulary

 Work with a partner to complete each activity.

1 democracy

The United States is a *democracy*. How do we select our leaders?

_____

2 privilege

Why might staying up late be a *privilege*?

_____

_____

3 commitment

Underline the base word in *commitment*.
Circle the suffix -*ment*
What does *commitment* mean?

_____

_____

4 amendments

Circle the synonym for *amendments*.

    damages   changes   mistakes

5 compromise

Don wants to swim. Bryan wants to bike. They decide to bike first and then swim. How is this an example of a *compromise*?

_____

_____

6 legislation

Which of the three words below has to do with *legislation*? Explain your answer.

    laws   bikes   movies

_____

_____

_____

7 eventually

What would you like to learn to do *eventually*?

_____

_____

8 **version**

Think of a movie you like. Draw two *versions* of a poster for that movie.

High-Utility Words

▶ Cause-and-Effect Words

Some words, such as *because* and *since,* show a cause. Some words, such as *so, therefore,* and *due to,* show an effect.

Circle the words that show cause and effect in the passage.

Tom was playing first base (since) it was his turn. Suddenly, it started to rain. His team kept playing because the rain was light. Then Tom's cap flew off due to the wind. It started to rain more. The players could not see the ball since there was so much rain. As a result, the game ended.

M Itani/Alamy

Read "A World Without Rules."
Use this page to take notes.

_____

_____

_____

_____

_____

_____

_____

_____

_____

_____

_____

_____

A WORLD WITHOUT RULES

? Essential Question

Why do we need government?

Read how government and laws help to protect us every day.

You may think rules were made to tell you what to do and to keep you from having fun. But what if we had no rules at all? Nobody would tell you what to do ever again! Sounds great, right? Let's see what it's like to live in a world without rules.

A Strange Morning

Let's start at home. Your alarm clock goes off. Why hurry? Without rules you don't have to go to school. **Eventually** you wander downstairs. Your little brother is eating cookies in the kitchen. Since there are no rules, you can have cookies for breakfast! Maybe you should have something healthy and **sensible** like a bowl of cereal. But you want cookies. You reach a **compromise** (KOM•pruh•mighz) and crumble the cookies over your cereal. Without rules, you will not have to brush your teeth anymore. However, you may have a cavity the next time you see the dentist.

A Community in Confusion

You decide to go to the playground because there is no law saying you have to go to school. Without traffic laws, cars speed by. Without crossing guards, there is no safe way to cross the street. But once you see the playground, you may not want to go there. Broken swings hang from rusty chains. Trash cans overflow with plastic bottles and bags. A huge tree branch lies across the slide. Since there are no rules, all government services are gone. As a result, nobody is in charge of taking care of the playground.

R. G. Roth

Text Evidence

❶ Connection of Ideas Ⓐ Ⓒ Ⓣ

Reread the first two paragraphs. **Draw boxes** around the questions in the first paragraph. What would it be like to live without rules? Give one example from the second paragraph.

_____

_____

_____

❷ Expand Vocabulary

Something that is **sensible** shows good sense. Why is it *sensible* to eat cereal for breakfast instead of cookies?

_____

_____

❸ Comprehension
Cause and Effect

Reread the last paragraph. **Circle** each cause. **Underline** each effect.

209

Text Evidence

❶ Expand Vocabulary

To **maintain** something is to take proper care of it. **Draw a box** around the detail that tells what needs to be *maintained* in parks.

❷ Comprehension
Cause and Effect

Reread the first paragraph. **Circle** the cause of the bad air. What effect does bad air have?

_____

_____

_____

❸ Connection to Ideas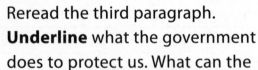

Reread the third paragraph. **Underline** what the government does to protect us. What can the government do to change a law?

_____

_____

_____

Now think about other things you love to do. Want to go to the beach? There will be no lifeguards there to keep you safe. Want to play soccer in the park? Your state and local governments are not around to **maintain** parks. So no one takes care of the playing fields. Feel like eating lunch outside? The air is bad because of pollution. As a result, you may have to stay inside.

Have you ever thought about another country invading our country? Remember, the government runs the army. Without a government, there is no army to protect us.

Back to Reality

Thankfully, this **version** of our world isn't real. We live in a **democracy** (di•MOK•ruh•see). We have the **privilege** (PRIV•uh•lij) of voting for the people that we want to run the country. Our government passes **legislation** (lej•is•LAY•shuhn), or laws, to help and protect us. If an old law no longer makes sense, the government can pass **amendments** to the law.

Community workers, such as crossing guards, police officers, and lifeguards, all work to keep you safe. Government groups have made a **commitment** to keep our air and water clean. And don't forget the armed forces. They were created to protect our nation.

Our government and laws were created to keep you safe. They are also there to **ensure** that everyone is treated fairly. Without them, the world would be a different place.

Text Evidence

1 Connection of Ideas **A C T**

Reread the fourth paragraph. **Circle** the details that tell what kind of community workers keep you safe. What do government groups do to keep us safe?

_____

_____

2 Expand Vocabulary

When you **ensure** something, you make certain that it happens. **Draw a box** around what the government *ensures*.

3 Comprehension
Cause and Effect

Reread the last paragraph. **Underline** the first sentence. Why were government and laws created?

_____

_____

_____

R. G. Roth

211

Respond to Reading

Discuss Work with a partner. Read the questions about "A World Without Rules" Use the discussion starters to answer the questions. Write the page numbers to show where you found text evidence.

❓Questions	Discussion Starters	Text Evidence
1 How does our government keep our playgrounds safe?	▶ Government services keep… ▶ I know this because…	Page(s): _____
2 How does the government keep our beaches and parks safe?	▶ Beaches are safe because… ▶ Parks are safe because…	Page(s): _____
3 How does the government make sure our air and water is clean?	▶ The government… ▶ I noticed that…	Page(s): _____

Mike Moran

212

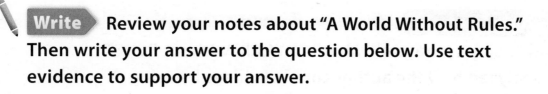

Write Review your notes about "A World Without Rules."
Then write your answer to the question below. Use text
evidence to support your answer.

What does the government do to keep us safe?

_____

_____

_____

_____

_____

_____

_____

_____

_____

_____

_____

Shared Read

Read an Analysis   **Connections Within a Text**

Read Sanjay's paragraph about "A World without Rules."
He analyzed how the author connects ideas by using
cause-and-effect relationships.

Student Model

> The author uses cause-and-effect relationships to present ideas in "A World Without Rules." The author gives examples that show what the effect of having no rules or laws would be on our world. Without traffic laws or crossing guards, the effect would be that you could not cross the street safely. Without government, the effect would be bad air and unclean water. If we lived in a world without laws, people would not be treated fairly. Rules and laws keep us safe. The author's use of cause-and-effect relationships helped me to understand why government and laws are important.

Topic Sentence

Circle the topic sentence. What is Sanjay going to write about?

Evidence

Draw a box around the cause-and-effect relationships Sanjay includes. What other information from "A World Without Rules" would you include?

Concluding Statement

Underline the concluding statement. Why is this sentence a good wrap up?

Leveled Reader

Write an Analysis **Connections Within a Text** Write a paragraph about "A Day in the Senate." Tell how the author uses cause-and-effect relationships to connect events.

_____

_____

_____

_____

_____

_____

_____

_____

_____

_____

_____

_____

Topic Sentence

☐ Include the title of the text you read.

☐ Tell how the author uses cause-and-effect relationships.

Evidence

☐ Give examples of cause-and-effect relationships.

☐ Make sure to include important details.

Concluding Statement

☐ Restate how the author used cause and effect relationships to connect events.

Essential Question

Why do people run for public office?

Go Digital!

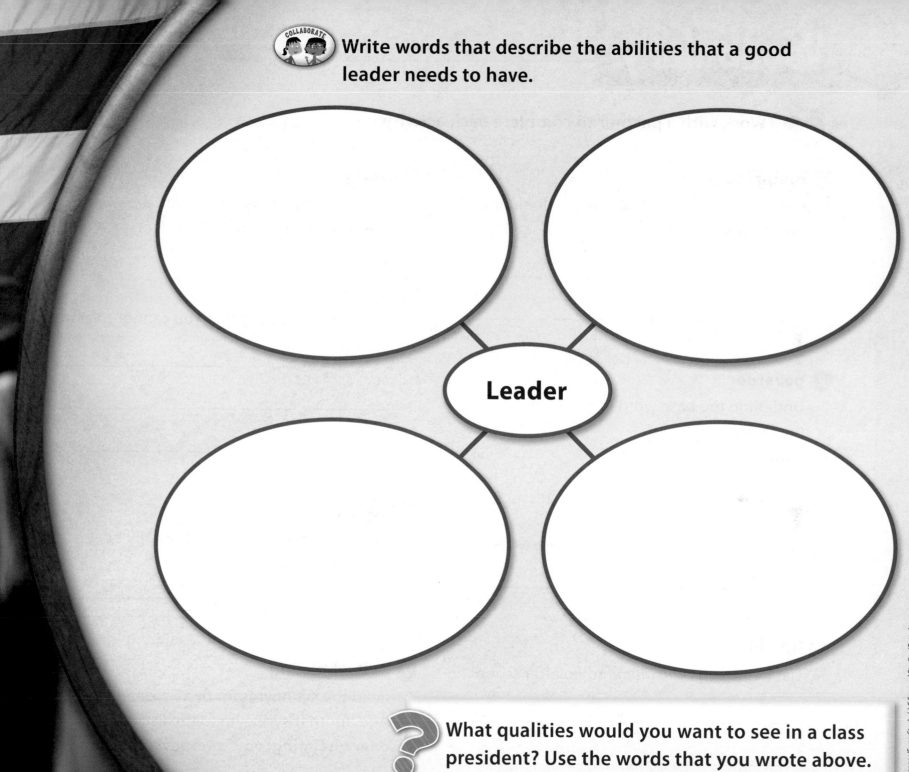

Write words that describe the abilities that a good leader needs to have.

Leader

What qualities would you want to see in a class president? Use the words that you wrote above.

Work with a partner to complete each activity.

1 campaign

List two things a politician might do during his or her *campaign*.

_____

_____

2 governor

Underline the base word in *governor*.
Circle the suffix *-or*
What does *governor* mean?

_____

_____

3 intend

List two things you *intend* to do after school.

_____

_____

4 weary

Act out how you feel when you are *weary*.
Use your body and face.

5 tolerate

Describe something that you cannot *tolerate*.

_____

_____

_____

6 opponent

Name a game in which you usually beat your *opponent*.

_____

7 overwhelming

Read the synonyms for *overwhelming*.
Add another synonym to the list.
overwhelming: vast, overpowering,

_____

8 accompanies

Draw somebody who *accompanies* you when you go to a movie.

High-Utility Words

▶ **Idioms**

An idiom is an expression whose meaning cannot be understood from the separate words in it.

Circle the idioms in the passage.

Matt plays with his new yo-yo. He knows that (practice makes perfect.) But Matt cannot get the hang of it. Matt's brother tells him, "You can do it. It's a piece of cake!" Matt is fed up with the yo-yo. He tries one more time. Out of the blue, he makes the yo-yo work! Matts spends the next hour playing with it. Time flies when you are having fun.

My Notes

Read "The TimeSpecs 3000."
Use this page to take notes.

_____

_____

_____

_____

_____

_____

_____

_____

_____

_____

_____

The TimeSpecs 3000

? Essential Question

Why do people run for public office?

Read how Miguel makes a decision to run for class president.

September 15

Dear Grandpa,

I just got back from our class trip to Washington, D.C. and I have a lot to tell you. The trip helped me decide to run for class president.

I owe it all to your invention, the TimeSpecs 3000! It helped me get some advice about my problem. I **intend** to tell you everything when I visit Saturday, but for now I've pasted my field notes into this e-mail. You can see how well your invention worked.

FIELD NOTES: **DAY 1**

I use the TimeSpecs 3000 at the Washington Monument. Our guide **accompanies** us everywhere. While she's talking, I put on the specs. The design needs tweaking because Ken whispered, "Nerdy glasses, dude!"

Suddenly, I'm seeing the Washington Monument in the past. I am watching the **ceremony** when they laid the cornerstone in 1848. Everyone's wearing old-fashioned clothes. When I take off the TimeSpecs 3000, I see my class is leaving. I go after them.

Chris Boyd

Text Evidence

❶ Comprehension
Point of View

Reread the first paragraph. **Circle** the pronouns. Who is Miguel writing to?

_____

_____

❷ Organization Ⓐ Ⓒ Ⓣ

Reread the second paragraph. **Underline** the sentence that tells the name of the invention. What did Miguel paste into his e-mail?

_____

_____

❸ Expand Vocabulary

A **ceremony** is a special event that celebrates something. **Draw a box** around the details that tell about the *ceremony*. When did the *ceremony* take place?

_____

_____

221

1 Expand Vocabulary

To be **immature** is to act childish. **Circle** the classmates' *immature* actions.

2 Organization Ⓐ Ⓒ Ⓣ

Reread the first two paragraphs. **Underline** the sentence that tells when Miguel puts on the TimeSpecs. What happens to Miguel after he puts on the specs?

_____

_____

_____

3 Comprehension
Point of View

Reread the second paragraph. **Draw a box** around the details that tell how Miguel feels when Lincoln's statue talks. Why is he speechless?

_____

_____

FIELD NOTES: **DAY 2**

We're back on the National Mall, which has a long reflecting pool. My teacher is finding it hard to **tolerate** my classmates' **immature**, childish behavior. They are yelling and throwing pebbles in the reflecting pool. I am **weary** of the noise. So I put on the TimeSpecs 3000 and look at the Lincoln Memorial.

I see how noble Lincoln's statue looks and start thinking again about whether I should run for class president. Suddenly, right out of the blue, I hear a voice. "Excuse me. You want to run for president?" I look up. Lincoln's statue is talking to me. It's so **overwhelming** that I just stand there. I am speechless.

Finally, I stammer, "President . . . Lincoln?"

"Maybe you should first run for mayor of your town," the statue says. "Or perhaps for **governor**? Once you get the hang of being in public office, run for president."

"Actually, it's for president of my 4th grade class," I say. The statue nods. "That's an excellent start."

While I have Lincoln's ear, I decide to get some advice. "I have a problem. I hate writing and giving speeches, but my **opponent**, Tommy, is great at both things."

"What kind of **campaign** would you run?" Lincoln asks.

"I have a lot of ideas," I tell him. "I want our school to get fruits and vegetables from the local farmers' market. We can serve them in the cafeteria. I also want to start a book drive for our school library."

"There is your speech," he says. "Tell people your ideas with honesty and **enthusiasm**. Show your excitement."

"Thanks, Mr. President," I say. "I can do that!"

Grandpa, I can't wait to see you on Saturday, when I will tell you about our visit to the Natural History Museum.

Your grandson and future class president,
Miguel

P.S. Don't wear the TimeSpecs 3000 while looking at dinosaur bones.

Chris Boyd

1 Comprehension
Point of View

Reread the first paragraph. **Underline** how Miguel feels about speeches. Why does he think this is a problem?

_____

_____

2 Expand Vocabulary

The word **enthusiasm** means showing interest or excitement. **Circle** what Lincoln tells Miguel to do with *enthusiasm*.

3 Organization Ⓐ Ⓒ T

Reread the sixth paragraph. **Draw a box** around the sentence that tells you the e-mail has returned to the present. What is Miguel going to tell Grandpa?

_____

_____

Respond to Reading

Discuss Work with a partner. Read the questions about "The TimeSpecs 3000." Use the discussion starters to answer the questions. Write the page numbers to show where you found text evidence.

❓ Questions | **Discussion Starters** | **🔍 Text Evidence**

Questions	Discussion Starters	Text Evidence
1 Who does Miguel talk to while he is wearing the TimeSpecs 3000?	▶ While Miguel is wearing the TimeSpecs 3000 he... ▶ I noticed that....	Page(s): _____
2 What problem does Miguel tell Lincoln about?	▶ Miguel tells Lincoln... ▶ I read that Lincoln asked...	Page(s): _____
3 What are two ideas Miguel has for his school?	▶ One idea Miguel has for his school is... ▶ Another idea is...	Page(s): _____

Mike Moran

224

Write Review your notes about "The TimeSpecs 3000."
Then write your answer to the question below. Use text
evidence to support your answer.

Why does Miguel decide to run for class president?

_____

_____

_____

_____

_____

_____

_____

_____

_____

_____

_____

Write About Reading

Shared Read

Read an Analysis **Point of View** **Read Alison's paragraph about "The TimeSpecs 3000." She wrote about how the author used a first-person narrator to tell a story.**

Student Model

The author of "The TimeSpecs 3000," uses a first-person narrator so that readers can experience events through Miguel's eyes. While visiting Washington D.C., Miguel wears special glasses. These special glasses let Miguel see people and events from the past. At the Lincoln Memorial, Lincoln speaks to Miguel. At first, Miguel is speechless. Then he tells Lincoln that he wants to run for class president. Lincoln gives Miguel good advice. Because the author used a first-person narrator, I felt like I was with Miguel experiencing everything he did.

Topic Sentence

Circle the topic sentence. What information does Alison include?

Evidence

Draw a box around the evidence that Alison cites. What other information from "The TimeSpecs 3000" would you add?

Concluding Statement

Underline the concluding statement. Why is this sentence a good wrap up?

Leveled Reader

Write an Analysis ▶ **Point of View** Write a paragraph about "Floozle Dreams." Tell how the author used a first-person narrator to tell the story.

_____

_____

_____

_____

_____

_____

_____

_____

_____

_____

_____

_____

Topic Sentence

☐ Include the title of the text you read.

☐ Tell about how the author used a first-person narrator.

Evidence

☐ Include details that show what the narrator is thinking.

☐ Tell how the use of first-person lets the reader see events through the narrator's eyes.

Concluding Statement

☐ Restate how the author used a first-person narrator to tell the story.

Talk About It

Weekly Concept Breakthroughs

Essential Question

How do inventions and technology affect your life?

Go Digital!

COLLABORATE Write words that describe different types of technology and how it affects your life.

Technology	Effect

 Describe one kind of technology and its effect on your life. Use words you wrote above.

CCSS Vocabulary

 Work with a partner to complete each activity.

1 squirmed

Circle one thing that will *squirm* if you try to hold it.

    a key   a book   a puppy

2 decade

How old will you be in one *decade*?

_____

3 gleaming

Read the synonyms below for *gleaming*. Add another synonym to the list.
gleaming: glimmering, sparkling

_____

4 technology

List two kinds of *technology* you use.

_____

_____

5 engineering

▸ Underline the base word in *engineering*

▸ Circle the ending, *-ing*.

▸ What does *engineering* mean?

_____

_____

6 directing

Pretend you are a crossing guard. Act out *directing* students to cross the street. Use your voice and your hands.

7 scouted

The girl was *scouting* the beach searching for seashells. How are the words *scouting* and *searching* related?

_____

_____

230

8 **tinkering**

Draw a picture of a person *tinkering* with a bike.

Pronouns

Indefinite pronouns refer to nouns in a general way. *Everywhere* **and** *anyone* **are examples of indefinite pronouns.**

Circle the indefinite pronouns in the passage.

Lee brings his camera (everywhere.) He takes pictures of anyone and everything. Everyone in Lee's family thinks he has talent. Lee wants to become a photographer. One day he hopes to meet someone who can help him make his dream come true. For now, Lee will keep snapping away!

Steve Prezant/age fotostock

My Notes

Read "A Telephone Mix-Up."
Use this page to take notes.

A Telephone Mix-Up

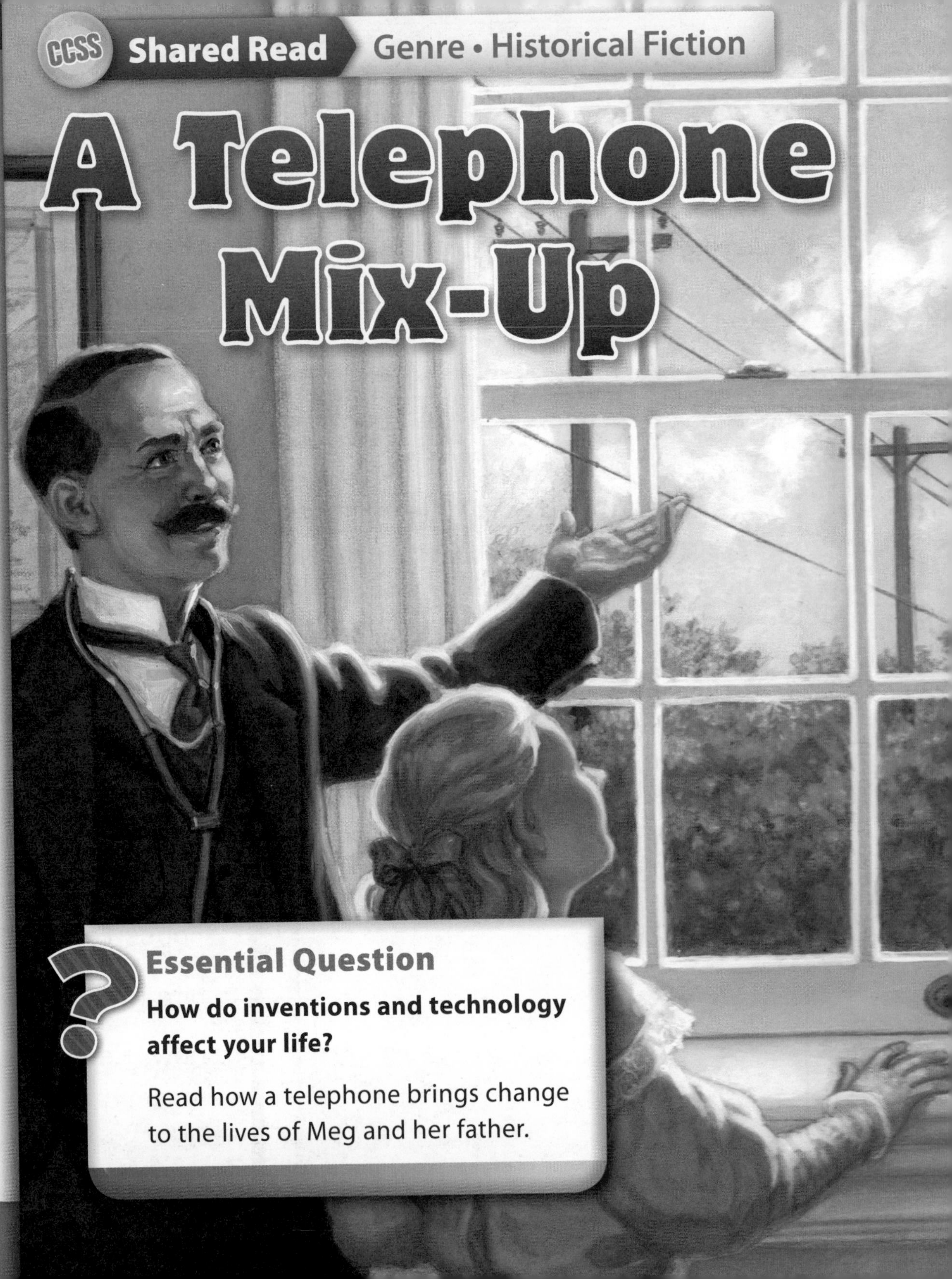

Essential Question

How do inventions and technology affect your life?

Read how a telephone brings change to the lives of Meg and her father.

"By tomorrow there will be eight telephones in Centerburg, Ohio, and one of them will be ours!" Dr. Ericksen said to his daughter, Meg. "I predict that before this **decade** is over, in another five years, there could be a hundred! That's how fast I see this **technology** spreading! When people need help, they'll call me on the telephone. **Envision** the lives it will save! Picture the amazing benefits!"

Meg knew that not everyone thought the telephone was an **engineering** miracle. Some people felt this newfangled machine would open a Pandora's box of troubles. It would cause people to stop visiting each other and writing letters.

Despite these concerns, progress marched on. Weeks earlier, Centerburg's first telephone had been installed in Mr. Kane's store, another at the hotel, and yet another at the newspaper office. Mrs. Kane was the town's first switchboard operator, **directing** all the calls.

The next morning, Meg wrote "October 9, 1905" on her slate. She **squirmed** in her seat, wishing the school day was over.

Tristan Elwell

Text Evidence

① Comprehension
Point of View

Reread the first paragraph. **Circle** Dr. Ericksen's prediction. What details tell how the doctor feels about this new technology?

_____

_____

② Expand Vocabulary

To **envision** means to think about something that is in the future. **Draw a box** around what Dr. Ericksen tells Meg to *envision*.

③ Sentence Structure Ⓐ Ⓒ Ⓣ

Reread the second paragraph. **Underline** the thing that people think will open a Pandora's box of troubles. What are people afraid will happen?

_____

_____

Text Evidence

1 Comprehension
Point of View

Reread the first paragraph. **Underline** the details that show what Meg thinks about when she looks at the wires. How does Meg feel about the telephone?

_____

_____

_____

2 Expand Vocabulary

Magnificence is the state of being very beautiful. **Circle** the thing that Dr. Ericksen describes as having such _magnificence_.

3 Sentence Structure (A)(C)(T)

Reread the last paragraph. **Draw a box** around the text that tells when Meg and her father saw Mr. Turner. What word in the sentence signals time?

_____

234

Walking home, Meg **scouted** the street, looking for the tall poles that were going up weekly. Thick wire linked one pole to another, and Meg knew each wire would carry the words of friends and neighbors. Conversations would zip over the lines.

Meg hurried into the house. There on the wall was a **gleaming** wooden telephone box with its heavy black receiver on a hook. Her father was smiling while **tinkering** with the shiny brass bells on top. "Isn't it impressive?" he asked. "Have you ever seen such **magnificence**?"

Suddenly the telephone rang loudly. Both Ericksens jumped.

Meg's father picked up the receiver and shouted, "Yes, hello, this is the doctor!"

"Again please, Mrs. Kane!" Dr. Ericksen shouted. "I didn't get the first part. Bad cough? Turner farm?"

"Can I go, Father?" Meg asked as Dr. Ericksen returned the receiver to the hook.

"Absolutely," he said, grabbing his medical kit and heading outside to his horse and cart.

When they got to the farm, they found Mr. Turner walking toward the barn.

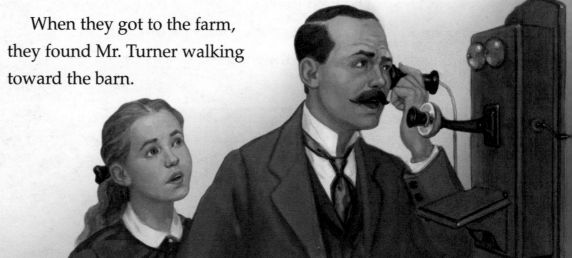

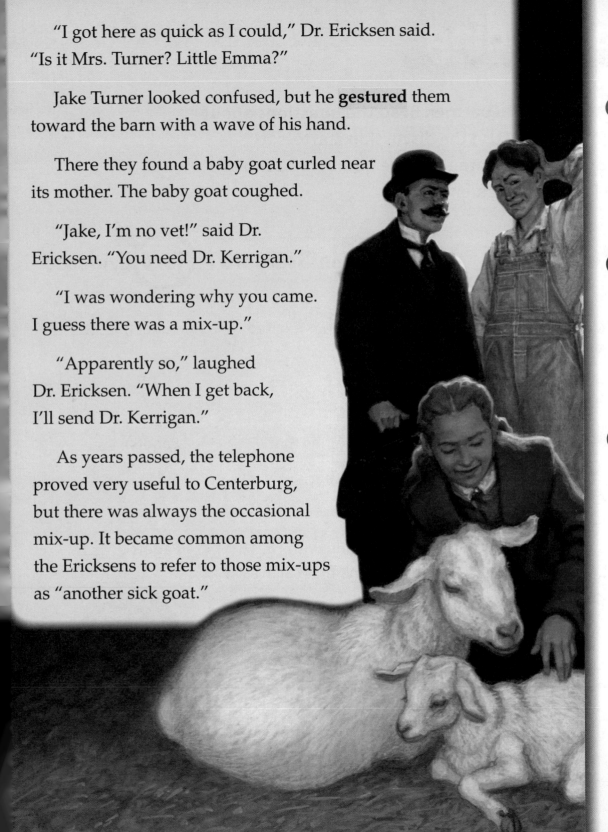

"I got here as quick as I could," Dr. Ericksen said. "Is it Mrs. Turner? Little Emma?"

Jake Turner looked confused, but he **gestured** them toward the barn with a wave of his hand.

There they found a baby goat curled near its mother. The baby goat coughed.

"Jake, I'm no vet!" said Dr. Ericksen. "You need Dr. Kerrigan."

"I was wondering why you came. I guess there was a mix-up."

"Apparently so," laughed Dr. Ericksen. "When I get back, I'll send Dr. Kerrigan."

As years passed, the telephone proved very useful to Centerburg, but there was always the occasional mix-up. It became common among the Ericksens to refer to those mix-ups as "another sick goat."

❶ Expand Vocabulary

A **gesture** is a body movement to express a feeling or a direction. **Circle** details that tell how Jake Turner *gestured*.

❷ Sentence Structure Ⓐ Ⓒ Ⓣ

Reread the fifth paragraph. **Underline** the text in quotation marks. Who is speaking?

_____

❸ Comprehension
Point of View

Reread the last paragraph. **Draw a box** around the words the narrator says about the telephone. How does the narrator feel about the telephone?

_____

_____

_____

235

Respond to Reading

Discuss Work with a partner. Read the questions about "A Telephone Mix-Up." Use the discussion starters to answer the questions. Write the page numbers to show where you found text evidence.

? Questions	Discussion Starters	Text Evidence
1 Why is Dr. Ericksen excited about having a telephone?	▶ Dr. Ericksen is excited because… ▶ He tells Meg…	Page(s): _____
2 What does Meg imagine when she sees the telephone poles and wires?	▶ Meg imagines that… ▶ I noticed that…	Page(s): _____
3 What was the mix-up with Dr. Ericksen's first telephone call?	▶ The mix-up with Dr. Ericksen's first call was… ▶ I know this because I read that…	Page(s): _____

Mike Moran

236

Write Review your notes about "A Telephone Mix-Up."
Then write your answer to the question below. Use text
evidence to support your answer.

How did the invention of the telephone affect Dr. Ericksen and Meg?

_____

_____

_____

_____

_____

_____

_____

_____

_____

Write About Reading

Shared Read

Read an Analysis **Genre** Read Rebecca's paragraph about "A Telephone Mix-Up." She wrote her opinion about how well the author used historical events from the past to develop a realistic story.

Student Model

Topic Sentence

Circle the topic sentence. What is Rebecca going to write about?

Evidence

Draw a box around the evidence that Rebecca includes. What other information from "A Telephone Mix-Up" would you include?

Concluding Statement

Underline the concluding statement. Why is this sentence a good wrap up?

In "A Telephone Mix-Up," I think the author did a good job of using the invention of the telephone to write a realistic story. When the telephone first comes to Meg's town, some people don't like it. They think people will stop writing letters and visiting each other. Meg's father is a doctor. He believes the telephone will help save lives. He has a phone put in their house. In my opinion, the author did a good job of writing a realistic story. I think it was true that some people did not like the telephone because they were afraid of the changes it would bring.

238

Leveled Reader

Genre Write a paragraph about "Ron's Radio." Tell how well the author used events from the past to create a realistic story.

_____

_____

_____

_____

_____

_____

_____

_____

_____

_____

_____

Topic Sentence

☐ Include the title of the text you read.

☐ Tell your opinion about how well the author used historical events in the story.

Evidence

☐ Include details the author used to make the story realistic.

☐ Tell how the invention of the radio was a real event.

Concluding Statement

☐ Restate how the author used real events and details to create realistic characters.

Talk About It

Weekly Concept Wonders in the Sky

Essential Question

How do you explain what you see in the sky?

Go Digital!

240

Write words that tell what you know about the moon.

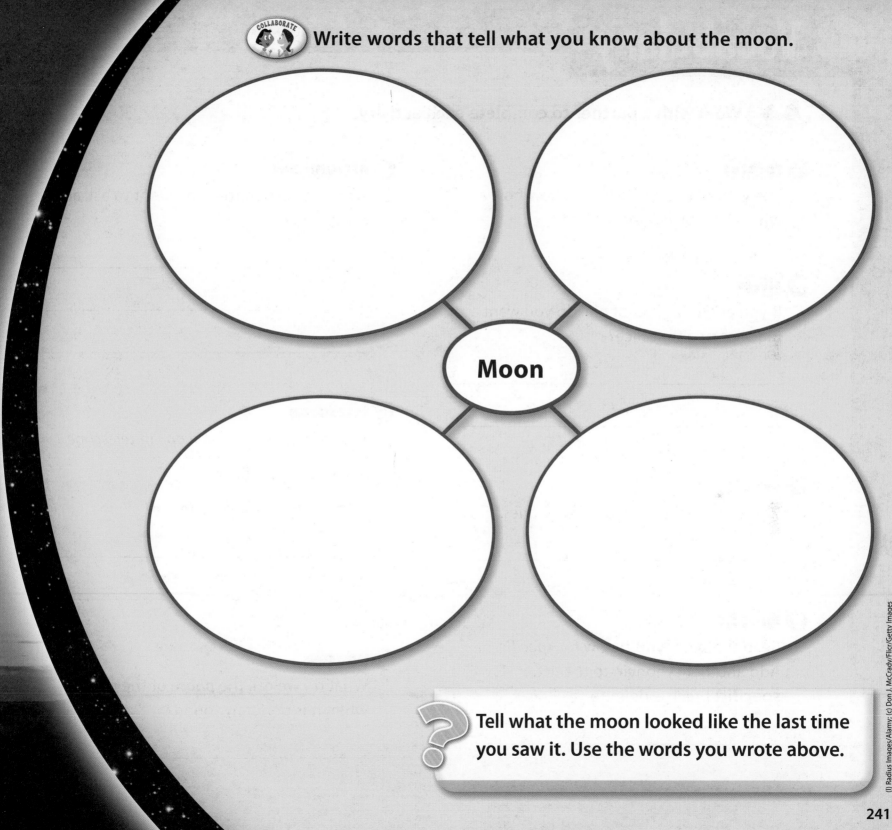

Moon

Tell what the moon looked like the last time you saw it. Use the words you wrote above.

Vocabulary

 Work with a partner to complete each activity.

1 rotates

Use your hands and arms to show how a wheel on a bike *rotates*.

2 sliver

If you ask for a *sliver* of pie, do you want a big slice or a thin slice?

_____

_____

3 series

Name a favorite book or movie *series*.

_____

4 specific

Read the synonyms below for *specific*. Add another synonym to the list.
specific: precise, definite,

_____

5 astronomer

Write a question that you want to ask an *astronomer*.

_____

_____

_____

6 telescope

▶ Underline the word *scope* in *telescope*.

▶ Circle the prefix *tele-*

▶ What does *telescope* mean?

_____

_____

7 phases

What do we call the *phase* of the moon when it is perfectly round?

_____

_____

8 crescent

Draw a picture of a *crescent* moon.

High-Utility Words

▶ **Suffixes**

The suffix *-ful* can stand for "full of" or "having the qualities of."

Circle words with the suffix *-ful* in the passage.

Maya loved going to the city at night. She and her family thought it looked (beautiful!) Colorful neon signs lit up the streets. Bright lights on the graceful buildings were plentiful. Lots of cheerful people were in the streets. The city was nothing like the peaceful town Maya lived in. That's why she liked to visit the city.

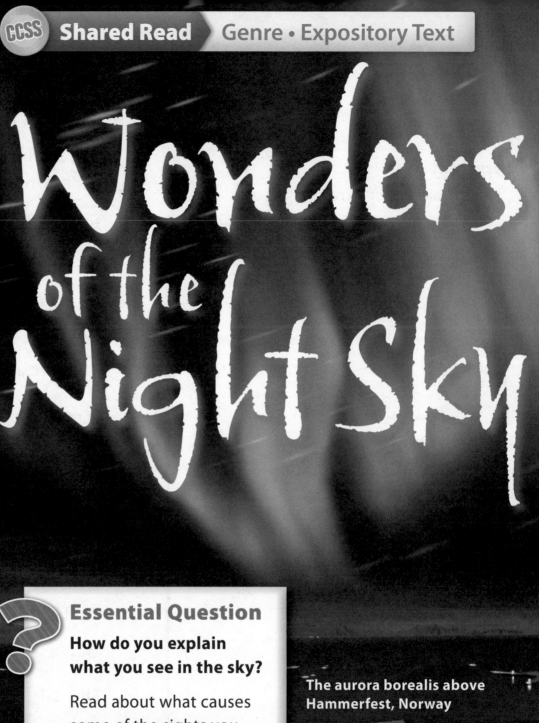

Wonders of the Night Sky

Essential Question

How do you explain what you see in the sky?

Read about what causes some of the sights you see in the sky.

The aurora borealis above Hammerfest, Norway

As Earth **rotates** on its axis, day becomes night. Suddenly, a gallery of lights is **revealed**! You may see a thin **crescent** moon or another of the moon's **phases**. You may even see a **series** of lights spread across the sky like ribbons. Scientists can help explain what we see.

Aurora Borealis

An amazing light show is seen near the North Pole. It is the **aurora borealis** (uh-RAWR-uh bawr-ee-AL-is) or "the northern lights." Brilliant bands of lights appear in the sky. They are green, yellow, red, and blue.

People once believed the lights were caused by sunlight. They believed sunlight reflected off polar ice caps. Then it bounced back and created patterns in the sky. In fact, the lights happen because of magnetic attraction.

The sun gives off electrically charged particles. These nearly invisible particles join a stream called a solar wind. As Earth orbits the sun, solar winds reach Earth's magnetic field. As a result, electric charges occur. These charges are sometimes strong enough to be seen from Earth. They cause the colorful aurora borealis.

Picture Press/Alamy

1 Expand Vocabulary

When something is **revealed**, it can now be seen. **Draw a box** around the details that tell what may be *revealed* in the night sky.

2 Genre Ⓐ Ⓒ Ⓣ
Expository Text

Reread the second paragraph. **Circle** the text that is in bold type. What information does the text in parentheses give you?

_____

_____

3 Comprehension
Cause and Effect

Reread the last paragraph. **Underline** the words that signal a cause-and-effect relationship. What happens when solar winds reach Earth's magnetic fields?

_____

_____

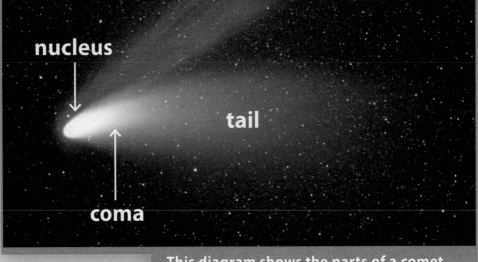

nucleus

tail

coma

This diagram shows the parts of a comet.
Comets' tails can be millions of miles long.

① **Genre** Ⓐ Ⓒ Ⓣ
Expository Text

Look at the diagram and read the
caption. **Draw a box** around the
purpose of the diagram. What is
the name for the head of a comet?

_____

② **Expand Vocabulary**

Streaks are long wavy lines.
Circle the details that tell why
people feared seeing *streaks* in
the night sky.

③ **Comprehension**
Cause and Effect

Reread the third paragraph.
Underline the result when a
comet comes closer to the sun.
What part of a comet do we
see from Earth?

_____

_____

_____

Comets

A comet is another light in the night sky. The word
comet comes from a Greek word. The word means,
"wearing long hair." The Greek philosopher **Aristotle**
(AR-uh-stot-uhl) thought comets looked like stars with hair.

Long ago, people feared these unknown **streaks**. They
believed the lines of light might bring war or sickness.
Today comets are not feared. We know they are made of
rock, dust, ice, and frozen gases.

Comets move around the sun in an oval-shaped orbit.
When a comet comes closer to the sun, the result is that
a "tail" of gas and dust is pushed out behind the comet.
This long tail is what we see from Earth.

Scientists think comets are some of the oldest things in
space. They track **specific** comets. They predict when we
will see them again.

Meteors

Have you ever seen shooting stars? Those streaks of light are not really stars at all. They are usually **meteors** (MEE-tee-erz). Meteors are the rocky debris and fragments that enter Earth's atmosphere. Sometimes Earth passes through an area in space with a lot of debris. This is when a meteor shower occurs. As a result, you may see hundreds of "shooting stars" during a meteor shower.

These days an **astronomer**, or anyone with a small, light **portable telescope**, can ask new questions about space. What do you see when you look at the night sky? You may see a **sliver** of the moon. Or you may see a fantastic light show. Either way, you are bound to see something amazing.

The Perseid meteor shower

Text Evidence

1 **Comprehension**
Cause and Effect

Reread the first paragraph. **Underline** what causes a meteor shower. What is the effect of a meteor shower?

_____

2 **Genre** ACT
Expository Text

Look at the page. **Draw a box** around the text feature that shows a meteor shower. What is the name of the meteor shower?

_____

3 **Expand Vocabulary**

Something that is **portable** is easy to carry or move. **Circle** the object mentioned in the text that is *portable*. Why is a *portable* telescope helpful?

_____

_____

247

Respond to Reading

Discuss Work with a partner. Read the questions about "Wonders of the Night Sky." Use the discussion starters to answer the questions. Write page numbers to show where you found text evidence.

?Questions

Discussion Starters

Text Evidence

1 Why were people afraid of comets long ago?

▸ People were afraid of comets because...

▸ I read that ...

Page(s): _____

2 What creates the long tail that we see on a comet?

▸ Comets move around...

▸ When a comet gets closer to the sun...

▸ When that happens...

Page(s): _____

3 What do scientists think about comets?

▸ Scientists think that comets...

▸ I read that ...

Page(s): _____

Mike Moran

Write Review your notes about "Wonders of the Night Sky." Then write your answer to the question below. Use text evidence to support your answer.

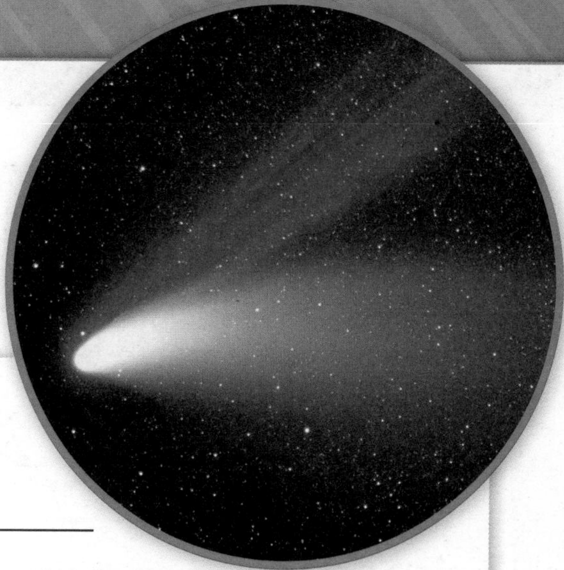

What is a comet?

Roger Ressmeyer/Photographer's Choice/Getty Images

Write About Reading

Shared Read

Read an Analysis **Text Features** Read Lee's paragraph about "Wonders of the Night Sky." She analyzes how the author uses headings to tell what each section of text is about.

Student Model

In "Wonders of the Night Sky," the author uses headings to tell what each section of the text is about. The first heading is "Aurora Borealis." This section explains what the aurora borealis are and what causes them. In the next section, the heading is, "Comets." This section includes a diagram of a comet. Since the author used headings, I knew what I'd be reading about in each section. The headings helped me to understand the text better.

Topic Sentence

Circle the topic sentence. What is Lee going to write about?

Evidence

Draw a box around the details that Lee includes. What other information from "Wonders of the Night Sky" would you include?

Concluding Statement

Underline the concluding statement. Why is this sentence a good wrap-up?

(br) Steve Cole/Photodisc/Getty Images

250

Leveled Reader

Write an Analysis   **Text Features** Write a paragraph about "Stargazing." Explain how the author uses headings to tell what each section of text is about.

_____

_____

_____

_____

_____

_____

_____

_____

_____

_____

_____

Topic Sentence

☐ Include the title of the text you read.

☐ Tell how the author uses headings to tell what each section of text is about.

Evidence

☐ Include one or more examples of these headings.

☐ Explain how the heading tells what the section of text is about.

Concluding Statement

☐ Restate how the author uses headings in the text.

251

Talk About It

Weekly Concept Achievements

Essential Question

How do writers look at success in different ways?

Go Digital!

252

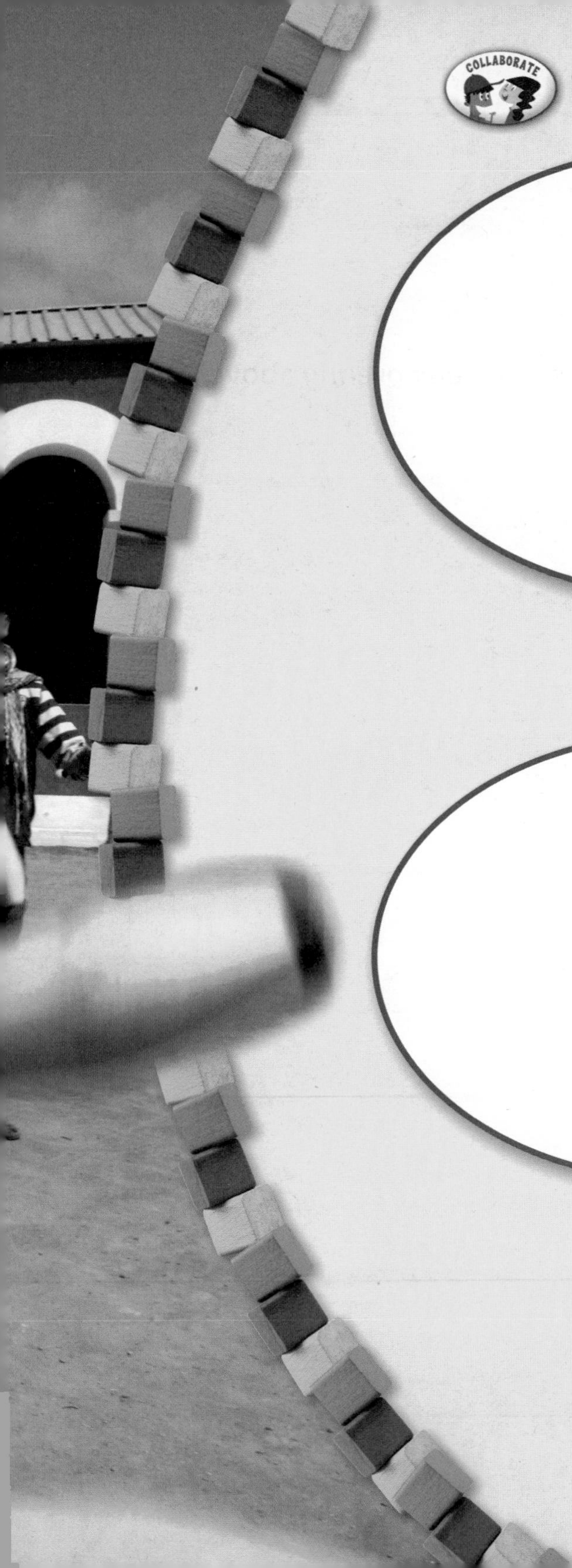

COLLABORATE **Write words that describe what success means to you.**

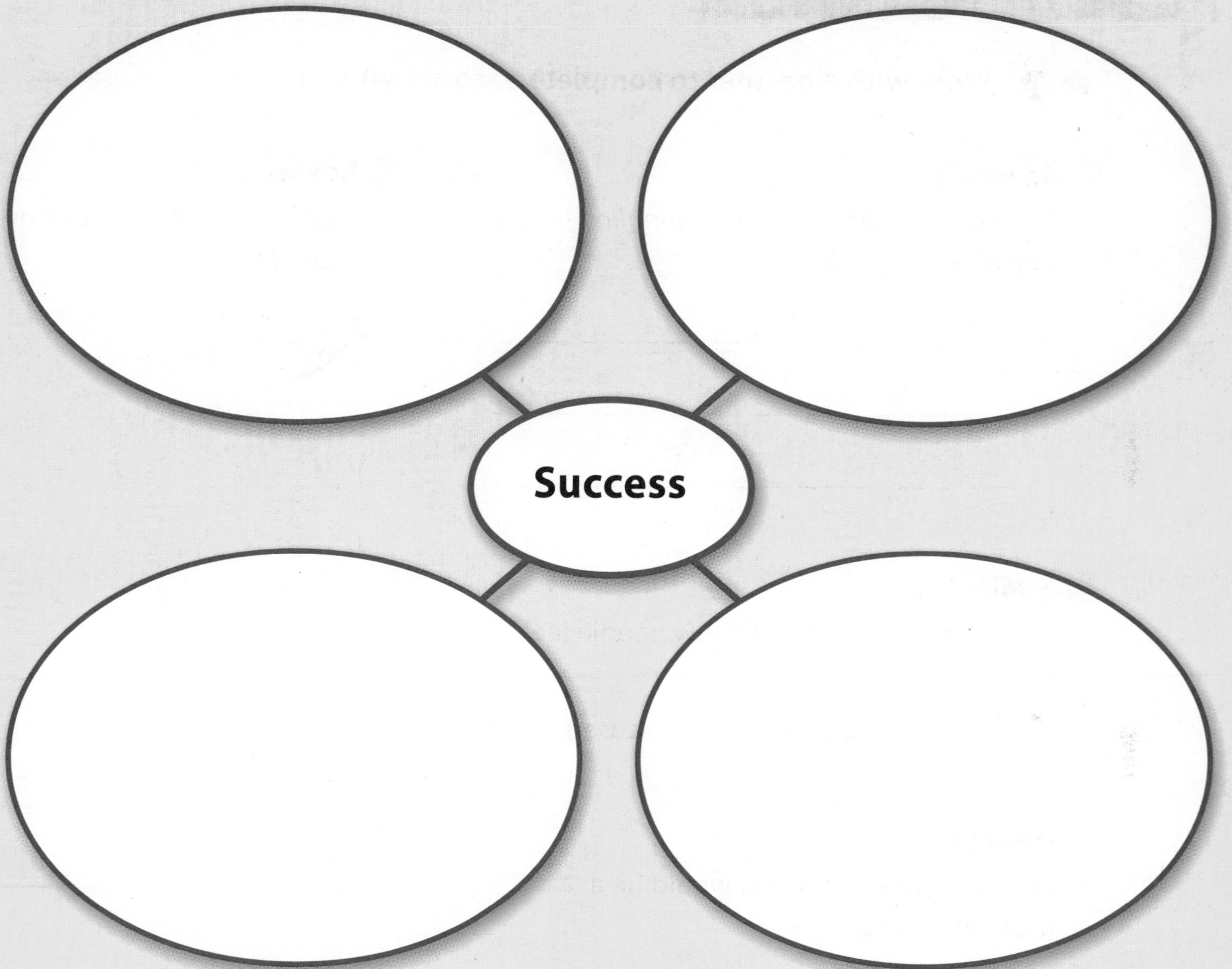

Success

Describe a time that you did something successfully. Use the words that you wrote above.

Work with a partner to complete each activity.

1 dangling

What do you sometimes see *dangling* from a tree after a storm?

_____

_____

_____

2 attain

Circle two words that tell how people feel when they *attain* a goal.

    proud   unhappy   pleased

3 triumph

Describe something that would be a *triumph* for you.

_____

_____

_____

_____

4 hovering

Draw a picture of a bee *hovering* above a flower.

254

Read the poem. Work with a partner to complete each activity.

The Play

When the cast list first went up,
I couldn't breathe. I strained to see
over the pushy crowd
of my classmates. My best friend
shrieked, "We got the leads!

We slap hands, our breath bursting
out of our mouths in a joyful yell.

Weeks later, on the wooden stage,
we take our bows in triumph.

The audience claps, their breath bursting
out of their mouths in a joyful yell.

5 stanza

A *stanza* is two or more lines of poetry that together form a unit of the poem. **Draw a box** around the second stanza.

6 denotation

The *denotation* is the definition of a word. What is the denotation of *shrieked*?

_____

_____

7 connotation

The *connotation* of a word is a feeling connected with it. Does the word *pushy* have a positive or negative connotation?

_____

8 repetition

When a word or phrase is repeated in a poem, it is called *repetition*. **Circle** a phrase in the poem that is repeated.

255

My Notes

Read the poems. Use this page to take notes.

_____

_____

_____

_____

_____

_____

_____

_____

_____

_____

_____

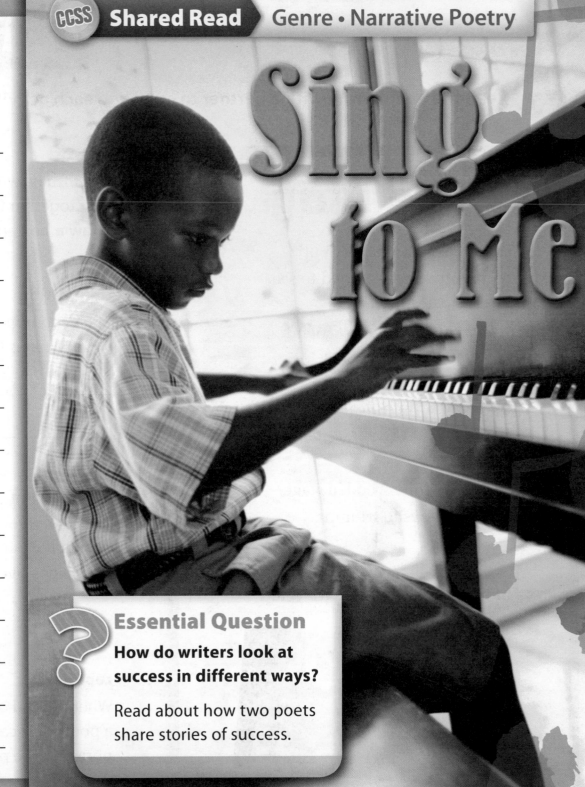

Sing to Me

Essential Question

How do writers look at success in different ways?

Read about how two poets share stories of success.

256

The cool white keys stretched for miles.
How would my hands pull
and sort through the notes,
blending them into music?

I practiced
and practiced all day.
My fingers reaching for a melody
that hung dangling,
like an apple just out of reach.

I can't do this.
I can't do this.

The day ground on,
notes leaping hopefully into the air,
hovering briefly, only to crash,
an awkward jangle, a tangle of noise
before slowly fading away.

My mom found me, forehead on the keys.
She asked, "Would you like some help?
It took months for my hands to do what I wanted."
She sat down on the bench,
her slender fingers plucking notes
from the air.

I can do this.
I can do this.

She sat with me every night that week,
working my fingers until their efforts
made the keys sing to me, too.

—Will Meyers

Text Evidence

① Genre ⒶⒸⓉ

Reread the second stanza. **Circle** what the narrator did all day. What is the narrator doing in this poem?

_____

_____

② Literary Elements
Repetition

Reread the poem. **Draw a box** around the first example of repetition. How is the narrator feeling?

_____

③ Comprehension
Theme

Reread the first stanza. Think about how the narrator feels. Reread the last stanza. How does the narrator feel now?

_____

_____

257

Text Evidence

1 Genre ACT

Reread the first stanza. **Underline** the words that help you identify the characters in the poem. Who are the two characters?

_____

_____

2 Comprehension
Theme

Reread the second stanza. **Draw a box** around the word that shows the narrator has tried to climb this tree more than once.

3 Literary Elements
Repetition

Look at the last three stanzas on this page. **Circle** the word that repeats in the same place in each stanza. What is the effect of the poet's use of repetition?

_____

_____

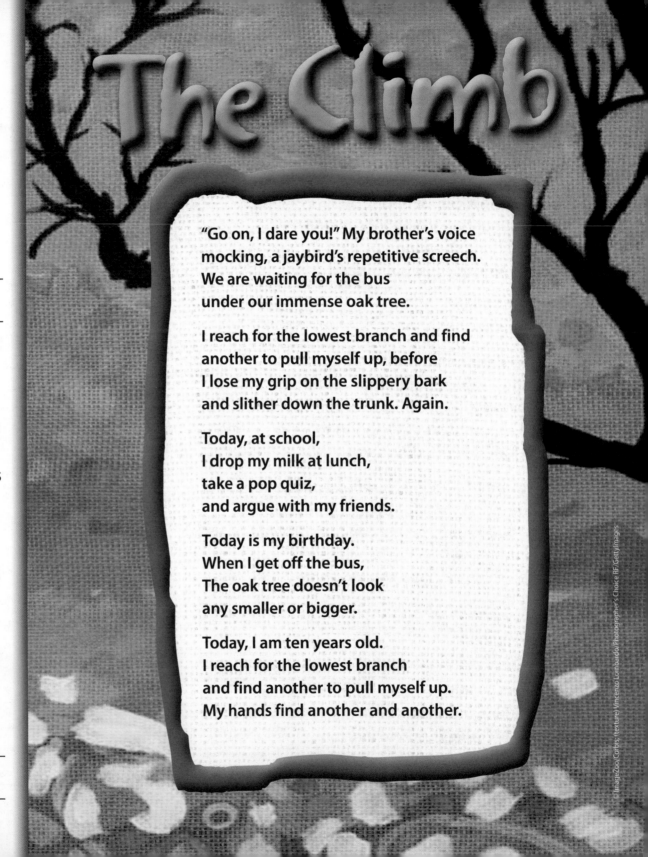

The Climb

"Go on, I dare you!" My brother's voice
mocking, a jaybird's repetitive screech.
We are waiting for the bus
under our immense oak tree.

I reach for the lowest branch and find
another to pull myself up, before
I lose my grip on the slippery bark
and slither down the trunk. Again.

Today, at school,
I drop my milk at lunch,
take a pop quiz,
and argue with my friends.

Today is my birthday.
When I get off the bus,
The oak tree doesn't look
any smaller or bigger.

Today, I am ten years old.
I reach for the lowest branch
and find another to pull myself up.
My hands find another and another.

Over and over among the red
outstretched leaves,
foot to branch: push!
hand to branch: pull!

My brother is rooted on the ground,
staring up at me,
until finally, I can't climb any higher,
or I will be a cloud.

— Sonya Mera

Text Evidence

1 Literary Elements
Stanza

Draw a box around the sixth
stanza of the poem.

2 Genre (A C T)

Circle the details in the last stanza
that tell you what the narrator's
brother is doing. What event has
made the narrator's brother stare?

_____

_____

3 Comprehension
Theme

Underline the details in the last
stanza that tell you the narrator
is successful in climbing the
tree. What has changed from the
beginning of the poem?

_____

_____

_____

259

Respond to Reading

 Discuss Work with a partner. Discuss the questions below about the poem "Sing to Me." Reread to find the answers. Write page numbers to show where you found text evidence.

 **Questions**  **Discussion Starters** **Text Evidence**

Questions	Discussion Starters	Text Evidence
1 What is the narrator's problem in the first four stanzas of "Sing to Me"?	▶ In "Sing to Me," the speaker is trying to… ▶ The narrator feels… ▶ I know this because I read…	Page(s): _____
2 What happens in the fifth stanza of the poem?	▶ In the fifth stanza… ▶ I noticed that…	Page(s): _____
3 What happens in the last stanza of the poem?	▶ In the last stanza… ▶ The narrator is now … ▶ I know this because I read…	Page(s): _____

Mike Moran

260

Write Review your notes about the poem "Sing to Me." Then write your answer to the question below. Use text evidence to support your answer.

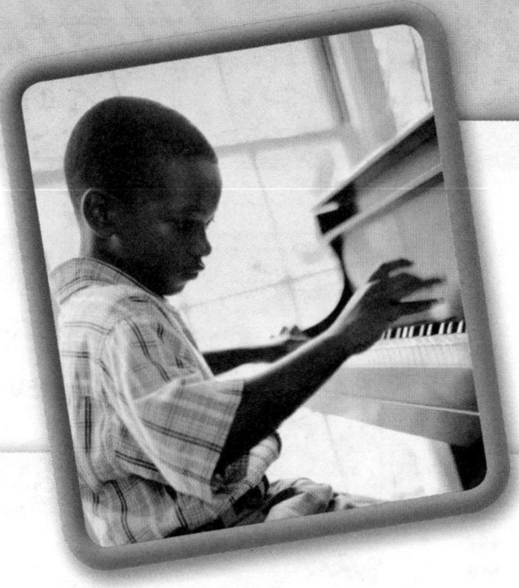

How does the narrator in "Sing to Me" attain success?

Tony Anderson/Taxi/Getty Images

Write About Reading

Shared Read

Read an Analysis > **Theme** Jon wrote about the poems "Sing to Me" and "The Climb." He analyzed how the authors developed the theme of each poem.

Student Model

In the poems of "Sing to Me" and "The Climb", the authors uses key details to develop the theme of each poem. For example, in "Sing to Me" the speaker practices all day. Still the melody is "like an apple just out of reach." Finally, the speaker's mother helps him. Eventually he is able to play the music. In "The Climb," the narrator has attempted to climb a tree many times but cannot do it. On the afternoon of the speaker's birthday, the speaker is able to climb the tree successfully. These details show how the authors develop the theme of achieving success in each of these poems.

Topic Sentence

Circle the topic sentence. What is Jon going to write about?

Evidence

Draw a box around the evidence that Jon includes. What other information from the poems would you include?

Concluding Statement

Underline the concluding statement. Why is this sentence a good wrap up?

262

(br) © ImageZoo/Corbis

Leveled Reader

Write an Analysis **Theme** Write a paragraph about "Try, Try Again." Analyze how the author uses key details to develop the theme.

_____
_____
_____
_____
_____
_____
_____
_____
_____
_____
_____
_____

Topic Sentence

☐ Include the title of the text you read.

☐ Tell whether the author uses key details to develop the theme.

Evidence

☐ Describe the theme of the text.

☐ Explain how key details help to develop this theme.

☐ Support your ideas with details.

Concluding Statement

☐ Restate how the author uses key details to develop the theme.

Figure It Out

The Big Idea

What helps you understand the world around you?

Talk About It

Weekly Concept Making It Happen

Essential Question

In what ways do people show they care about each other?

Go Digital!

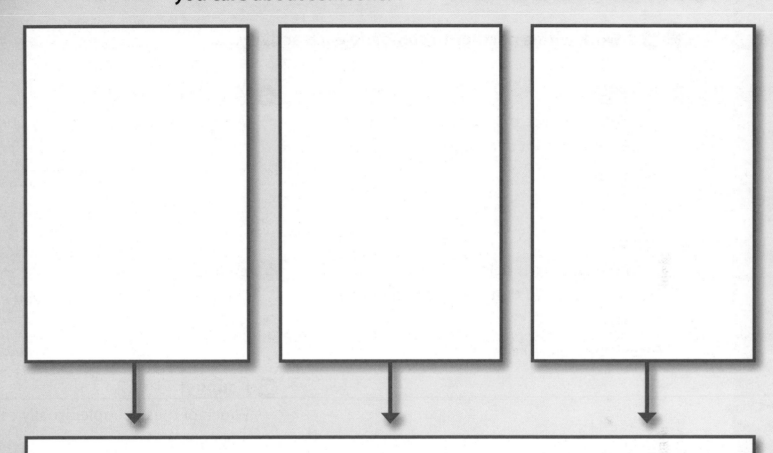

COLLABORATE Write words that describe three ways that you can show you care about someone.

Show You Care

 Tell about one way you can show that you care about a friend. Use the words you wrote above.

Work with a partner to complete each activity.

1 emotion

Read the sentence below out loud. Say the sentence with a lot of *emotion*.

We did it!

2 fussy

Read the antonyms below for *fussy*.
Add another word that means the opposite of *fussy*.

fussy: easygoing, calm,

_____

_____

3 encircle

Underline the word *circle* in *encircle*.
Draw a line under the prefix *en-*.
What does *encircle* mean?

_____

_____

_____

4 portraits

Where would you find family *portraits*?

_____

_____

5 express

Use your face to show how you *express* unhappiness.

6 bouquet

Which of these people usually carries a *bouquet*?

    scientist   cook   bride

7 sparkles

What can a driver do to make sure his or her car *sparkles*?

_____

_____

8 whirl

Draw a picture of a ride at an amusement park that will *whirl* when it starts.

High-Utility Words

▶ **Compound Words**

Compound words are made up of two or more smaller words.

Circle the compound words in the passage.

Jason and I went to the (football) game this afternoon. The best part of the night wasn't the game or the popcorn. It was the fans. The turnout for the game was huge. Many fans wore school colors. One teenage fan had his face painted blue and white! The fans went wild whenever our team made a touchdown.

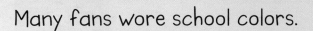

269

My Notes

Read "Sadie's Game." Use this page to take notes.

_____

_____

_____

_____

_____

_____

_____

_____

_____

_____

_____

_____

_____

270

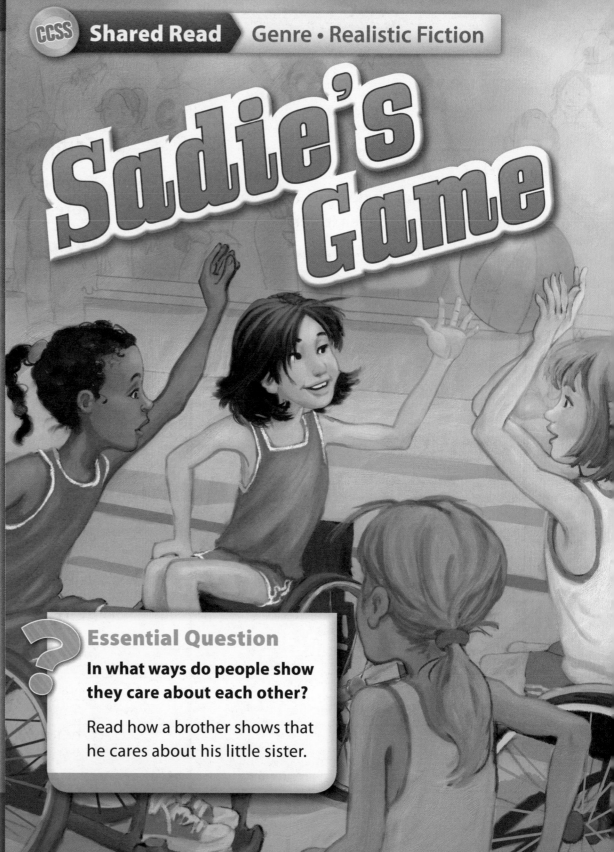

Sadie's Game

? Essential Question

In what ways do people show they care about each other?

Read how a brother shows that he cares about his little sister.

The referee's whistle signaled Sadie's second foul of the game. It was only the first quarter, and Sadie had already **collided** twice with another player's wheelchair. After this last crash, the coach waved her off the court as the upset crowd jeered behind her. She had never seen a crowd **express** such disappointment before.

Sadie watched her teammates **whirl** and spin in front of her. Her **emotions** were all over the place, and it showed in her basketball playing. If only she and her brother had not argued this morning. "Why can't you be at my game, Richie?" Sadie had asked. "Don't I matter to you anymore?"

James Bernardin

1 Expand Vocabulary

To **collide** is to crash into something. **Underline** the detail that tells what Sadie *collided* twice with during the game. What did the coach do after she *collided*?

_____

_____

2 Organization Ⓐ Ⓒ Ⓣ

Reread the last paragraph. **Draw a box** around the words that tell you when Sadie and her brother argued.

3 Comprehension
Problem and Solution

Reread the last paragraph. **Circle** details that tell about Sadie's basketball playing during the game. What is Sadie's problem?

_____

_____

_____

Text Evidence

1 **Organization** (A)(C)(T)

Reread the first paragraph. **Draw a box** around the details that tell what Sadie loved to do before her accident. What did Richie teach Sadie to do again after her accident?

_____

_____

2 **Expand Vocabulary**

A person's **priorities** are the things that are most important to that person. **Circle** Richie's new *priorities*.

3 **Organization** (A)(C)(T)

Reread the last paragraph. **Underline** what Sadie saw when she looked at her mother. Her mother's smile is a clue that something good is going to happen. What happens next?

_____

_____

Richie was Sadie's world. They both loved sports, especially basketball. Sadie had loved to play basketball before her accident. Richie taught her to play again afterward. The days when she did not want to get out of bed, he would bully and coax her, talking her into getting up. He even borrowed a wheelchair for himself. Together they would roll across the court, zipping, passing, and dribbling.

But lately Richie preferred to hang out with his new high school friends. Sadie would watch as Richie polished his new car. He was as **fussy** as a mother cat cleaning her kittens. When he drove away, tears would cloud Sadie's eyes.

Mama was her sun. Her arms would reach out and **encircle** her in a warm embrace. "Sadie," she would say, "your brother still loves you. He has new **priorities** now. Other things may come first, but he cares about you." Sadie still felt hurt.

Sadie saw her coach frown. She searched for her mother, expecting disappointment in her eyes, but instead she saw a big smile. It was the same smile she saw in **portraits** of her mother at home. Sadie followed her mother's gaze to find Richie jogging toward her, holding a colorful **bouquet** of flowers tied with a ribbon. Richie's eyes **sparkled**, and his smile gleamed. He bowed and handed his little sister the flowers as though she were a queen.

"We're losing. How do you know we're going to win?" Sadie asked.

"I don't," Richie said, "but it's not important. What I know is you're like a **whirlwind** on the court, always moving. There is no way I am going to miss your big game!" He put his hand on her shoulder. "It's great to have a lot of new friends, but I realized that you're my best friend."

Sadie smiled. Those words meant more to her than "I'm sorry" ever could. She rested the flowers on her lap and went back out onto the court. She decided to play the rest of the game with the bouquet in her lap. With her brother watching from the sidelines, Sadie stole the ball from an opponent. Then she dribbled her way to the net, making the first of many amazing shots for the team.

James Bernardin

Text Evidence

1 Expand Vocabulary

A **whirlwind** is a rapidly moving column of air. **Draw a box** around the details that tell you why Sadie is like a *whirlwind*.

2 Organization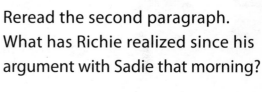

Reread the second paragraph. What has Richie realized since his argument with Sadie that morning?

_____

_____

_____

3 Comprehension
Problem and Solution

Reread the last paragraph. **Underline** details that describe Sadie's playing when she returns to the court. What has changed since the beginning of the story?

_____

_____

273

COLLABORATE

Discuss Work with a partner. Read the questions about "Sadie's Game." Use the discussion starters to answer the questions. Write page numbers to show where you found text evidence.

? Questions   **Discussion Starters**   **Text Evidence**

1 What does Richie teach Sadie to do again after her accident?	▶ After Sadie's accident, Richie teaches Sadie to… ▶ I also read that…	Page(s): _____
2 How does Richie surprise Sadie at the game?	▶ Richie surprises Sadie at the game when he… ▶ I read that…	Page(s): _____
3 What does Richie say to Sadie that shows that he cares?	▶ Richie tells Sadie that… ▶ I noticed that…	Page(s): _____

Mike Moran

Write Review your notes about "Sadie's Game."
Then write your answer to the question below. Use text
evidence to support your answer.

How did Richie show that he cares about his younger sister, Sadie?

_____

_____

_____

_____

_____

_____

_____

_____

_____

_____

James Bernardin

275

Shared Read

Topic Sentence

Circle the topic sentence. What is Carla going to write about?

Evidence

Draw a box around the evidence that Carla includes. What other information from "Sadie's Game" would you include?

Concluding Statement

Underline the concluding statement. Why is this sentence a good wrap up?

Read an Analysis ▶ **Problem and Solution** Read Carla's paragraph below about "Sadie's Game." She analyzes how the author uses problem and solution in a story to develop the plot.

Student Model

In "Sadie's Game," the author uses problem and solution to develop the plot. Sadie's problem is that she is not playing well in the basketball game because she is upset. She had an argument with her brother, Richie, that morning. Sadie thinks Richie spends too much time with his new friends. She is hurt that he doesn't spend more time with her. In the end, Richie solves Sadie's problem. He comes to the game. He surprises Sadie with flowers. Because Richie is there, Sadie plays better. The author uses Sadie's problem and its solution to develop the plot of the story.

Leveled Reader

Write an Analysis **Problem and Solution** Write a paragraph about "Saving Stolen Treasure." Explain how the author uses problem and solution to develop the plot.

_____

_____

_____

_____

_____

_____

_____

_____

_____

_____

_____

Topic Sentence

☐ Include the title of the text you read.

☐ Tell how the author used problem and solution to develop the plot.

Evidence

☐ Describe the problem.

☐ Include evidence to explain how the problem was solved.

Concluding Statement

☐ Restate how the author used problem and solution to develop the plot.

Talk About It

Weekly Concept On the Move

Essential Question

What are some reasons people moved west?

Go Digital!

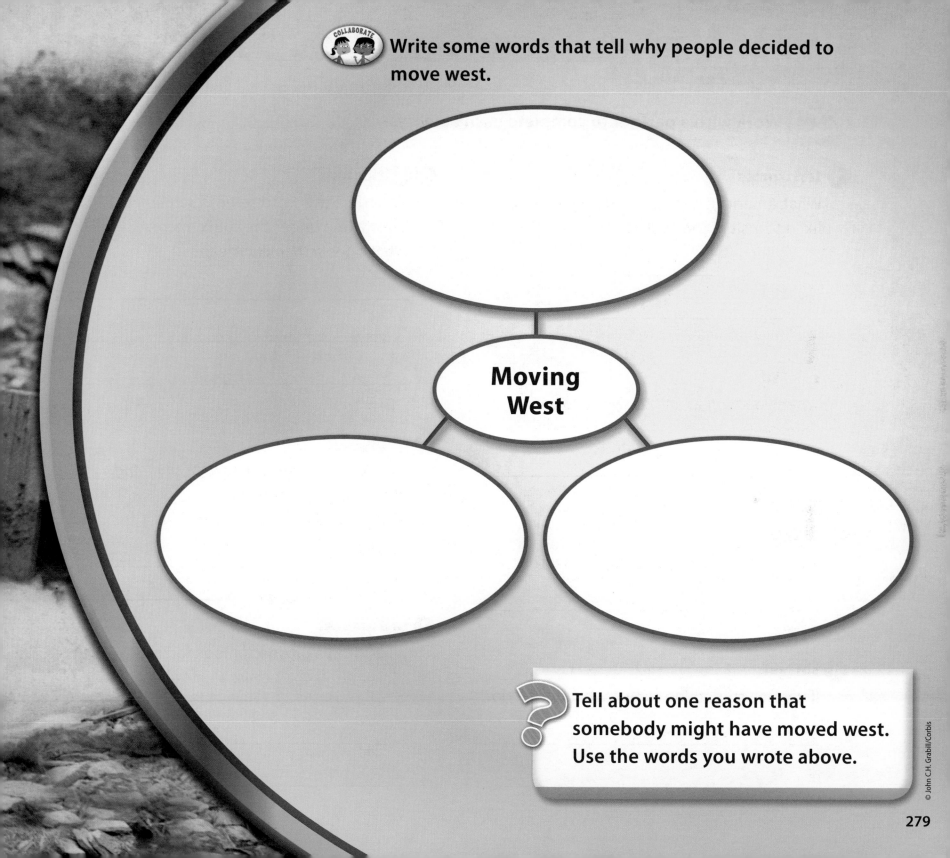

COLLABORATE Write some words that tell why people decided to move west.

Moving West

? Tell about one reason that somebody might have moved west. Use the words you wrote above.

© John C.H. Grabill/Corbis

279

Work with a partner to complete each activity.

1 territories

What American *territories* would you have liked to visit in the 1800s?

_____

_____

2 scoffed

When you *scoff* at an idea what do you think of it?

_____

3 topple

What can cause a lamp to *topple* over?

_____

4 shrivel

If you see something *shrivel*, what does it do?

_____

_____

5 settlement

Underline the word *settle* in *settlement*. Draw a line under the suffix *-ment*. What does *settlement* mean?

_____

_____

_____

6 plunging

Read the synonyms below for *plunging*. Write another synonym.

plunging: diving, dropping,

_____

7 prospector

What does a *prospector* look for?

_____

_____

8 **withered**

Draw a picture of a plant. Then draw a plant that has *withered*.

High-Utility Words

▶ **Homographs**

Homographs are words that are spelled the same but have different meanings.

Circle the homographs in the passage.

Tess decided to (row) a boat out to the lighthouse. There was a (row) of boats on the shore. She chose the second one and pushed it into the sea. She gave a wave to her dog on the shore. A second later, a big wave came and lifted up the boat and pushed her towards the lighthouse.

My Notes

Read "My Big Brother, Johnny Kaw." Use this page to take notes.

_____

_____

_____

_____

_____

_____

_____

_____

_____

_____

_____

_____

_____

_____

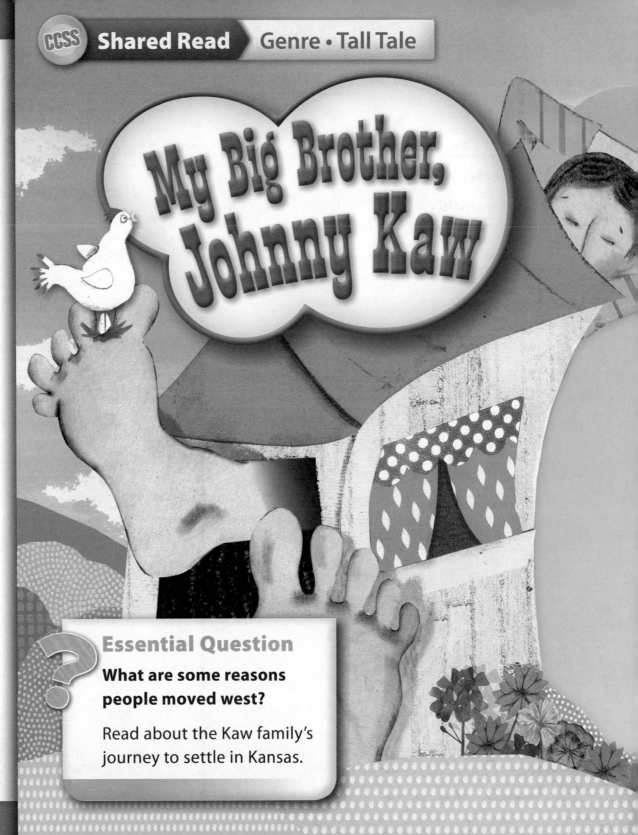

My Big Brother, Johnny Kaw

Essential Question

What are some reasons people moved west?

Read about the Kaw family's journey to settle in Kansas.

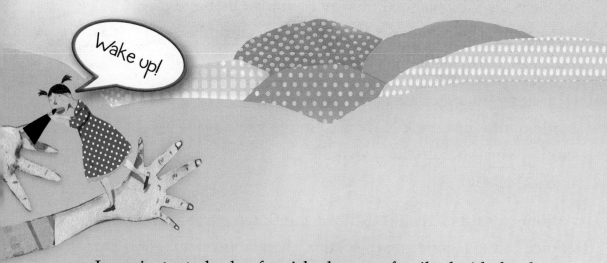

Wake up!

I was just a tadpole of a girl when my family decided to leave the city. My daddy said, "There are **territories** out west with wide open spaces. The Kaw family needs room to grow!"

He was talking about my brother. At fifteen, Johnny was so tall that when he stretched out in bed his head hung out the front door and his legs hung out the back. His feet reached all the way to the chicken coop where the hens laid eggs between his toes.

Mama loaded the wagon with our **belongings**. Daddy hitched up the oxen. We began to head west with everything we owned, but soon Johnny hollered for everybody to stop.

"We'll never get there with these slowpokes pulling us!" Johnny **scoffed**. He unhitched the team and put one ox on each shoulder.

"Don't let them **topple** off!" Daddy hollered.

"Tadpole can watch them!" Johnny said. He set me on top of his head where I had to hang on to Johnny's red hair to keep from falling off. Then Johnny began pulling the wagon.

Josee Basaillon

Text Evidence

❶ Genre Ⓐ Ⓒ Ⓣ
Tall Tale

Reread the second paragraph. **Draw a box** around the details that make Johnny seem larger than life.

❷ Expand Vocabulary

Your **belongings** are the things that belong to you, such as clothing and books. Reread the third paragraph. **Circle** the phrase that has the same meaning as *belongings*.

❸ Comprehension
Cause and Effect

Reread the fourth paragraph. **Underline** the sentence that tells what Johnny did with the oxen. What caused him to do this?

_____

_____

_____

_____

283

Text Evidence

1 Genre ACT
Tall Tale

Reread the first paragraph. **Circle** the details that tell you what Johnny did with the wagon. According to this story, who created the Kaw River?

_____

_____

2 Comprehension
Cause and Effect

Reread the third paragraph. **Draw a box** around the sentence that tells what Johnny did with the mountains after he cut them down. What was the effect of Johnny's actions?

_____

_____

3 Expand Vocabulary

To give **assistance** to others is to help them. **Underline** the details that tell why the neighbors needed *assistance*.

Kaw!

He pulled the wagon one way then the other and dug a big gully. The next night a big rain came and filled it up. Now they call that gully the Kaw River.

Johnny pulled our wagon to a Kansas **settlement** where people were trying to grow crops. "These mountains are in the way," one settler said.

Johnny said he would fix it. He cut down a tree and carved it into a giant, sharp scythe. Then he used it to cut the mountains off at the base. He hauled them west and piled them in a row. Today folks call them the Rocky Mountains.

Everybody in Kansas asked us to stay. So we built a house and started planting wheat.

One summer it was dry. All of the wheat had started to **shrivel** up. Our neighbors asked for Johnny's **assistance**. "We need help. Our crops have almost **withered** away," they said. "We need rain!"

Johnny looked at the clouds. He took his big hoe and poked holes in the clouds and down came the rain in buckets!

One morning at the riverbank, Mama was **plunging** our clothes in the water to clean them. A **prospector** rode up. He said he was going to California to find gold. "Trouble is," he said, "there's not one trail that's good enough to get there."

Mama said, "Let me talk to my son."

Johnny was happy to help. For a week he hiked back and forth, dragging giant bags of wheat everywhere, **clearing** trails of trees, brush, and boulders. The gold rush folks were delighted to have good paths. They named them the Oregon Trail, the Santa Fe Trail, and the Chisholm Trail.

I'm glad our family ended up in Kansas. Neighbors say this is a bad place for tornadoes. So far we haven't seen one. I can't wait, though! Johnny plans to lasso that tornado and ride it like a bucking bronco, and he's promised me a ride!

Josee Basaillon

❶ Expand Vocabulary

To **clear** is to remove things that are in the way. **Circle** the things Johnny was *clearing* from the trails.

❷ Comprehension
Cause and Effect

Reread the first three paragraphs. **Draw a box** around the effects of Johnny clearing the trails. What caused Johnny to clear the trails?

_____

_____

_____

_____

❸ Genre A C T
Tall Tale

Reread the last paragraph. **Underline** the sentence that tells about something only a larger-than-life character can do.

Respond to Reading

Discuss Work with a partner. Read the questions about "My Big Brother, Johnny Kaw." Use the discussion starters to answer the questions. Write page numbers to show where you found text evidence.

❓Questions

Discussion Starters

🔍Text Evidence

Questions	Discussion Starters	Text Evidence
① Why did the Kaw family decide to leave the city?	▶ The Kaw family left the city because… ▶ I know this because I read…	Page(s): _____
② What problem did Johnny help the people in a Kansas settlement solve?	▶ The people in Kansas… ▶ Johnny solved the problem by…	Page(s): _____
③ Why did the Kaw family settle in Kansas?	▶ As a result, the people of Kansas… ▶ I read that the Kaw family…	Page(s): _____

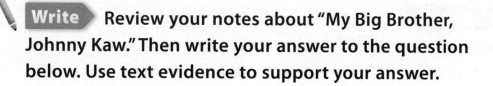

Write Review your notes about "My Big Brother, Johnny Kaw." Then write your answer to the question below. Use text evidence to support your answer.

Why did the Kaw family move to Kansas?

_____

_____

_____

_____

_____

_____

_____

_____

_____

_____

Write About Reading

Shared Read

Read an Analysis **Genre** Read the paragraph Colin wrote about "My Big Brother, Johnny Kaw." He expressed his opinion on how well the author used exaggeration to develop the main character.

Student Model

In "My Big Brother, Johnny Kaw," I think the author does a good job of using exaggeration to show that the main character is larger-than-life and very strong. Johnny carries oxen on his shoulders. He pulls a wagon all the way to Kansas. He cuts down mountains. When there is no rain for a long time, Johnny pokes holes in the clouds with a giant hoe. The author's use of exaggeration helped me to understand that Johnny is so strong that he is a larger-than-life tall tale character.

Topic Sentence

Circle the topic sentence. What is Colin going to write about?

Evidence

Draw a box around the evidence that Colin includes. What other information from "My Big Brother, Johnny Kaw" would you include?

Concluding Statement

Underline the concluding statement. Why is this sentence a good wrap up?

288

Leveled Reader

Write an Analysis **Genre** Write a paragraph about "The Adventures of Sal Fink." Write your opinion on how well the author uses exaggeration to develop Sal's character.

_____

_____

_____

_____

_____

_____

_____

_____

_____

_____

Topic Sentence

☐ Include the title of the text you read.

☐ Tell how well the author uses exaggeration to develop the main character.

Evidence

☐ Describe the main character.

☐ Include details that show how exaggeration is used to develop the main character.

Concluding Statement

☐ Restate how the author used exaggeration to develop the main character.

Talk About It

Weekly Concept Inventions

Essential Question

How can inventions solve problems?

Go Digital!

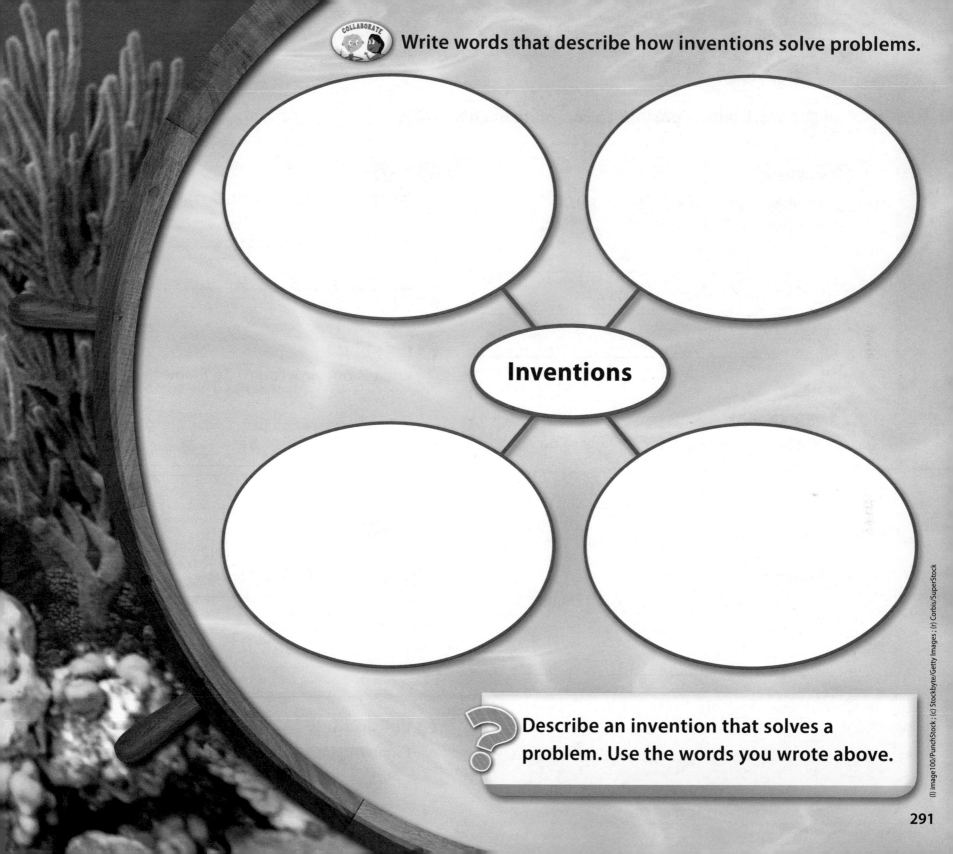

COLLABORATE **Write words that describe how inventions solve problems.**

Inventions

? Describe an invention that solves a problem. Use the words you wrote above.

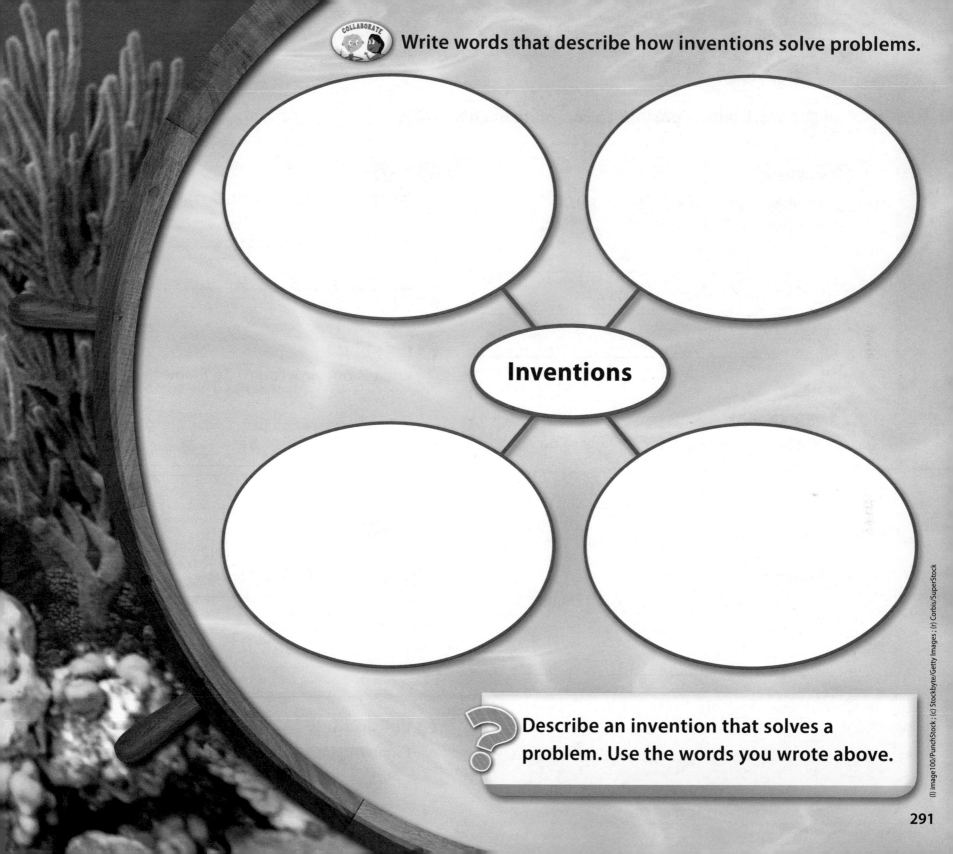

Vocabulary

 Work with a partner to complete each activity.

1 mischief

What kind of *mischief* can a puppy get into in a closet full of shoes?

_____

_____

_____

2 experiment

In what class are you most likely to do an *experiment* using electricity?

_____

3 hilarious

Do you laugh at something you think is *hilarious*? Why or why not?

_____

_____

4 dizzy

What can make a person *dizzy*?

_____

_____

5 procedure

What is one *procedure* you follow in school?

_____

_____

6 nowadays

What do people use *nowadays* to check facts or find information?

_____

_____

7 politician

Circle the person who is a *politician*.

doctor   artist   governor

8 **genuine**

Draw a picture of something with a *genuine* diamond in it. Tell your partner about what you drew.

High-Utility Words

Suffix -*ment*

The suffix -*ment* is a word part. It is added to the end of a word. It changes a word's meaning.

Circle the words with the suffix -*ment* in the passage.

There is (excitement) at the fire department. The city government has just voted to get the firefighters new equipment. Everyone is in agreement. The firefighters need new gear. The replacement gear will be stronger and lighter. It will be an improvement over the old heavy gear.

M. Harris/Iconica/Getty Images

Read "Stephanie Kwolek: Inventor." Use this page for notes.

_____

_____

_____

_____

_____

_____

_____

_____

_____

_____

_____

Stephanie Kwolek:
INVENTOR

Essential Question

How can inventions solve problems?

Read how Stephanie Kwolek invented a super strong fiber that saves lives.

Kevlar® is used in vests for police and police dogs.

If you could invent a material for a superhero, what would it be like? It would be light, bullet-resistant, and fireproof, right? Chemist Stephanie Kwolek invented something like this. It's called Kevlar®. Superheroes don't wear it. But heroes like police officers and firefighters do.

Becoming a Chemist

Math and science always interested Stephanie. She was not a student who caused **mischief**. She worked hard in high school. Stephanie's teachers praised her. They encouraged her to study chemistry in college. Stephanie wanted to go to medical school, but she could not **afford** to pay for it.

So Stephanie took a job at a textile lab. She planned to save money for medical school. At the lab, she discovered a **genuine** love of chemistry. She learned to make chain-like molecules called polymers. These polymers could be spun into fabrics and plastics.

Stephanie enjoyed doing **experiments** so much that she decided not to go to medical school.

Text Evidence

① **Expand Vocabulary**

To **afford** something is to have money to pay for it. **Circle** what Stephanie could not *afford*.

② **Comprehension**
Problem and Solution

Reread the second and third paragraphs. **Underline** Stephanie's problem in the second paragraph. What step did Stephanie take to solve her problem?

_____

_____

③ **Genre** Ⓐ Ⓒ Ⓣ
Biography

Reread the section "Becoming a Chemist." How are the events in this section organized?

_____

_____

_____

295

Text Evidence

1 Expand Vocabulary

To **reinforce** something is to make it stronger by giving it more support. **Circle** what the scientists wanted to *reinforce* tires with.

2 Comprehension
Problem and Solution

Reread the first paragraph. **Underline** the text that states the problem. What steps did Stephanie take to help solve the problem?

_____

_____

_____

3 Genre Ⓐ Ⓒ Ⓣ
Biography

Look at the time line. **Draw a box** around the entry that tells what year Stephanie got her chemistry degree. What year did Stephanie discover the fibers for Kevlar®?

_____

A Strange Liquid

In 1964, the United States was facing a gas shortage. Scientists wanted to help. They thought that if you could **reinforce**, or strengthen, tires with light fiber instead of heavy wire, cars and airplanes would use less gas. Stephanie's boss asked her to work on making a new fiber. Stephanie experimented by mixing polymers. Polymer mixtures, or solutions, are usually thick. Stephanie's solution was watery.

Stephanie brought her strange liquid to a worker. His job was to spin the liquids into fibers. He looked at Stephanie's mixture and laughed. He thought it was **hilarious** that she believed it could be made into fiber. Stephanie asked him to spin it and he finally agreed. He followed the **procedure**. Soon a strong fiber began to form. Stephanie was so thrilled, she felt **dizzy** with excitement.

STEPHANIE KWOLEK'S TIME LINE

1923	1946	1964	1971	1995
Born in Pennsylvania	Earned a degree in chemistry	Discovered the fibers for Kevlar®	Kevlar® is marketed	Inducted into the Inventor's Hall of Fame

Kevlar® is used in this solar racing car.

Stronger than Steel

Stephanie tested the fiber and found that it was fireproof. It was stronger and lighter than steel, too. Stephanie believed the fiber could be turned into a useful material. She was right. The material became known as Kevlar.

Firefighters wear suits made from Kevlar®.

After Stephanie's discovery, it took almost a decade of teamwork to develop Kevlar. Some people worked on getting a patent for Kevlar. Others thought of ways to use and sell it. **Nowadays**, Kevlar® is widely used. The President and other **politicians** stay safe wearing **protective** Kevlar® clothing. So do firefighters and police officers. Kevlar® is also used in tires, bicycles, spacecraft, and skis. By developing Kevlar, Stephanie helped create protective clothing and equipment that is light and strong.

Stephanie's invention has saved many lives over the years. She was inducted into the National Inventors Hall of Fame for her work. Her photograph has appeared on a book cover and in advertisements for Kevlar. She says that she never expected to be an inventor. But she is happy that her work has helped people.

Text Evidence

1 Genre Ⓐ Ⓒ Ⓣ
Biography

Look at the photograph and caption. What information do the photograph and caption add?

_____

_____

2 Comprehension
Problem and Solution

Reread the first paragraph. **Underline** the details that tell about Kevlar®. Think about Stephanie's problem on page 296. How did she solve it?

_____

_____

3 Expand Vocabulary

Something that is **protective** protects someone or something from being hurt. **Circle** details that tell who wears Stephanie's fiber as *protective* material.

Discuss Work with a partner. Discuss the questions below about "Stephanie Kwolek: Inventor." Reread to find the answers. Write page numbers to show where you found text evidence.

? Questions **Discussion Starters** **Text Evidence**

❶ What did Stephanie invent?	▶ Stephanie invented... ▶ When she tested... ▶ I noticed that...	Page(s): _____
❷ What is made from the fiber, Kevlar®?	▶ Kevlar® is used to make... ▶ I read that...	Page(s): _____
❸ Why is Kevlar® an important invention?	▶ Stephanie's invention has... ▶ I also read that Stephanie...	Page(s): _____

Mike Moran

Write Review your notes about "Stephanie Kwolek: Inventor." Then write your answer to the question below. Use text evidence to support your answer.

What did Stephanie invent and why is it important?

_____

_____

_____

_____

_____

_____

_____

_____

_____

Write About Reading

Shared Read

Read an Analysis **Text Features** Read the paragraph Terri wrote about "Stephanie Kwolek: Inventor." She gave her opinion on how well the author used photographs and captions to provide more details about the topic.

Student Model

In "Stephanie Kwolek: Inventor," I think the author did a good job of using photos and captions to give more details. One photo shows a police dog wearing a Kevlar® vest. Another shows a Kevlar® police vest. One of the photos shows what firefighters' suits look like when they are made from Kevlar®. The captions told what was being shown in each photo. The photos and captions helped me to understand what Kevlar® is used for. That is why I think the author did a good job of using photos and captions to add more information.

Topic Sentence

Circle the topic sentence. What is Terri going to write about?

Evidence

Draw a box around the evidence that Terri includes. What other information from "Stephanie Kwolek: Inventor" would you include?

Concluding Statement

Underline the concluding statement. Why is this sentence a good wrap up?

Leveled Reader

Text Features Write a paragraph about "The Inventive Lewis Latimer." Write your opinion of how well the author uses photographs and captions.

_____

_____

_____

_____

_____

_____

_____

_____

_____

_____

_____

Topic Sentence

☐ Include the title of the text you read.

☐ Give your opinion about how well the author uses photographs and captions to give more details about the topic.

Evidence

☐ Include specific photos and captions the author uses.

☐ Explain why these are helpful.

Concluding Statement

☐ Restate your opinion.

Talk About It

? **Essential Question**

What can you discover when you look closely at something?

Go Digital!

302

Write words that tell why something looks different when you look at it closely.

Close-Up

 Pick an object and look closely at it. Describe what you see. Use the words you wrote above.

Vocabulary

CCSS

 Work with a partner to complete each activity.

1 typical

What do you do on a *typical* weekend?

_____

_____

2 gritty

If you get something *gritty* on your hands, what does it feel like?

_____

_____

3 microscope

How does something very tiny look under a *microscope*?

_____

4 humid

Show how you might feel and move on a very warm, *humid* day.

5 dissolves

Read the synonyms below for *dissolves*. Add another synonym.

dissolves: vanishes, melts away,

_____

6 cling

What is something a monkey can *cling* to?

_____

_____

7 mingle

At school, where do you *mingle* with your friends?

_____

_____

_____

_____

8 magnify

Draw something tiny. Then draw how it looks when you *magnify* it with a magnifying glass.

High-Utility Words

Sequence Words

Sequence words are words that signal the order in which something happens.

Circle the sequence words in the passage.

Using a microscope is easy. First, you take a glass slide with something on it. Next, you place it under the microscope. Then you adjust the focus knobs on the slide. After the slide is in focus, get ready to be amazed. Finally, you look at the slide and marvel at what you see.

Francesco Carta fotografo/Flickr/Getty Images

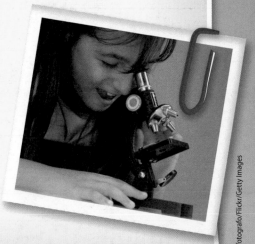

Read "Your World Up Close."
Use this page to take notes.

Your World Up Close

? Essential Question

What can you discover when you look closely at something?

Read about a tool that allows us to see everyday objects up close.

Compare these gritty grains of sugar with the magnified sugar crystal.

Does the picture on the left show a diamond? Or a glass prism? Look closer. Take a step back. You are *too* close.

It is a picture of a sugar crystal. This extreme close-up was taken by an electron microscope, a tool that can **magnify** an item to many times its actual size.

Pictures taken with electron microscopes are called photomicrographs. The word *micro* means small. We are seeing a small part of the sugar crystal up close.

Photomicrography dates back to 1840. That is when a scientist, Alfred Donné, first photographed **images** through a **microscope**. Around 1852, a pharmacist made the first camera that took photomicrographs. Then in 1882, Wilson "Snowflake" Bentley became the first person to use a camera with a built-in microscope. He photographed snowflakes and showed that there is no such thing as a **typical** snowflake. Each is unique. Nowadays, we use electron micrographs.

Bentley's photographs showed that snowflakes are shaped like hexagons.

Text Evidence

❶ Sentence Structure Ⓐ Ⓒ Ⓣ

Reread the second paragraph. **Underline** the detail that tells what was used to take the photo of the sugar crystal. What does the word *tool* refer to in the second sentence?

_____

_____

_____

❷ Expand Vocabulary

An **image** is a picture or likeness of something. **Circle** the text that tells how Alfred Donné made his *images*.

❸ Comprehension
Sequence

Reread the fourth paragraph. **Draw a box** around the event that happened in 1852. What year did Bentley use a camera with a built-in microscope?

_____

Text Evidence

1 Sentence Structure (A)(C)T

Reread the first paragraph. In the last sentence, what word does the pronoun *it* stand for? **Underline** the word.

2 Expand Vocabulary

When people have a **disease**, they are sick or ill. **Circle** what helps scientists to see what causes sickness and *diseases*.

3 Sentence Structure (A)(C)T

Reread the last sentence on the page. **Draw a box** around what we have learned. How have we learned this?

_____

_____

_____

_____

The microscopes you use at school do not show much detail. An electron microscope is much more powerful. It allows scientists to see things we can't see with our eyes alone, such as skin cells.

The picture below is a close-up of human skin. It shows the detail an electron microscope can capture. The more an image is magnified, the more detail you see. The most magnification a photomicrograph can capture is about 2 million times the original size.

Magnified images help scientists see what causes sickness and **diseases**. Scientists have learned how illnesses behave. Looking through microscopes, we have learned what is inside a cell or how a snowflake **dissolves** into a drop of water.

This fingerprint is magnified by an electron microscope.

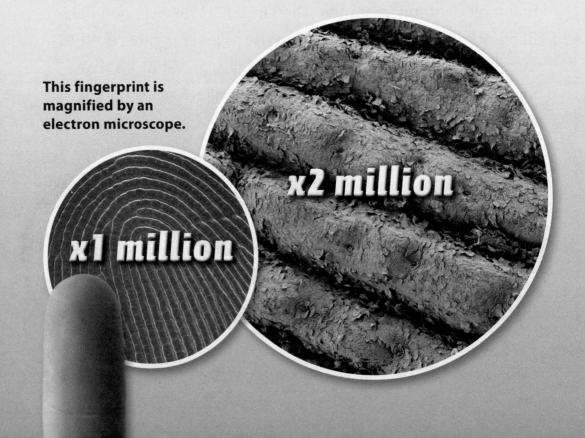

x1 million

x2 million

Mold on a strawberry looks like grapes under an electron microscope.

Scientists use electron micrographs to see how things change over time. For example, how does a piece of fruit **decay**? First the fruit looks fresh. After a few days it softens. Next specks of mold appear. These small spots **cling** to the fruit. Days pass. Eventually the fruit is covered in mold. We can see these changes under the microscope far earlier than when we use just our eyes.

Suppose it is a **humid** day. You **mingle** outside with friends. What would the sweat on your skin look like magnified? The possibilities are endless if you examine your world up close.

Text Evidence

1 Expand Vocabulary

If food **decays**, it rots and cannot be eaten. **Draw a box** around the first sign of *decay* in a piece of fruit.

2 Sentence Structure Ⓐ Ⓒ Ⓣ

Reread the last sentence in the first paragraph. **Circle** the words that come before the word *than*. What does this first part of the sentence tell us?

_____

_____

3 Comprehension
Sequence

Reread the first paragraph. **Underline** the words that signal a sequence of events. What does this sequence of events tell about?

_____

_____

_____

Respond to Reading

 Discuss Work with a partner. Read the questions about "Your World Up Close." Use the discussion starters to answer the questions. Write the page numbers to show where you found text evidence.

 **Questions**

Discussion Starters

 **Text Evidence**

Questions	Discussion Starters	Text Evidence
1 What do electron microscopes do?	► Electron microscopes… ► I know this because I read . . .	Page(s): _____
2 What have images from electron microscopes helped scientists to see?	► Images from electron microscopes have … ► Over the years, scientists have…	Page(s): _____
3 What is another way electron microscopes are helpful to scientists?	► Electron microscopes help scientists… ► For example…	Page(s): _____

Write Review your notes about "Your World Up Close." Then write your answer to the question below. Use text evidence to support your answer.

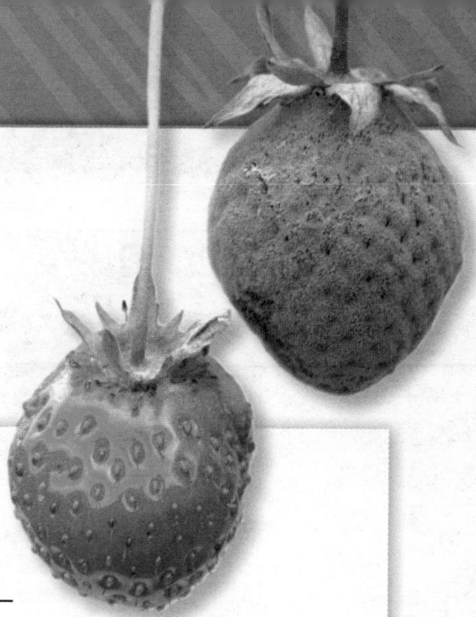

How do electron microscopes help scientists?

Petals and posies/Alamy

Write About Reading

Shared Read

Read an Analysis ▸ **Key Details** Read the paragraph Derek wrote about "Your World Up Close." He analyzed how the author uses key details to support the main idea.

Student Model

Topic Sentence

Circle the topic sentence. What is Derek going to write about?

Evidence

Draw a box around the evidence that Derek includes. What other information from "Your World Up Close" would you include?

Concluding Statement

Underline the concluding statement. Why is this sentence a good wrap up?

In "Your World Up Close," the author uses key details to support the main idea that electron microscopes allow us to learn about new things. An electron microscope can make things look two million times bigger. It helps scientists learn about diseases and how they are caused. Scientists use electron microscopes to understand how fruit changes when it decays. These are some examples of key details the author uses to support the main idea.

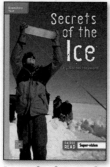

Leveled Reader

Write an Analysis **Key Details** Write a paragraph about "Secrets of the Ice." Write about the key details the author uses to support the main idea.

_____

_____

_____

_____

_____

_____

_____

_____

_____

_____

_____

_____

_____

Topic Sentence

☐ Include the title of the text you read.

☐ Tell how the author used key details to support the main idea.

Evidence

☐ Include specific details the author uses to support the main idea.

☐ Explain how the details support the main idea.

Concluding Statement

☐ Restate how the author uses key details.

Talk About It

Essential Question

How can learning about the past help you understand the present?

Go Digital!

Write words that describe the different ways people learn about the past.

The
Past

Describe one way that people learn about the past. Use the words you wrote above.

COLLABORATE

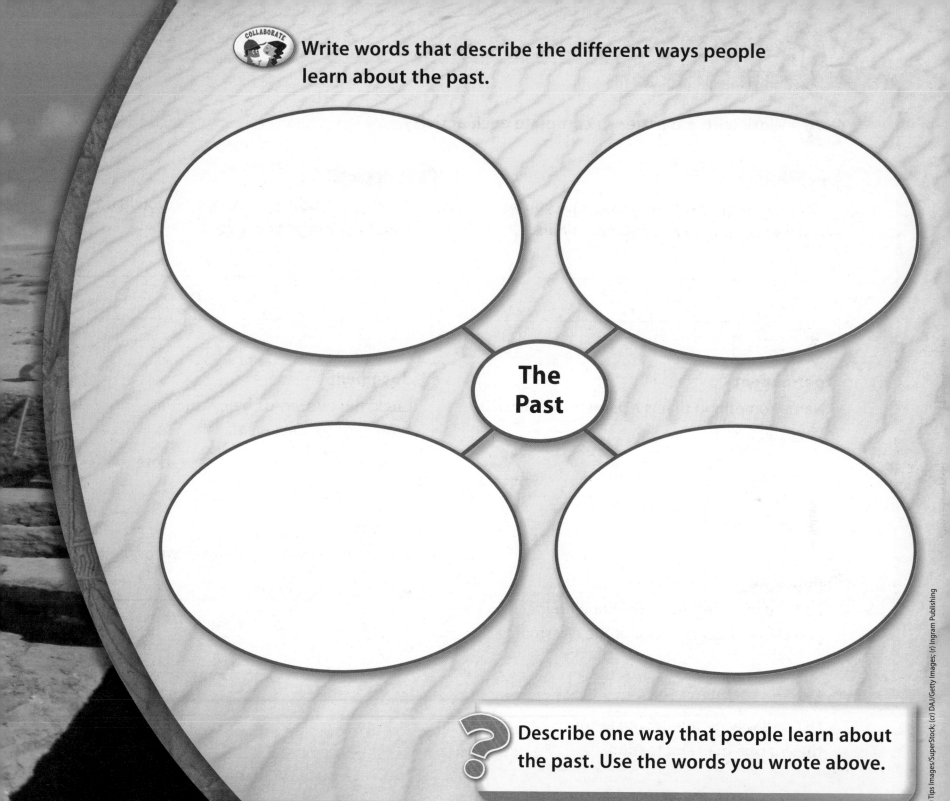

CCSS Vocabulary

 Work with a partner to complete each activity.

1 expedition

List two things you would take with you if you were going on a hiking *expedition*.

_____

_____

2 permanent

Name something that is a *permanent* part of your classroom.

_____

_____

3 evidence

Pretend you are a detective looking for clues and *evidence* on the floor of the classroom.

4 era

List one way people stayed in touch before the *era* of e-mail and texting.

_____

5 archaeology

When you study *archaeology* do you learn about the future or the past?

_____

_____

6 document

Circle the two words below that are synonyms for *document*.

record   shout   note

7 uncover

▶ Underline the word *cover* in *uncover*.

▶ Circle the prefix *un-*.

▶ What does *uncover* mean?

_____

_____

_____

316

8 **tremendous**

Draw a picture of a tree that has a *tremendous* number of branches on it.

High-Utility Words

▶ **Suffixes**

Adding the suffix *-ment* to the end of a word changes the meaning of the word.

Circle the words with the suffix *-ment* in the passage.

My friend said she would have liked to live in an early (settlement) out West. I looked at her in amazement. I explained that the roads back then had no pavement. If you had an ailment, you'd have trouble finding a doctor. Also, there was very little entertainment back then. We continued our disagreement until lunchtime.

My Notes

Read "Where It All Began."
Use this page for notes.

Where It All Began

Essential Question

How can learning about the past help you understand the present?

Read about the Jamestown settlement.

Building the Jamestown settlement in 1607

Take a tour of Jamestown, Virginia.

They thought they were lost. Three ships had sailed from England on December 20, 1606. The **expedition** was bound for Virginia, carrying 144 people.

Finally, on April 26, 1607, the ships sailed into Chesapeake Bay. The settlers built a fort on an island in a river. They named the fort after their king, James. Jamestown became the first successful, **permanent** English settlement in the New World.

The Struggle to Survive

"Ignorance is bliss" is a well-known proverb, or saying. And for the 104 men and boys who came ashore, this was true. They were faced with **tremendous** problems. The water was unsafe to drink and food was **scarce**—there was very little to eat. Two weeks after the settlers arrived, 200 Indians attacked them.

Text Evidence

❶ Organization Ⓐ Ⓒ Ⓣ

Reread the first paragraph. **Underline** the details that tell where the ships sailed from and when. Where were the ships going?

_____

❷ Comprehension Sequence

Reread the first two paragraphs. **Circle** the dates that help you understand when these events took place. What happened after the ships finally arrived in Chesapeake Bay?

_____

_____

❸ Expand Vocabulary

When something is **scarce**, there is a limited amount of it. **Draw a box** around the detail that tells what was _scarce_ in Jamestown.

319

Text Evidence

1 Expand Vocabulary

People or things that are **local** come from the nearby area. What did John Smith want to trade for with the *local* tribes?

_____

_____

2 Organization Ⓐ Ⓒ Ⓣ

Reread "The Real-Life Pocahontas" sidebar. **Circle** the dates that tell when Pocahontas was born and when she died.

3 Comprehension
Sequence

Reread "The Real-Life Pocahontas" sidebar. **Underline** where Pocahontas and John Rolfe went after they got married. What happened on the way back from London?

_____

_____

John Smith, a military man, became head of the colony in 1608. He found **local** tribes in the area willing to trade food for English goods. Smith was tough. "He that will not work, shall not eat," he told the colonists. Smith knew that an attitude of every man for himself would hurt the settlement.

Pocahontas saved Captain John Smith's life.

Pocahontas became a friend to John Smith. She was the daughter of Chief Powhatan. He ruled 14,000 Algonquian-speaking peoples in the western Chesapeake area.

The Real-Life Pocahontas

Princess Matoaka was born around 1595. Her father, Chief Powhatan, called her Pocahontas. She saved John Smith's life twice.

Pocahontas married a planter, John Rolfe. In early America, settlers and Indians didn't marry. It was the first marriage in that **era** between an Englishman and a Native American. Rolfe, Pocahontas, and their son visited London, but Pocahontas fell ill on the ship back and died in March 1617.

320

Map of Settlement of Virginia 1607–1700

Ohio
Pennsylvania
New Jersey
Maryland
Delaware
West Virginia
Virginia
Kentucky
Jamestown
North Carolina

N W E S

MAP KEY

← Immigration (English, French, Italians, Poles, and Africans)

■ Extent of European Settlement, 1700

● Village

■ Fort

▲ Indian Reservation

★ Capital

(tl) © PoodlesRock/Corbis; (bl) © W. Langdon Kihn/National Geographic Society/Corbis (tr) Mapping Specialists; (cr) Courtesy of APVA Preservation Virginia

Taking a Closer Look

Archaeologists digging in Jamestown have discovered Indian artifacts along with English ones, **evidence** that Indians lived in the fort. "It must have been a very close relationship," says William Kelso, an expert in early American **archaeology**.

Kelso has worked for 10 years to **document** this site. His team has **managed** to successfully **uncover** more than 1 million artifacts and map out the fort and a burial ground.

Dr. William Kelso working on the archaeological dig in Jamestown

Jamestown left a record of greed and war, but it was also the start of representative government. The settlers gave America a solid base to build upon.

Text Evidence

① Organization Ⓐ Ⓒ Ⓣ

Reread the first paragraph. **Underline** the details that tell you what archaeologists have discovered in Jamestown. When do the events described in "Taking a Closer Look" take place?

_____

_____

② Expand Vocabulary

If you **managed** to do something, you had success in getting it done. **Circle** the details that tell what William Kelso's team *managed* to uncover at Jamestown.

③ Organization Ⓐ Ⓒ Ⓣ

Reread the last paragraph. **Draw a box** around the details that tell what started in Jamestown. What did the settlers give America?

_____

_____

Discuss Work with a partner. Discuss the questions below about "Where It All Began." Reread to find the answers. Write page numbers to show where you found text evidence.

? Questions	**Discussion Starters**	**Text Evidence**
❶ What is Jamestown and when was it founded?	▶ Jamestown is…. ▶ Jamestown was founded in….	Page(s): _____
❷ What have William Kelso and his team done at Jamestown?	▶ Archaeologist William Kelso and his team have found…. ▶ They have mapped…. ▶ I know this because I read….	Page(s): _____
❸ Why is Jamestown an important site for archaeologists?	▶ Jamestown left a record of…. ▶ Jamestown was the first…. ▶ I know this because I read….	Page(s): _____

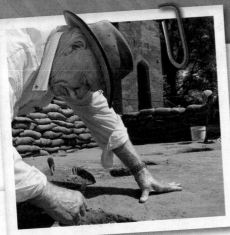

Write Review your notes about "Where It All Began." Then write your answer to the question below. Use text evidence to support your answer.

Courtesy of APVA Preservation Virginia

Why is the Jamestown site important?

Write About Reading

Shared Read

Student Model

Topic Sentence

Circle the topic sentence. What is Tim going to write about?

Evidence

Draw a box around the evidence that Tim includes. What other information from "Where it All Began" would you include?

Concluding Statement

Underline the concluding statement. Why is this sentence a good wrap up?

I think that the author of "Where it All Began" did a good job of supporting the position that Jamestown is an important part of America's history because it was the first permanent English settlement in the New World. The author tells what life was like when Jamestown was first founded. Life was hard for the settlers. Indians attacked them. Food was scarce. The author says that even though Jamestown was a hard place to live, it was the start of government by representation. I think the author did a good job of using details to support her position.

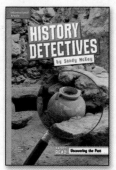

Leveled Reader

Write an Analysis **Author's Point of View** Write a paragraph about "History Detectives." Tell how well the author supported his or her position on a topic.

_____

_____

_____

_____

_____

_____

_____

_____

_____

_____

_____

Topic Sentence

☐ Include the title of the text you read.

☐ Tell whether the author did a good job of supporting a position.

Evidence

☐ Give key pieces of evidence from the text.

☐ Explain how this evidence supports the author's position.

☐ Support your ideas with details.

Concluding Statement

☐ Restate your opinion.

Past, Present, and Future

Sean Gallup/Getty Images News/Getty Images

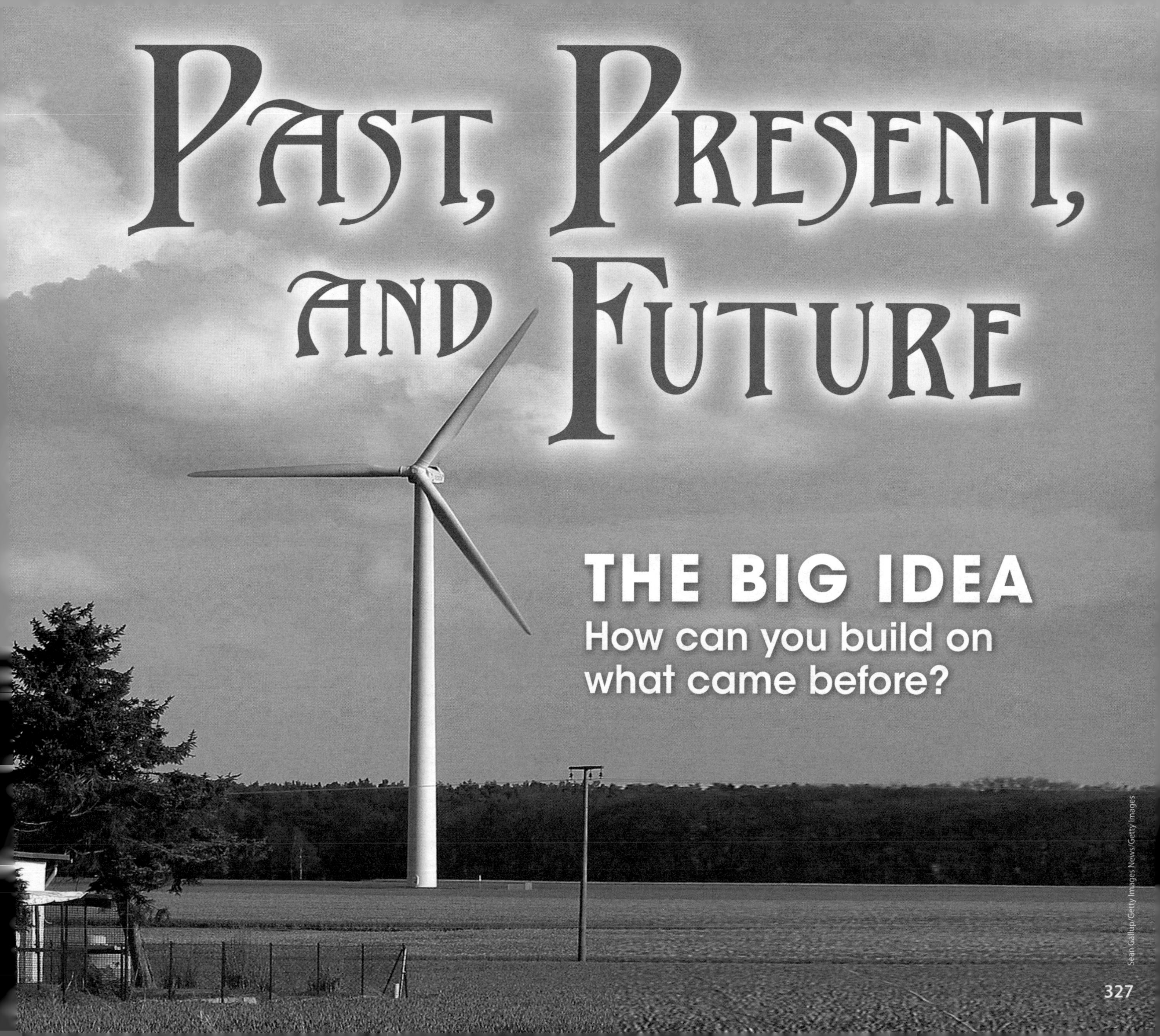

THE BIG IDEA

How can you build on what came before?

Talk About It

Weekly Concept Old and New

Essential Question

How do traditions connect people?

Go Digital!

COLLABORATE

Write words that describe traditions from your culture and other cultures.

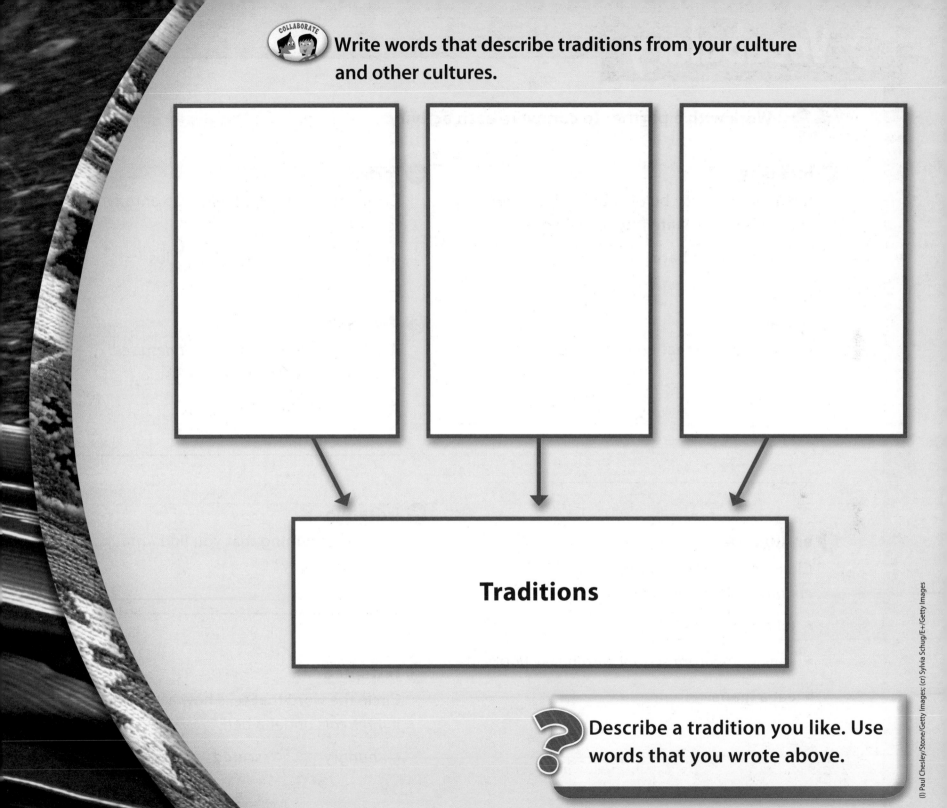

Traditions

? **Describe a tradition you like. Use words that you wrote above.**

Work with a partner to complete each activity.

1 **intensity**

Read the sentence below out loud. Say the sentence with an *intensity* of feeling.

The test was so hard!

2 **honor**

Name a holiday that *honors* a leader.

_____

_____

_____

3 **endurance**

Circle the thing that someone needs *endurance* in order to do.

▶ take a long nap

▶ walk home from school with heavy books

▶ eat a grape

4 **forfeit**

Circle the word below that is an antonym for *forfeit*.

give up   win   lose

5 **despised**

Read the synonyms below for *despised*. Add another synonym to the list.

depised: unloved, detested,

_____

6 **irritating**

What is something that you find *irritating* when you study?

_____

7 **retreated**

Circle the word that tells how a cat is feeling if it *retreats* under a bed.

hungry   scared   playful

8 **ancestors**

Draw a picture of one of your *ancestors*.

High-Utility Words

Prepositions

Prepositions are words that show *when*, *where*, or *how* something happens.

Circle the prepositions in the passage.

I waited (inside) the train station. I stood near the stairs and remembered Chad's last visit. I hadn't seen him for a year. Would I still have fun with him? The train pulled into the station. Chad hopped off the train and walked across the platform. He had a big smile on his face. He hadn't changed a bit!

Hill Street Studios/Blend Images/Alamy

My Notes

Read "A Surprise Reunion." Use this page to take notes.

A Surprise Reunion

? Essential Question

How do traditions connect people?

Read how a brother and sister are reunited after many years apart.

332

hief Cameahwait looked with **intensity** across the Shoshone camp. The tribe was preparing for the Rabbit Dance. The dance was done to **honor** the rabbit. Rabbit was an important food source. The Shoshone had long used traditions such as this dance to mark special occasions and to remember their **ancestors**.

In the distance, children played with a rawhide ball. They rolled the ball into a circle drawn in the dust. If the ball rolled outside the circle, a child had to **forfeit** a turn. Cameahwait smiled as he remembered the games he once played.

But beneath his smile was pain. Cameahwait missed his little sister. She had been snatched from camp during a raid long ago. He **despised** those who had taken her. He closed his eyes. He pictured the games they had played together. She had an **irritating** habit of following him everywhere, he remembered, and she had been very demanding. He loved her strong, **assertive** manner. What had become of her?

David McCall Johnston

Text Evidence

❶ Organization ACT

Reread the last paragraph. What important event do you learn about that happened in the past? **Draw a box** around the sentence that tells about that event.

❷ Comprehension
Theme

Reread the last paragraph. **Circle** the detail that tells about Chief Cameahwait's smile. How does he feel about his little sister?

_____

_____

_____

_____

❸ Expand Vocabulary

People who are **assertive** are forceful and confident. **Underline** details about Cameahwait's sister that show how *assertive* she is.

333

Text Evidence

1 **Organization** Ⓐ Ⓒ Ⓣ

Reread the first paragraph. **Draw a box** around the details that tell what Cameahwait returned to. What was Cameahwhait thinking about before he was interrupted?

_____

_____

2 **Expand Vocabulary**

To move things from one place to another is to **transport** them. **Circle** the word that tells what Captain Lewis needed to *transport*.

3 **Organization** Ⓐ Ⓒ Ⓣ

Reread the second paragraph. **Underline** the words that tell when these events took place. Reread the third paragraph. When do these events take place?

_____

_____

"It is time to ride," Hawk-That-Soars said, interrupting Cameahwait's thoughts. Cameahwait returned to the present. He turned and mounted his horse.

A man named Captain Lewis had approached the Shoshone days before. Lewis had come in peace, so Cameahwait welcomed him and his party. Lewis told the Shoshone he was part of a group with a mission: the group was to explore the land between the Missouri River and the great ocean. Lewis then asked for a favor. The rest of his party was waiting at the river with a supply boat. He needed the strength and **endurance** of the Shoshone horses to **transport** supplies across the difficult land. In return, Lewis offered the Shoshone food and other goods.

Cameahwait's party arrived at Lewis's camp. There they met Captain Clark.

"Let's sit and discuss how we may help each other," said Clark. They went inside a large tent. Buffalo blankets were spread around. Lewis addressed the chief. "We travel with a woman who knows your language."

A woman with long, dark braids entered the tent. As her eyes adjusted to the dim light, she nodded to the chief. "I am Sacagawea," she said.

Cameahwait could not believe his eyes! He examined her face. He watched as her expression slowly changed. He knew this was the same sweet face of his lost sister.

Sacagawea ran to him. Tears filled her eyes. The pain and sadness that Cameahwait had carried over the years **retreated** to a forgotten place.

"My brother!" she cried. "Is it really you?"

Lewis and Clark were happy to have been partners in this **reunion** between brother and sister. Chief Cameahwait promised them whatever help and resources they needed.

"You have given me a great gift," Cameahwait told them. "You have reunited me with my beloved sister. Our people will sing and tell stories so that all may remember and honor this day for generations to come."

Text Evidence

❶ Comprehension
Theme

Reread the first two paragraphs. **Circle** the detail that tells how Cameahwait knew the woman was his sister. How does he feel?

_____

_____

❷ Expand Vocabulary

A **reunion** is a meeting of friends or family after a period of time. **Underline** the detail that tells who the *reunion* was between.

❸ Comprehension
Theme

Reread the last paragraph. In the future, how will Cameahwait remember this day?

_____

_____

_____

335

Discuss Work with a partner. Discuss the questions below about "A Surprise Reunion." Reread to find the answers. Write page numbers to show where you found text evidence.

? Questions | **Discussion Starters** | **Text Evidence**

? Questions	Discussion Starters	Text Evidence
1 What happened to Chief Cameahwait's little sister?	▶ Chief Cameahwait's little sister was… ▶ I read that…	Page(s): _____
2 Why is remembering the past important to Chief Cameahwait?	▶ Memories of the past helped Cameahwait remember… ▶ I know this because I read…	Page(s): _____
3 What happened when Lewis and Clark reunited Chief Cameahwait with his sister?	▶ Cameahwait said his people would remember his reunion with his sister for… ▶ To remember the day, the Shoshone people would create…	Page(s): _____

Write Review your notes about "A Surprise Reunion." Then write your answer to the question below. Use text evidence to support your answer.

How does Chief Cameahwait feel about his sister?

_____

_____

_____

_____

_____

_____

_____

_____

_____

_____

Write About Reading

CCSS

Shared Read

Read an Analysis ▶ **Theme** Read Enzo's paragraph below about "A Surprise Reunion." He analyzed how the author communicated the theme of the story.

Student Model

Topic Sentence

Circle the topic sentence. What is Enzo going to write about?

Evidence

Draw a box around the evidence that Enzo includes. What other information from "A Surprise Reunion" would you include?

Concluding Statement

Underline the concluding statement. Why is this sentence a good wrap up?

The theme of "A Surprise Reunion" is about how traditions and family connect people. Chief Cameahwait's little sister was kidnapped when she was a child. When he thinks about his sister, he remembers how she followed him around and how demanding she was. He has not seen her in years, but he still misses her. When they are reunited, Cameahwait recognizes his sister instantly. I think the theme of this story is that even when people are separated for a long time, traditions and family create a strong, lasting bond.

David McCall Johnston

338

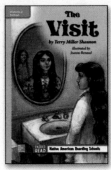

Leveled Reader

Write an Analysis **Theme** **Write a paragraph about "The Visit." Analyze how the author communicated the theme of the story.**

Topic Sentence

- ☐ Include the title of the text you read.
- ☐ Ask yourself "how" or "why" questions.
- ☐ Tell what you think the theme is.

Evidence

- ☐ Explain why you think this is the theme.
- ☐ Use text evidence to support your ideas.
- ☐ Support your ideas with details.

Concluding Statement

- ☐ Restate why you think this is the theme of the text.

Talk About It

Essential Question

Why is it important to keep a record of the past?

Go Digital!

340

Write words that tell about ways to keep a record of the past.

The Past

 Describe one way that your family has kept a record of the past. Use the words you wrote above.

Work with a partner to complete each activity.

1 treacherous

Circle the words below that are synonyms for *treacherous*.

    safe   unsafe   dangerous

2 detested

Write one food that you *detest* eating.

_____

3 obedience

How does a dog show *obedience,* if its master tells it to sit?

_____

_____

4 eldest

Who is the *eldest* person in your family?

_____

_____

5 discarded

If you found a *discarded* banana peel, where would you put it?

_____

_____

6 ignored

Name a kind of alarm that should not be *ignored*.

_____

_____

7 refuge

Where can you take *refuge* on a hot, sunny day?

_____

_____

8 depicts

Draw a picture that *depicts* your favorite food.

High-Utility Words

▶ **Homophones**

Homophones are words that sound alike but are spelled differently. They also have different meanings.

Circle the homophones in the passage.

I (heard) that Mrs. Jensen kept a diary about her life on the farm. She wrote about the (herd) of cows. And she told about her two hens, too. She began working before the sun came up. Her son helped her. I know the work was hard, but she had no complaints about it.

Lynn Betts, USDA Natural Resources Conservation Service

My Notes

Read "Freedom at Fort Mose."
Use this page to take notes.

Freedom at FORT MOSE

? Essential Question

Why is it important to keep a record of the past?

Read how a boy uses a diary to tell about his life of freedom in a new place.

344

In September of 1754, twelve-year-old Lucius Jackson and his family had been living at Fort Mose in St. Augustine, Florida for a year. They were part of a group who had escaped from a plantation in South Carolina. They knew Fort Mose was a place of **refuge** for runaways. People were willing to suffer and **endure** the **treacherous** journey there for the promise of freedom. While he was at Fort Mose, Lucius kept a diary.

17th September 1754

It has been raining for a week now. This weather reminds me of learning to read back in Charleston. When the rains came, we couldn't work in the fields and had to stay in the cabins. Mr. Slocum, the landowner, **detested** getting his boots wet, so he rarely came to check on us. He thought all we knew was work and **obedience**. Miss Celia took a risk writing letters and words on the dirt floor for us children to learn. As the **eldest** person in our cabin, she said it was a risk she was willing to take. Learning to read was easy for me because I liked turning letters into words and words into ideas. I believe that reading is a gift. Mr. Samuel Canter believes this, too. He is a farmer who lives nearby and who gave me this fine diary. He said, "Lucius, in years to come people can read about this place and understand what we risked to gain freedom."

Neil Shigley

Text Evidence

1 Expand Vocabulary

When you **endure** something, you suffer through it. **Circle** the detail that tells what runaways had to *endure* to get to Fort Mose.

2 Sentence Structure Ⓐ Ⓒ Ⓣ

Reread the first paragraph. **Underline** the sentence that tells the name of the main character and where he has been living. What year does the story take place?

_____

3 Comprehension
Theme

Reread the second paragraph. **Draw a box** around the sentence that tells what Lucius thinks about reading. How do you think Lucius feels about writing?

_____

_____

_____

Text Evidence

1 Expand Vocabulary

A **duty** is a job that you must do. **Circle** the details of Lucius's *duty* while on patrol with his father.

2 Comprehension
Theme

Reread the first two paragraphs. **Draw a box** around what Lucius's family was seeking a year ago. How does Lucius describe their feelings when they arrived?

_____

_____

3 Sentence Structure ⒶⒸⓉ

Reread the second sentence in the last paragraph. **Underline** the detail that tells what Lucius has to do first. What happens next?

_____

_____

_____

8th October 1754

Last night, I went on patrol with my father. My **duty** is to walk along the wall of the fort looking for anything unusual. It has been a while since we came under attack, but we cannot let down our guard. We also listen for people who may be seeking freedom, as we did a year ago.

While on patrol, I thought about the night my family came to Fort Mose, and how scared, but hopeful, we felt as we entered through the big gates.

I must stop writing now. It is my turn to gather palm fronds, which we lay in the sun to dry. Once they are dried, we use them to repair huts and build new ones. Each week, more people come to the fort. Our priest, Father de Las Casas, keeps the records. There are almost a hundred people now.

Nell Shigley

26th October 1754

Last week, a family arrived from Virginia. They were starved and weak beyond belief. My mother gave them clean clothes to replace the ones they had been wearing. Their old clothes were **discarded**. I tried to talk to the boy who is about my age, but he **ignored** me.

Later, I tried again to speak to the boy, whose name is Will. I showed him this diary and explained that it **depicts** as **accurately** as possible what life at Fort Mose is like. He seemed surprised and asked, "You know how to read and write?"

"Yes," I told him. He looked at me in silence, but I could see a question in his eyes. "Do you want to learn?" I asked.

"Is it not dangerous?" he asked quietly, looking around to see if anyone could hear us.

I smiled, remembering how long it took me to understand what freedom meant.

"Will, here at Fort Mose you are free to learn, and I am free to teach you."

We began our lessons right away.

Text Evidence

❶ Expand Vocabulary

To be **accurate** is to make few or no mistakes. **Circle** the phrase that shows what Lucius tries to write about *accurately* in his diary.

❷ Sentence Structure Ⓐ Ⓒ Ⓣ

Reread the second paragraph. **Draw a box** around the text in quotation marks. Who is speaking?

_____

❸ Comprehension
Theme

Reread the last five paragraphs. **Underline** what Will asks Lucius. What does freedom mean at Fort Mose?

_____

_____

_____

Respond to Reading

 **Discuss** Work with a partner. Discuss the questions below about "Freedom at Fort Mose." Reread to find the answers. Write page numbers to show where you found text evidence.

? Questions	**Discussion Starters**	**Text Evidence**
1 Why did Mr. Samuel Canter say that Lucius should keep a diary?	▶ Samuel Canter thought people in the years to come could... ▶ I know this because I read...	Page(s): _____
2 According to Lucius's diary, how did he learn to read and write?	▶ When it rained, Miss Celia took a risk and... ▶ Lucius learned to read and write this way because...	Page(s): _____
3 What did you learn about life at Fort Mose from Lucius's diary?	▶ When new families came to Fort Mose, they arrived... ▶ Everyday life at Fort Mose included... ▶ I know this because I read...	Page(s): _____

348

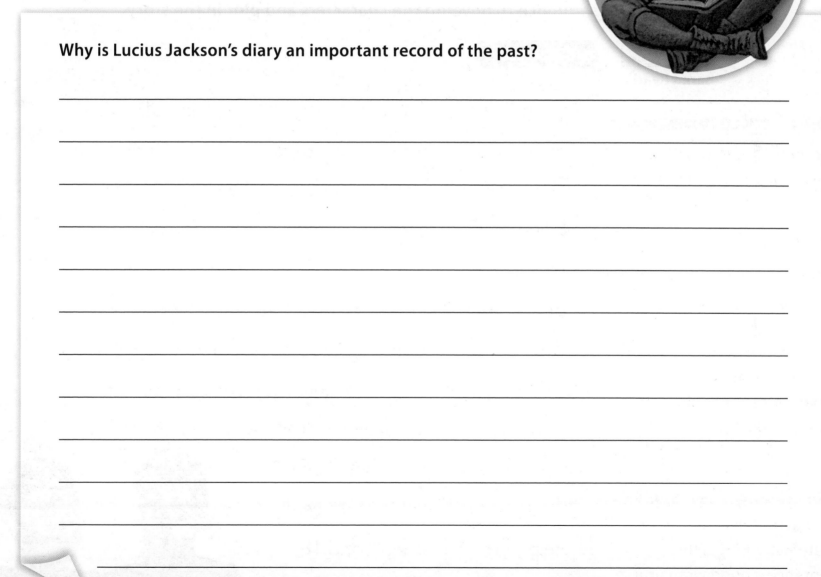

Write Review your notes about "Freedom at Fort Mose." Then write your answer to the question below. Use text evidence to support your answer.

Why is Lucius Jackson's diary an important record of the past?

_____

_____

_____

_____

_____

_____

_____

_____

_____

_____

Neil Shigley

Write About Reading

Shared Read

Read an Analysis Sequence of Events Read the paragraph below about "Freedom at Fort Mose." Maggie gives her opinion about how well the author used sequence to develop the characters and plot in the story.

Student Model

Topic Sentence

Circle the topic sentence. What is Maggie going to write about?

Evidence

Draw a box around the evidence that Maggie includes. What other information from "Freedom at Fort Mose" would you include?

Concluding Statement

Underline the concluding statement. Why is this sentence a good wrap up?

In "Freedom at Fort Mose," I think the author did a good job of using the sequence of events to develop the characters and plot. Lucius's family has been living at Fort Mose for a year. In his diary, he writes about how he and his family felt when they arrived at the fort. Then a family arrives from Virginia. There is a boy named Will. Lucius shows Will his diary. Will asks Lucius if it is dangerous to learn to read and write. Lucius explains that he is free to learn to read and write at Fort Mose. The clear sequence of events really helped me to understand the characters and the plot.

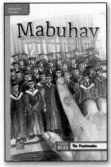

Leveled Reader

Write an Analysis **Sequence of Events** Write a paragraph about "Mabuhay." Give your opinion about how well the author used sequence of events in the story to develop the characters and plot.

_____

_____

_____

_____

_____

_____

_____

_____

_____

_____

Topic Sentence

☐ Include the title of the text you read.

☐ Tell your opinion about how well the author used sequence to develop characters and plot.

Evidence

☐ Explain how the sequence of events helped develop the characters and plot.

☐ Use details to support your ideas.

Concluding Statement

☐ Restate your opinion.

351

Talk About It

? Essential Question

How have our energy resources changed over the years?

Go Digital!

Write words about different kinds of energy sources.

Energy
Resources

Describe a renewable energy source. Use the words you wrote above.

CCSS Vocabulary

 Work with a partner to complete each activity.

1 incredible

Name the most *incredible* thing you have seen an athlete do.

_____

_____

2 consequences

Circle a *consequence* of not getting enough sleep at night.

▶ having lots of energy

▶ not having any energy

3 renewable

▶ Underline the word *new* in *renewable*.

▶ Circle the prefix *re-*.

▶ Draw a box around the suffix *-able*.

▶ What does *renewable* mean?

_____

_____

4 efficient

Tom has a piano recital tomorrow. What would be an *efficient* use of his time?

_____

5 installed

What equipment would you like to see *installed* on your school playground?

_____

6 consume

Circle the thing below that *consumes* electricity.

    carrot   lamp   rock

7 coincidence

Beth and Niki wore the same shirt on purpose. Tell why this is *not* a coincidence.

_____

_____

8 converted

Draw a picture of what a milk carton would look like if you *converted* it into a vase.

High-Utility Words

Linking Words

Some linking words link the main part of a sentence to another group of words.

Circle the linking words in the passage.

I defended electric cars (when) we had an energy debate. I said we need them because we depend on gas too much. Since my friend took the other side, she said electric cars take too long to charge. Although they are popular, electric cars are expensive. We both had good arguments!

My Notes

Read "The Great Energy Debate." Use this page to take notes.

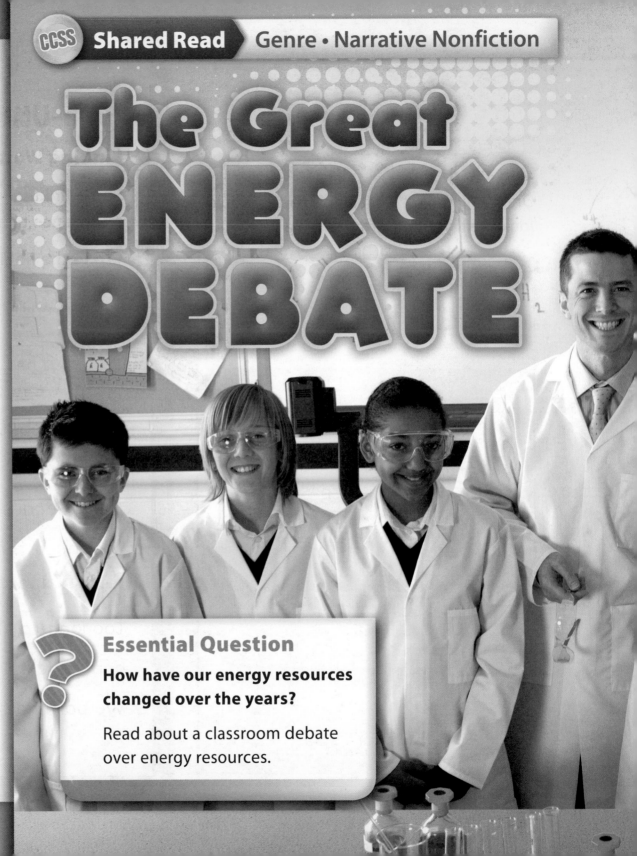

The Great ENERGY DEBATE

? **Essential Question**

How have our energy resources changed over the years?

Read about a classroom debate over energy resources.

Our energy debate will be an **incredible** event. Our teacher will not tell us which side we will be on until the day before the debate. We'll have to study and preplan arguments for both sides.

The debate is about different energy sources. One team will talk about the benefits of an energy source and the other team will talk about its **drawbacks**, or problems. We need to understand the **consequences** of each resource and how they affect the environment, as well as the costs.

Text Evidence

❶ Connection of Ideas Ⓐ Ⓒ Ⓣ

Reread the first paragraph. What will the teacher not tell the students? **Draw a box** around the sentence in the first paragraph that explains this. What do the students need to do to prepare for the debate?

_____

_____

_____

_____

❷ Expand Vocabulary

Reread the second paragraph. A **drawback** is a problem or a difficulty. **Circle** the word that means almost the same thing as *drawbacks*.

❸ Comprehension
Main Idea and Key Details

Reread the second paragraph. **Underline** key details that tell about the topic of the debate.

357

Text Evidence

1 **Connection of Ideas** A C T

Reread the sidebar "What Is Energy?" **Draw a box** around the sentences that tell about coal and how we use it to produce energy. How do we change sunlight into electrical energy?

_____

_____

_____

2 **Comprehension**
Main Idea and Key Details

Reread the first paragraph of the main text. **Underline** a key detail that explains why fossil fuels are nonrenewable resources.

3 **Expand Vocabulary**

When you are **hypercritical,** you point out all the things that are wrong with something. **Circle** two details that tell why it easy to be _hypercritical_ of fossil fuels.

What Is Energy?

Energy is the ability to do work or make a change. We use wind, sun, fossil fuels, and biofuels to produce energy. Coal is a fossil fuel. Burning coal produces heat energy that is changed into electrical energy. We use that energy to light our houses. Solar energy comes from the sun. Solar panels change sunlight into electrical energy.

We will talk about gasoline as an energy source. I will say gasoline is made from oil, a fossil fuel. Fossil fuels are formed over millions of years. But here is the problem: we use them far faster than it takes them to form. They are nonrenewable resources. If we keep using them, there will be none left. Plus, burning these fuels pollutes the air!

Those problems make it easy to be **hypercritical** of fossil fuels. However, most cars and factories use this kind of fuel.

We will debate the use of wind energy. I will say it is a **renewable** energy source. Unlike fossil fuels, wind will never run out. One large wind turbine can make enough energy for a whole city, and it doesn't damage the environment! Turbines can be put all over the world to capture wind energy. Then that energy is **converted** into electrical energy. However, wind is not as **efficient** as other energy sources. Only about 30 or 40 percent of all wind energy is changed into electricity. It is expensive to have wind turbines **installed** worldwide.

This debate is important. The United States makes up about 5 percent of the **entire** world's population. Yet we **consume** about 30 percent of all the world's energy. It is not a **coincidence** that students are asked to take part in these debates. We will have to make hard decisions when we are adults. The debate will be difficult, but I am ready!

Text Evidence

❶ Connection of Ideas Ⓐ Ⓒ Ⓣ

Reread the page. **Draw a box** around the benefits of wind energy. What is one of the drawbacks of wind energy?

_____

_____

❷ Expand Vocabulary

The word **entire** means the whole thing. **Underline** a word in the last paragraph that means the same as *entire*.

❸ Comprehension
Main Idea and Key Details

Reread the last paragraph. **Circle** the key details that tell why this debate is important. What will the students need to do when they are adults?

_____

_____

 **Discuss** Work with a partner. Discuss the questions below about "The Great Energy Debate." Reread to find the answers. Write page numbers to show where you found text evidence.

❓ Questions	Discussion Starters	🔍 Text Evidence
❶ How long did it take for fossil fuels to form?	▶ Fuels such as oil are called… ▶ These fuels took millions. . .	Page(s): _____
❷ What will happen if we keep using fossil fuels?	▶ Fossil fuels are nonrenewable because… ▶ I know this because I read…	Page(s): _____
❸ What are some energy sources that we can use instead of fossil fuels?	▶ An energy source that can be captured using turbines is… ▶ Solar panels capture energy from… ▶ These energy sources are renewable because…	Page(s): _____

Mike Moran

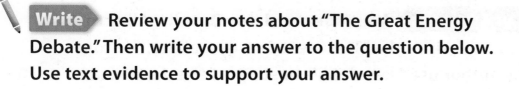

Write Review your notes about "The Great Energy Debate." Then write your answer to the question below. Use text evidence to support your answer.

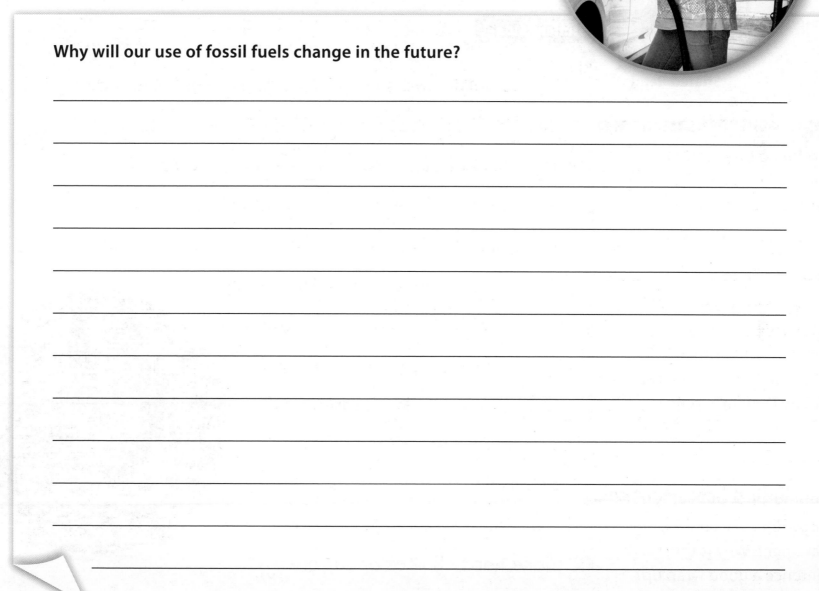

Why will our use of fossil fuels change in the future?

_____

_____

_____

_____

_____

_____

_____

_____

_____

_____

Write About Reading

CCSS

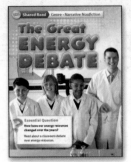

Shared Read

Read an Analysis ▸ **Main Idea and Key Details** Alberto wrote an analysis of the "The Great Energy Debate." He told how the author used key details to support the main idea.

Student Model

Topic Sentence

Circle the topic sentence. What is Alberto going to write about?

Evidence

Draw a box around the evidence that Alberto includes. What other information from "The Great Energy Debate" would you include?

Concluding Statement

Underline the concluding statement. Why is this sentence a good wrap up?

The author uses key details to support the main idea in "The Great Energy Debate." America uses a great deal of energy. Some energy sources are renewable and some are nonrenewable. Each source has its pros and cons. For example, fossil fuels take millions of years to form. Eventually, we will run out of them. On the other hand, renewable energy sources, such as wind energy, can be expensive. The author uses key details to support the main idea that today's students will have to make hard choices about energy.

Hal Bergman/Photodisc/Getty Images

362

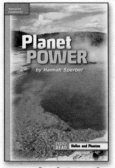

Leveled Reader

Write an Analysis **Main Idea and Key Details** **Write a paragraph about "Planet Power." Explain how the author uses key details to support the main idea.**

Topic Sentence

- [ ] Include the title of the text you read.
- [ ] Tell whether the author uses key details to support a main idea.

Evidence

- [ ] Describe some of those details.
- [ ] Explain how they support the main idea.

Concluding Statement

- [ ] Restate how the key details were used to support the main idea.

Talk About It

Weekly Concept Money Matters

? Essential Question

What has been the role of money over time?

Go Digital!

Write words that describe the different kinds of things that represent money.

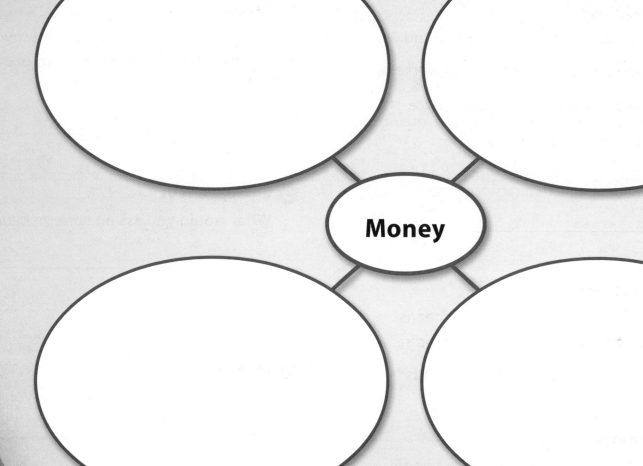

Money

 Describe what you use to pay for things. Use the words you wrote above.

CCSS Vocabulary

 Work with a partner to complete each activity.

1 **marketplace**

The word *marketplace* is a compound word.

▶ Underline the word *market* in *marketplace*.

▶ Draw a box around the word *place*.

What is a *marketplace*?

_____

_____

2 **merchandise**

Circle the synonym below that means almost the same thing as *merchandise*.

buyer   store   goods

3 **economics**

In a system of *economics* where people barter for things, what do they do? Circle the answer below.

▶ They trade for things.

▶ They use paper money to buy things.

4 **invest**

To make money, would you *invest* your allowance in a lemonade stand or a video game?

_____

5 **entrepreneur**

What would you ask an *entrepreneur*?

_____

_____

6 **global**

List a country you might visit if you were a *global* traveler.

_____

7 **transaction**

What kind of *transaction* can you make at a bank?

_____

8 currency

Draw an example of United States *currency*.

High-Utility Words

▶ **Comparative Endings *-er* and *-est***

The endings *-er* and *-est* are added to the end of words to compare things. The ending *-er* is added to compare two things. The ending *-est* is added to compare more than two things.

Circle the words in the passage that end with *-er* and *-est*.

The (closest) bank is a mile from our house. My parents have a saving account there. I have a smaller account at the same bank. Last year, I saved over $100.00. This year, I'm saving money even faster. Dad says the smartest kids get into the habit of saving. Saving is easier than I thought!

My Notes

Read "The History of Money." Use this page to take notes.

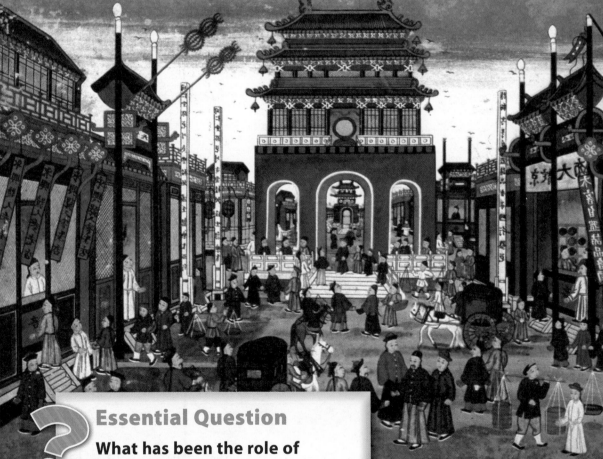

THE HISTORY of MONEY

Essential Question

What has been the role of money over time?

Read about the history of money.

A painting of a commercial center in Beijing, China, in 1840

W hat makes money valuable? A dollar bill is only a piece of paper. You cannot eat or wear it. So why do people want it? Think about the proverb, "Money doesn't grow on trees." Money is valuable because it is hard to get.

Bartering

Pretend you're a goat herder visiting a **marketplace** in China in 1200 B.C. The **merchandise** ranges from cattle to tools. You need a piece of rope. How will you pay for it? You do not want to trade a goat for a rope. The goat is worth too much! Instead, you trade goat milk for the rope. This system of **economics** is called bartering. But what if the rope merchant does not want goat milk?

Early Currency

No need to cry over spilt milk. Luckily, you sold goat milk earlier in exchange for ten cowrie shells, the first system of **currency** in China. You give two cowrie shells to the rope merchant. This is an easier way to buy and sell things. Cowrie shells are lightweight and **durable**—they last a long time—and are easy to take with you. This idea of currency is catching on in Thailand, India, and Africa.

You start saving your extra shells to **invest** in another goat. The shells you spend to buy the goat will pay off later when you sell the milk it produces. This type of business decision makes you an **entrepreneur**. You are growing a business.

(bkgd) The Granger Collection, New York; (r) McGraw-Hill Education

Text Evidence

❶ Organization **A C T**

Reread the second paragraph. **Underline** the details that name an early system of economics and when and where people used it.

❷ Expand Vocabulary

Something that is **durable** is strong and doesn't wear out. **Circle** the phrase that means *durable*. Why was it important that cowrie shells be *durable*?

_____

_____

_____

_____

❸ Comprehension
Main Idea and Key Details

Reread the last paragraph. **Draw a box** around the sentences that give key details about how an entrepreneur grows a business.

❶ Expand Vocabulary

When something **emerges**, it appears or becomes known. Where did metal coins first *emerge*?

_____

❷ Organization Ⓐ Ⓒ Ⓣ

Reread the last paragraph. **Draw a box** around the date that metal coins first appeared. When did gold and silver coins become popular in Europe and the Middle East?

_____

_____

_____

❸ Comprehension
Main Idea and Key Details

Underline the key details that describe metal coins when they first appeared in China.

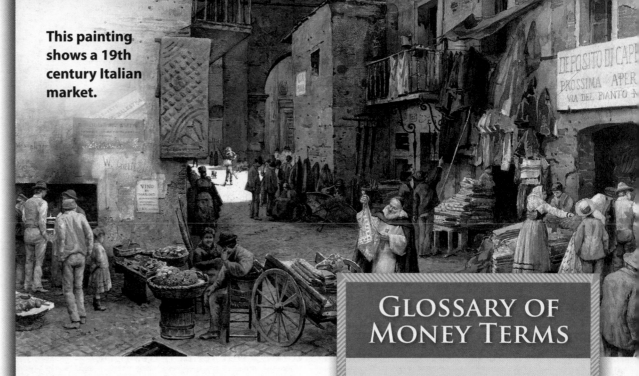

This painting shows a 19th century Italian market.

New Kinds of Currency

If you are at a marketplace in Rome around 900 B.C., you can use salt as currency. The idiom "to be worth one's salt" is still used today.

Another form of currency, metal coins, first **emerged** in China around 1000 B.C. When coins first appeared, they varied in shape, size, and worth. By the 7th century B.C., coins made of silver and gold became popular in Europe and the Middle East. These coins were usually round. After being weighed to determine their value, coins were stamped with designs that stated their worth.

GLOSSARY OF MONEY TERMS

BARTERING (BAR-tur-ing)
Trading by exchanging food, services, or goods instead of using money.

CURRENCY (KUR-uhn-see)
Any form of money that a country uses.

ECONOMY (ee-KON-uh-mee)
A system of managing money, goods, and services.

MARKETPLACE (MAR-kit-plays)
A place where goods are bought and sold.

Paper Money

There are two reasons the use of paper money developed in China in the 10th century. A bag of coins is heavy. There was also not enough metal to make the coins. European paper money first appeared in Sweden at the beginning of the 17th century. Italy used paper money about 90 years later. Paper money **represented**, or stood for, the gold or silver a person had in the bank. Today, the value of paper money is printed on it.

Modern Money

In today's **global** economy, sending money electronically is common. Many people use a credit or debit card to make a digital **transaction**. Numbers on a computer screen represent dollars and cents. No paper money is exchanged.

As easy as it is to spend money today, saving money is important. When considering spending money, think of the proverb, "A penny saved is a penny earned."

Text Evidence

❶ Comprehension
Main Idea and Key Details

Reread "Paper Money." **Underline** key details that tell why and when paper money was developed.

❷ Expand Vocabulary

Something that **represents** another thing takes the place of it. **Circle** the detail that tells what paper money originally *represented*.

❸ Organization Ⓐ Ⓒ Ⓣ

Review all the headings. **Draw a box** around the heading that tells how we use money today. Think about the headings. How is the information in this text organized?

_____

_____

_____

_____

Respond to Reading

 Discuss Work with a partner. Discuss the questions below about "The History of Money." Reread to find the answers. Write page numbers to show where you found text evidence.

 **Questions**    **Discussion Starters**   **Text Evidence**

1 What was the problem with bartering, or trading for goods, at a marketplace?

▶ Sometimes people at the marketplace did not like...

▶ I know this because I read...

Page(s): _____

2 What made currency an easier way to buy and sell?

▶ Currency could be exchanged for...

▶ Currency was also easier to...

Page(s): _____

3 How could currency be used for investing?

▶ People could save...

▶ Then they could use the currency to...

▶ I know this because I read...

Page(s): _____

Mike Moran

372

Write Review your notes about "The History of Money." Then write your answer to the question below. Use text evidence to support your answer.

Why did currency replace bartering, or trading, for goods?

_____

_____

_____

_____

_____

_____

_____

_____

McGraw-Hill Education

Write About Reading

CCSS

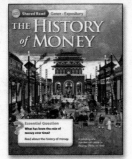

Shared Read

Read an Analysis Text Features Seth wrote an analysis about "The History of Money." He gave his opinion about how well the author used text features to provide more details about a topic.

Student Model

Topic Sentence

Circle the topic sentence. What is Seth going to write about?

Evidence

Draw a box around the evidence that Seth includes. What other information from "The History of Money" would you include?

Concluding Statement

Underline the concluding statement. Why is this sentence a good wrap up?

In "The History of Money," the author uses a glossary as a text feature to give more details about the topic. The glossary has money terms that are used in the text. Each term is defined and its pronunciation is given. The glossary makes it easy to quickly refer to each of the terms. These money terms are key to understanding the text. I think the author did a good job of using a text feature to provide more details about the topic.

374

Leveled Reader

Write an Analysis **Text Features** Write an analysis of "The Bike Company." Tell your opinion about how well the author used text features.

_____

_____

_____

_____

_____

_____

_____

_____

_____

_____

_____

Topic Sentence

☐ Include the title of the text you read.

☐ Tell how well you think the author used text features to give more details about a topic.

Evidence

☐ Describe the text features.

☐ Explain how these features give more details.

Concluding Statement

☐ Restate how well you think the author used text features to give more details.

Talk About It

Weekly Concept Finding My Place

Essential Question

What shapes a person's identity?

Go Digital!

376

 Write words that describe your personality and what activities you enjoy.

My Identity

 Describe something that you like to do. Use the words you wrote above.

Vocabulary

 Work with a partner to complete each activity.

1 mist

Circle the synonym below for the word *mist*.

snow   mud   spray

2 roots

Who could you ask about your family's *roots*?

_____

_____

3 individuality

▶ Underline the word *individual* in *individuality*.

▶ Draw a box around the suffix *-ity*.

▶ What does *individuality* mean?

_____

_____

_____

_____

4 gobble

Draw a picture of a dog as it *gobbles* up its food.

 Read the poem. Work with a partner to complete each activity.

MY HOUSE

Washed up on the tables in my house,

you'll find paintbrushes, squashed tubes

of azure blue, cadium red, and rusty orange.

These are my father's tools.

Scattered on the floor, the chairs,

are books, everywhere books!

They peer out from under the sofa,

and fight for space on the shelves.

Around it all, my mother's voice,

a warm ocean surrounding

the island of my house.

---

5 imagery

Imagery is the use of words to create a picture in the reader's mind. **Underline** one example of imagery in "My House."

6 personification

Personification is when human characteristics are given to anything that is not human. **Circle** an example of personification in "My House."

7 metaphor

A *metaphor* compares two things without the use of *like* or *as*. **Draw a box** around a metaphor in "My House."

8 free verse

Free verse poems do not have a consistent meter or rhyme scheme. How do you know "My House" is a free verse poem?

_____

_____

Andrew Paterson/Alamy

Read the poems. Use this page to take notes.

_____

_____

_____

_____

_____

_____

_____

_____

_____

_____

_____

_____

_____

? Essential Question

What shapes a person's identity?

Read how poets talk about important experiences.

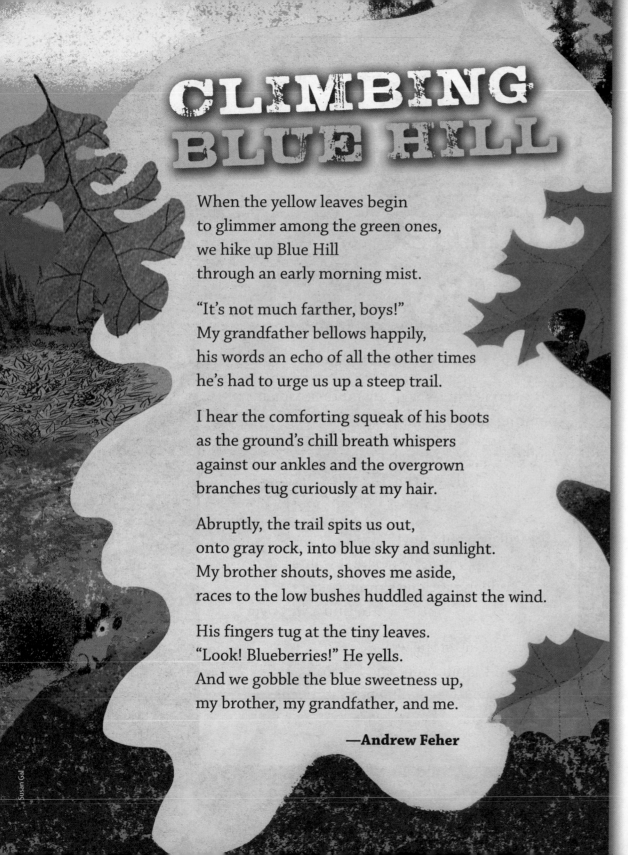

CLIMBING BLUE HILL

When the yellow leaves begin
to glimmer among the green ones,
we hike up Blue Hill
through an early morning mist.

"It's not much farther, boys!"
My grandfather bellows happily,
his words an echo of all the other times
he's had to urge us up a steep trail.

I hear the comforting squeak of his boots
as the ground's chill breath whispers
against our ankles and the overgrown
branches tug curiously at my hair.

Abruptly, the trail spits us out,
onto gray rock, into blue sky and sunlight.
My brother shouts, shoves me aside,
races to the low bushes huddled against the wind.

His fingers tug at the tiny leaves.
"Look! Blueberries!" He yells.
And we gobble the blue sweetness up,
my brother, my grandfather, and me.

—Andrew Feher

Susan Gal

Text Evidence

❶ Connection of Ideas **A C T**

Reread the first stanza. **Draw a box** around the details that tell you that summer is almost over. What time of day is it?

_____

❷ Literary Elements
Personification

Reread the third stanza. **Circle** the details that describe the overgrown branches. What human quality does the poet give to the branches?

_____

❸ Comprehension
Theme

Reread the second stanza. **Underline** the details that show the boys and their grandfather have hiked together before. What happens in the last stanza?

_____

_____

381

Text Evidence

1 Connection of Ideas (A)(C)(T)

Draw a box around the girl's name in the title. Reread the first five lines. What is the mother pointing to in the poem?

_____

_____

2 Literary Elements
Personification

Reread the poem. **Circle** an example of personification. What human characteristic does the poet give the ivy?

_____

_____

3 Comprehension
Theme

Think about the poem. Why do you think the mother named her daughter, Ivy?

_____

_____

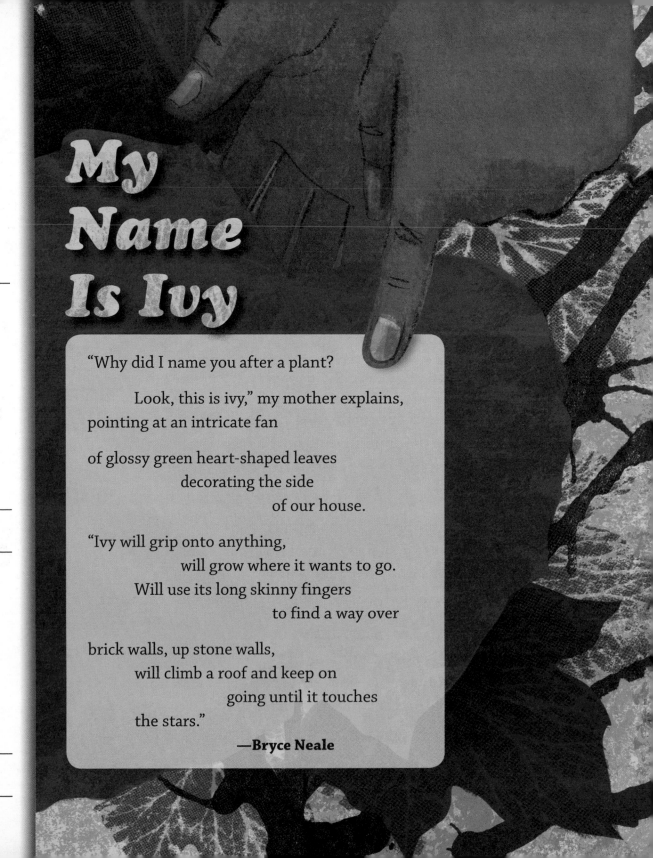

My Name Is Ivy

"Why did I name you after a plant?

    Look, this is ivy," my mother explains,
pointing at an intricate fan

of glossy green heart-shaped leaves
        decorating the side
                of our house.

"Ivy will grip onto anything,
        will grow where it wants to go.
    Will use its long skinny fingers
            to find a way over

brick walls, up stone walls,
    will climb a roof and keep on
        going until it touches
  the stars."

—**Bryce Neale**

Collage

Grandma gave me her eyes.
"Eyes of a panther," Grandpa whispers.

Grandpa gave me his nose.
"A bumpy, rocky road of a nose," Grandma scoffs.

Dad gave me his long skinny toes.
"My roots reach back to the lemurs," he jokes.

Mama gave me her lopsided smile.
"Don't ever lose it," she warns.

I gave them my heart.
"It's big enough to hold you all," I say.

— **Maria Diaz**

Susan Gal

Text Evidence

1 Literary Elements
Metaphor

Circle the metaphor in the second stanza. What two things are being compared?

_____

_____

2 Connection of Ideas A C T

Underline the details that tell what the narrator's family members gave her. What did the narrator give her family members?

_____

3 Comprehension
Theme

Draw a box around the title of the poem. How is the narrator like a collage?

_____

_____

383

Respond to Reading

 **Discuss** Work with a partner. Discuss the questions below about the poem "Collage." Reread to find the answers. Write page numbers to show where you found text evidence.

?Questions | **Discussion Starters** | **Text Evidence**

1 What did the narrator in "Collage" get from her grandparents?	▶ The narrator's grandparents gave her individuality by… ▶ I know this because I read…	Page(s): _____
2 What did the narrator's parents give her?	▶ The narrator's parents gave her… ▶ Her mother told her…	Page(s): _____
3 What does the narrator give to her family in return?	▶ The narrator in "Collage" gives… ▶ The narrator tells her family… ▶ I know this because I read…	Page(s): _____

Mike Moran

384

Write Review your notes about "Collage." Then write your answer to the question below. Use text evidence to support your answer.

How does the narrator in "Collage" feel about her family?

_____

_____

_____

_____

_____

_____

_____

_____

_____

_____

Shared Read

Read an Analysis > **Word Choice** Tina wrote about the poems "Climbing Blue Hill" and "Collage." She shared her opinion on which poet did a better job of using precise language.

Student Model

Topic Sentence

Circle the topic sentence. What is Tina going to write about?

Evidence

Draw a box around the evidence that Tina includes. What other information from the poems would you include?

Concluding Statement

Underline the concluding statement. Why is this sentence a good wrap up?

After reading "Climbing Blue Hill" and "Collage," I think the author of "Climbing Blue Hill" did the best job of using precise language. The first line of the poem says, "When the yellow leaves begin/to glimmer among the green ones." The word "glimmer" makes me think of shiny gold leaves. "Comforting squeak" is another example of the precise language the poet uses. In "Collage," the poet uses words like "long" and "skinny." These words are not as precise and do not create a picture in my mind. I think that the author of "Climbing Blue Hill" did a better job of using precise language.

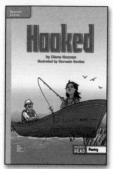

Leveled Reader

_____

_____

_____

_____

_____

_____

_____

_____

_____

Topic Sentence

☐ Include the title of the text you read.

☐ Look at the author's use of precise language.

Evidence

☐ Tell what the description you chose is about.

☐ Use details to explain how word choice helped to make the description more vivid.

Concluding Statement

☐ Restate which description was the most vivid because of the author's choice of words.